The Writer Uprooted

Edited by Alvin H. Rosenfeld

Jewish Literature and Culture
Series Editor, Alvin H. Rosenfeld

Indiana University Press   Bloomington · Indianapolis

THE
WRITER
UPROOTED

Contemporary
Jewish Exile
Literature

This book is a publication of

Indiana University Press
601 North Morton Street
Bloomington, IN 47404-3797 USA

http://iupress.indiana.edu

Telephone orders   800-842-6796
Fax orders   812-855-7931
Orders by e-mail   iuporder@indiana.edu

Library of Congress Cataloging in-Publication Data

The writer uprooted : contemporary Jewish exile
literature / edited by Alvin H. Rosenfeld.
     p. cm. — (Jewish literature and culture)
 Includes bibliographical references and index.
 ISBN 978-0-253-35144-9 (cloth : alk. paper) —
ISBN 978-0-253-21981-7 (pbk. : alk. paper)
1. American literature—Jewish authors—History and
criticism. 2. American literature—20th century—History
and criticism. 3. Jewish authors—Europe, Eastern. 4.
Exiles' writings—History and criticism. 5. Immigrants—
United States. 6. Identity (Philosophical concept)
in literature. 7. Jews—United States—Intellectual
life. I. Rosenfeld, Alvin H. (Alvin Hirsch), date
PS153.J4W62 2008
810.9'8924—dc22

                              2007052690

1 2 3 4 5   13 12 11 10 09 08

This book is dedicated to two treasured friends:
ALICE GINOTT COHN
who knows the challenges of exile
and
TED COHN
who lovingly helps her meet them

Contents

Introduction

— Alvin H. Rosenfeld

According to the Hebrew Bible, the story of mankind unfolds between the poles of exile and redemption—the pains of being cast out and the pleasures of homecoming. Adam, banished from the paradisal garden, stands forth as the original exile. Abraham, the first of the patriarchs, is also the first to leave his native country and experience the trials of life in a new land. Born in that land, his son Isaac stays put, but famine drives Isaac's son Jacob into Egypt; and Jacob's favorite son, Joseph, is expelled by his brothers into that land of darkness and restriction, which becomes forever after the symbol of exile incarnate. Moses, the liberator of his people from bondage in Egypt and the carrier of the divine promise of return, glimpses the Promised Land from afar but is kept from setting foot on its soil. Those who are privileged to enter and reside there enjoy periods of sovereignty and prosperity, only to be uprooted by war and be scattered across the earth.

And so the story goes over many generations of Jewish existence, which, prior to the establishment of the modern state of Israel, was too often marked by banishment and the wanderings of forced dispersion.

It is little wonder, then, that the Jew—the most pliant of symbols to mythmakers everywhere—has been adopted as the paradigmatic emblem of exile. From Chaucer to James Joyce and beyond, the wanderer in literature—through countries, cities, other minds—has been figured as the Jew, whose vicissitudes have been taken to exemplify the modern condition of personal displacement and cultural dispossession and loss.

The chapters of this book address this condition in its most contemporary manifestations. Classical Judaism's theological understanding of exile as a form of divine punishment ("For our sins were we banished from the land") is absent from the pages that follow, for, in the main, the authors represented here do not think about their condition so much in religious terms as they do in historical, political, and psychological ones. These writers also reveal that, for all of the difficulties it presents, exile can have a creative side and over the centuries has been a major source of intellectual and artistic production. Eliminate from literature the writers who have changed lands and languages and what remains would be a much thinner and poorer record of human experience. From earliest times to today, the list of literary exiles—Isaiah, Ovid, Virgil, Petrarch, Dante, Voltaire, Heine, Shelley, Byron, Keats, Conrad, James, Joyce, Eliot, Pound, Auden, Yeats, Nabokov, Beckett, Ionescu, Kundera, Solzhenitsyn, Brodsky, Milosz, Rushdie, Ishiguro—is both long and distinguished. Some of those just named—and the above list could be increased substantially—were voluntary exiles; others were forced to leave their native cities or lands and lived abroad involuntarily. But whether they are thought of today as banished writers or émigrés, expatriates, or refugees, all have known and recorded the experiences of radical disruption and displacement that define the condition of exile and the challenges, both anguished and comic, of adjusting to the strangeness of life elsewhere.

As a nation of immigrants, America has been generally hospitable to newcomers and has welcomed people from a hundred different countries to its shores. In the decades between 1880 and the mid-1920s, Jews from Eastern Europe comprised one of the largest and most creative of America's immigrant groups, and the novels, stories, memoirs, poems, and plays of Jewish authors of this era and their immediate descendants added greatly to the richness and range of twentieth-century American writing. One thinks of such early authors as Mary Antin, Abraham Cahan, Anzia Yezierska, Henry Roth, and Ludwig Lewisohn and of such later writers as Saul Bellow, Bernard Malamud, Cynthia Ozick, Isaac Bashevis Singer, and Philip Roth. The works of these writers and numerous others like them provided new strains of social and political consciousness, philosophical and religious reflection, urbanity, and humor that enlivened American literature and connected it to some of the most vital traditions of European culture. When one adds the work of certain notable essayists and critics—Irving Howe, Alfred Kazin, Leslie Fiedler, Lionel Trilling, and Philip Rahv, among them—it is clear that the contributions of American Jews to American literary culture have been significant.

In the view of some scholars, this once-flourishing tradition of American Jewish creativity inevitably would run its course, exhausted by the absorptive powers of Americanization itself. In this view, the immigrant experience may have triggered an outburst of writing by American Jews, but as these authors and their descendants became part of the country's social and cultural mainstream, they would lose touch with the catalytic energies that inspired them to write in the first place. Those who see this story in these terms, therefore, tend to be elegiac in their assessments of the place of Jews in American letters and conclude that, with the growing distance from immigrant-era experience, the sources that fed this strain of creativity would be depleted.

This projection of cultural decline is being challenged in our own day by an interesting and largely unanticipated phenomenon—the arrival in North America of a new generation of Jewish immigrant authors. A selective short list would include Gary Shteyngart, Lara Vapnyar, and Ilya Kaminsky (originally from Russia); Henryk Grynberg, Eva Hoffman, and Louis Begley (Poland); Norman Manea, Elie Wiesel, Marguerite Dorian, Andrei Codrescu, and Nina Cassian (Romania); Arnost Lustig and Bronislava Volková (the Czech Republic); David Bezmozgis (Latvia); Walter Abish (Germany); David Albahari (Serbia); Alan Isler (Great Britain); André Aciman (Egypt); and Roya Hakakian (Iran). As indicated, most of these come from the countries of Eastern Europe and have arrived in the past thirty years or so. Some continue to write in their native tongues; others quickly adapted to English. But whatever their choice of a literary language, it is already apparent that this cohort of writers is highly talented and is refashioning older immigrant narratives in newly creative ways. Some of the questions these writers raise about Old World–New World experience are familiar: How does one adapt to a new and often bewildering cultural environment? Which values from one's former life can survive in this very different place, and which are expendable? What does one become in becoming an American, and what does one cease to be in taking on a new, hybrid identity?

Issues like these are part of the common fate of all newcomers to this country and, indeed, help to define and redefine the American ethos. As these questions are formulated in the literature being produced by this latest wave of foreign-born Jewish authors, though, some surprising answers emerge. They do so in part because, while the countries in which these writers grew up—Russia, Poland, Hungary, Romania, Latvia, Czechoslovakia—may bear the same names as the countries that produced the earlier generation of immigrant Jews, they were, in fact, very different places socially, culturally, and politically. Nor is the America to which the newer writers have come identical to the

America that received large numbers of European immigrants in the late nineteenth and early twentieth centuries. There are commonalities that belong to the immigrant experience as such, but the sensibilities at play are hardly the same and, consequently, the literary renderings of such experience are quite different.

In addition to and, in many cases, in advance of the immigrant experience, though, there is the experience of exile, including that version of it that numerous East European writers knew intimately: inner exile. To most Americans, this is a foreign, if not an altogether unknown, experience; but especially for those who suffered the double tyrannies of both Nazism and communism, the homeland was often no haven at all from oppression, and one's only chance for mental and spiritual survival was to dwell, for a time, within. Some immersed themselves in poetry and music; others took recourse to riddles and a range of other mind games. Such survival strategies are memorably recorded in the contributions to this book by Manea, Grynberg, Volková, and Ozsváth. At best, though, these were only temporary solutions, and ultimately departure from one's native city or town became a necessity. While they may not have been physically banished from their homelands, then, the separation of these writers from their places of origin confronted them with many of the same trials that others have had to face who were physically forced out. The traumas of dispossession and dislocation that accompany the difficult passage from what once was home to a place that Norman Manea has called "Exileland" is a prominent feature of this literature and sets it apart from much of the literature written by the earlier generation of American Jewish writers.

"How [do] you become a Jew after the Holocaust, after Communism, and after exile? Are these, by definition, essentially Jewish traumas?" Manea asks. The history that gives rise to such questions was not part of the experience of Jewish writers of earlier decades. Nor has it directly shaped the sensibilities of such younger writers as Lara Vapnyar, Gary Shteyngart, David Bez-mozgis, and Ilya Kaminsky, who grew up hearing about but did not personally have to contend with the severe testings of the Nazi Holocaust and Stalinist oppression at its worst. The generational differences here are crucial and add contrasting, often comic, elements to the narratives of the Jewish literary exile. It is still too soon to know, but as they continue to explore the bafflements and enticements of a life that moves between two countries, two cultures, and two or more languages, one senses that this emerging generation of foreign-born Jewish novelists, short-story writers, and poets may contribute some new and especially interesting dimensions to American literature in the years ahead.

Together with the work of figures like Manea, Grynberg, and others represented in this book, they are also destined to add to that growing corpus of writings by Jewish authors elsewhere that crosses national borders and is beginning to take on a global character. The contributions of the American-based writers to this emerging transnational Jewish literature are fascinating to observe. They also raise a number of compelling questions: What, for instance, is one to make of the fact that one of Romania's most formidable intellectuals does his writing—in Romanian—from an apartment on New York City's Upper West Side? The sounds that reach him there are in English, Spanish, Chinese, Korean, Hebrew—almost every language but his native one; yet Norman Manea is widely regarded as one of Romania's most interesting and innovative literary stylists. Has his situation as an exile writer furthered or impeded his art? Or how does one explain the fact that one of Poland's most prolific authors—Henryk Grynberg—manages to keep his Polish language and Polish Jewish sensibility alive while living in McLean, Virginia, a place as remote from the author's origins as one can be but one from which he has written more than twenty books? Or how does a remarkably inventive Czech poet—Bronislava Volková—and a devoted and increasingly prolific Yiddish poet—Dov-Ber Kerler (who writes under the pen name "Boris Karloff")—keep their art supple and creative in Bloomington, Indiana, where Czech and Yiddish are hardly ever heard? Are the answers to these and numerous other questions to be found, as Geoffrey Hartman suggests, in searching out the hidden links between continuities in the work and discontinuities in the lives of these authors? Is the frequent emphasis on place—the lost, abandoned, or rejected place—a function of the exile writer's continuing sense of radical displacement? And what do these writers take to be the Jewish element in the experiences they record and the ideas they develop in response to them?

There are no readily available answers to any of these questions, for this is an area of literary and cultural history that still awaits serious investigation. If the present book serves as a prod to such study, it will have achieved one of its main purposes. And if it moves readers to discover the poetry and prose being produced by the writers featured in this volume, another one of its largest aims will have been fulfilled.

The Writer Uprooted originated in an unusual conference held at Indiana University in March 2006. To the best of my knowledge, this was the first time that a number of this country's most interesting Jewish émigré authors had ever been assembled to talk seriously about common experiences and common concerns. Originating in six different countries and living today in a variety of American cities, most had never met before, yet the conversations that opened up among them over their days in Bloomington—about the burdens that accompany cultural rupture and separation but also the possibilities of reorientation, recovery, and renewal—were intimate, open, honest, intense, and full of compelling insights. Exile, it emerged, was a metaphysical as well as a geographical condition, and coping with it was not easy. Yet while the presentations dealt with a difficult order of human experience, they were uniformly moving, and, at times, even riveting. Given the rare qualities of creative intelligence on display, in the end, they were also uplifting.

The present book reflects the intellectual essence of that exciting gathering and offers readers an opportunity to become engaged with some of the many challenging themes it brought to the fore.

I wish to thank the following departments, programs, and administrative offices at Indiana University for their support, without which neither the conference nor this book would have been possible: the Office of the Vice Provost for Research for a New Frontiers in the Humanities New Perspectives grant; the Robert A. and Sandra S. Borns Jewish Studies Program; the Dorit and Gerald Paul Program for Jewish Culture and the Arts; the Lilly Library; the Office of International Programs; the Department of English; the Polish Studies Center; the Russian and East European Institute; the Department of West European Studies; the Department of Comparative Literature; and Indiana University Press. Special thanks go to Melissa Deckard, Patricia Ek, Melissa Hunt, Carolyn Lipson-Walker, and Barbara Krawcowicz for their invaluable assistance in helping me organize the conference and prepare the manuscript of this book.

The Writer Uprooted

Nomadic Language

— Norman Manea

Kafka did not often write about the country in which he was born, but he did write about the language—that is, the homeland—which he came to inhabit. In this connection, he spoke about "impossibilities" and of the use of the German language as the "self-tormenting usurpation of an alien property." In a letter to Max Brod, he lists three impossibilities for a Jew writing in German or, in fact, in any other language. He considers these impossibilities as a matter of "the Jewish question or of despair in relation to that question." Kafka saw himself as a product of the impossible, which he recreated continuously as poetry, that is, as life, with a magical and austere fixation. His three impossibilities are as follows: the impossibility of not writing, of writing in German, and of writing differently, which means, probably, of writing in a language other than German. To these he adds a fourth, comprehensive impossibility: namely, "the impossibility of writing per se." Actually, this last point entails the impossibility of living per se, the impossibility "to endure life"—as a diary entry tells us. "My whole being is directed toward literature . . . the moment I abandon it, I cease to live. Everything I am, and am not, is a result of this," he confesses. Few people have had their homeland as dramatically located in writing as the Jewish Franz Kafka writing in Prague in German — his paradoxical way of "crossing over to the side of the world" in the struggle with himself. "I am nothing but literature and can and want to be nothing else," he often repeated.

It may seem surprising that Kafka did not mention a fifth impossibility, one which is the most kafkaesque of all: E. M. Cioran, who held that you would do better to write operettas than to write in a foreign language. And yet it would be more suggestive to call it "the snail's impossibility": that is, the impossibility of continuing to write in exile, even if the writer takes along his language as the snail does his house. Such an extreme situation seems borrowed from the very premise of Kafka; and our clownish forerunner K. could not but be attracted by such a farcical hypothesis of self-destruction.

For the mature adult, exile reformulates tardily the premise of initiation and becoming, reopens the gate of life's extreme risks and potential, putting into question all the steps of past experience. Moreover, for those prematurely traumatized, never truly free from the psychosis of the provisory, from the threat of being thrown once again into the chaos of the unknown, exile suddenly releases all the old fears. One does not so much lose a precarious and dubious stability as discovers oneself deeper in the abyss of never-ending instability. The writer, always a "suspect," as Thomas Mann said, an exile par excellence, conquers his homeland, through language. To be exiled also from this last refuge represents a multiple dispossession, the most brutal and irredeemable decentering of his being.

In the beginning was the Word, the ancients told us. In the beginning for me, the word was Romanian. The doctor and all those who assisted my difficult birth spoke Romanian. Romanian was spoken in my home, where I spent most of my time with Maria, the lovely peasant young woman who took care of me and spoiled me, in Romanian. Of course these were not the only sounds around me. German, Yiddish, Ukrainian, and Polish were spoken in Bukovina, as was a peculiar dialect, a Slavic mixture typical of the Ruthenians. It is notable that the family quarrel between Yiddish, the earthly-plebeian language of exile, and Hebrew, the holy-chosen language, peaked at the 1908 Czernowitz conference when the celebrated triumph of Yiddish ("The Jews are one people, their language is Yiddish") gave no sign of the spectacular and definitive domination that Hebrew would attain with the founding, four decades later, of the state of Israel. When my grandfather asked at my birth if the newborn had nails, trying to gauge my chances of survival, he presumably asked in Yiddish, although he knew Hebrew and spoke fluent Romanian. The books sold in his bookshop were, in fact, Romanian. At five, when I was deported to the Transnistria concentration camp, along with the rest of Bukovina's Jewish population, I spoke only Romanian. With my first expulsion beyond the Dniestr, the Romanian language was also banished.

The Yiddish poet Itzik Manger once said: "When the great calamity overwhelmed the German-assimilated Jew, when a brutal sergeant-major cult roared: 'Out, Jew!' the German Jew woke from his self-justifying dream, from his trance of German culture, and began to run. But in himself, and with himself, he carried a bastard: a foreign language; a foreign body." In my case, a brutal Romanian, not German, sergeant-major cult roared: "Out, Jew," but the Romanian language I carried wasn't a bastard or a foreign body; it was my only language. It also was, of course, the language of that brutal sergeant-major cult, and this I was already aware of at too early an age.

In the camp I learned Yiddish from the elderly captives and Ukrainian from native children in the neighborhood. After liberation by the Red Army I attended a Russian school for one year. When we returned to Romania in 1945, I enrolled in a Romanian school, but my parents soon arranged for me to be privately tutored—in German. What we experienced during those years of terror in "Trans-tristia" had originated, they knew quite well, in Hitler's Berlin, but they were also aware of, even though they were not particularly well educated to, the difference between recent horror and the longer view, between hatred and culture. I studied Hebrew for only one year, when I was roughly thirteen, in order to be formally accepted among the "men" of the tribe. Surprisingly, traces resurface, even today, when I least expect them. In high school I learned French and Russian, but none of the languages I had taken up ever became fully internalized. Echoes of my subconscious "cosmopolitanism" sound only occasionally these days when, suddenly and without effort on my part, the proper turn of phrase occurs to me in a conversation held in one of these half-familiar, still foreign languages, even when I have access to them. In the end, I feel at home in only one language.

Writing seems a childish pursuit, as we well know, even when done with the excessive seriousness to which children are prone.

My long road to this immaturity began one July day in 1945, several months after our return from the camps. An edenic summer in a small Moldavian town. The enchanted banality of the normal, the overwhelming joy of finally feeling secure. A perfect afternoon: sun and stillness. In the room's half-light, I listened to a voice that was mine and yet not my own. The green book of Romanian folktales I had been given just before I reached the solemn age of nine spoke directly to me. It was then, I think, that I experienced the wonder of the word, the magic of literature: both wound and balm, disease and therapy. The language to which I was subjected in the Transnistria camps was a cacophony that mingled despair with barked orders from the guards, that brutal sergeant-major roaring. Yiddish, German, Ukrainian, Russian: all the camp's idioms rushed into the chasm it had rent in my life.

In 1945, the survivors and their nomadic language were repatriated. An impoverished language, anemic, hesitant, and confused, it needed, as I did, the nutrients of normality. I made all sorts of rediscoveries: food, games, school, clothing, relatives, but above all I was mad for books, newspapers, magazines, posters. I discovered new words and new meanings, my language absorbed them quickly and with great excitement. Early, too early, I dreamed of joining the clan of word wizards, the secret sect I had just discovered.

My first literary attempt was, of course, an "amorous discourse," as Roland Barthes would say. In 1947, in the lowest high school class at the Jewish Lyceum in Suceava—a private school that was to be banned a year later—I dedicated my childish rhetoric to the blond girl whose name followed mine in the class registry: Manea, Norman; Norman, Bronya. I read that solemn declaration, full of pathos, to Bronya and a small group of bewildered classmates. And then, in the first year of the "dictatorship of the Proletariat," I continued with the same childish enthusiasm to write poems in honor of the Revolution, of Stalin, of world peace—terrible poems, of course, which may compete, I would say, with the terrible poems written at that time by mature and renown poets all around the world. Yet, I was already searching for something "different," something that would transcend daily trivialities, eager as I was to uncover my true self among all the individuals who inhabited me. The one-Party system of the socialist dictatorship took over, gradually, any private ownership: land and banks, industry and schools, farms and hospitals and newspapers, apartments and kindergartens, stadiums and pharmacies and libraries, agriculture and culture—everything. We all were owned by the state, and the wooden official language of the Party dominated our daily life, sometimes our nightlife, too. Some people could still find a shelter in their family library. That was not my case. Coming back from our nomadic ordeal, we didn't have much of anything. The bookstore of my grandfather was gone as was he himself, buried in a nameless grave in Ukraine. Hunting for books took many useless detours and traps in order to find, finally, after a great waste of time and energy, the authors I was looking for. Yet, reading saved me from the deadening effect of the dictatorship's new language. My imagination was inflamed by German romanticism; I immersed myself in English and French realism; but above all I was mesmerized by the great Russian literature, at the time extensively and superbly translated in Romania. Tolstoy and Goncharov, Gogol and Pushkin, Chekhov and many others. It was not until the "liberalization" period of the 1960s that I would experience the true Dostoyevsky and the great modernists, Joyce, Proust, Faulkner, the Latin Americans, and the surrealists, as well as modern Romanian writers, who had finally been rehabilitated and republished after years of a stupid ban. Reading preserved me from ideological idiocy and grotesque opportunism, first as an unhappy student at the polytechnic and then as an unhappy engineer. The naive illusion that a solid, practical profession might save me from socialist demagogy and terror was soon dispelled.

My first story, "Pressing Love," published in 1966 in a small avant-garde literary journal banned after six issues, was filled with coded erotic anxiety. I had timidly tried to reestablish a thematic and linguistic normality. The official press immediately condemned the text as apolitical, absurd, aestheticizing, and cosmopolitan.

Soon after, I finally heard my voice in my own book, which coincidentally also had a cover as green as that of the folktale book I discovered at my return, in 1945, from my first exile.

I found the refuge I had so long desired. I was finally at home.

I had protected my language as well as I could from the pressures of official speech; now I had to defend it from suspicious and hostile censors who would massacre or eliminate sentences, paragraphs, and chapters, in my following books. In that period, the tedious jargon of power that had reigned for years gradually opened the floodgates for the dictator's endless stream of a new-old nationalism. Everything was oriented toward the head clown: television, the press, laws, the party "debates," preschool education, cheering and athletic events, philatelist conferences.

Twenty years after my first published story, an apolitical, strictly literary text, and before my flight to the West, in 1986, my allegorical novel *The Black Envelope* put strong political accents on daily life under socialist misery and terror at a time when the dictatorship was encouraging the "aesthetical" approach to writing in order to avoid daily reality in favor of a more magnificent one.

Even if he didn't mention exile as one of his dear "impossibilities," Kafka did think about migration, expatriation. For that guinea pig of the impossible, expatriation was not just an extravagant variation of his estrangement. Expatriation had been sometimes an immediate, urgent, even demonic summons. "Filthy brood—is what I heard them call the Jews," he tells us in one of his letters. "The heroism involved in staying put in spite of it all is the heroism of the cockroach," he adds.

Kafka did think of that fifth impossibility not only when he dreamt, in his last years, of settling in the Holy Land. "I'm here at the General Insurance Company and yet I hope to sit sometime, in some far-away countries, at a window of the office of sugar plantations or to look to Muslim cemeteries," he had once written. Salvation through self-destruction seemed always to him a greatly appealing burlesque. "What I call foolish is the idea that Tibet is far from Vienna" — such words are indeed his. "I'm reading a book about Tibet; at a description of a settlement near the Tibetan border in the mountains my heart grows suddenly heavy, this village seems so hopelessly deserted, so far from Vienna. Would it really be far?" Kafka asks Milena, asking himself too, and knowing too well that the desert is, in fact, not far away at all, but dangerously close to Vienna, to Prague, to the General Insurance Company where he worked, to his family house, to the room and desk of his solitude.

Neither sugar-cane plantations, nor Muslim cemeteries, nor the Great Wall of China of his famous story were far away. It is not necessary to imagine Kafka in the Middle-Eastern desert, or in Communist China, or in Brazil, where that thoroughly un-kafkaesque Viennese Jew Stefan Zweig would commit suicide, in order to authenticate one of the most expressive twists of the twentieth century. Even imagining Kafka in the world capital of exiles, New York, the New York of his character Karl Rossman, or next door in Newark, "in a room in the house of an elderly Jewish lady on the shabby lower stretch of Avon Avenue," as Philip Roth suggested, would not add a lot to our knowledge about his or our predicament. In his nocturnal room in Prague, Kafka, the exile par excellence, had already been in these and many other distant or nonexistent places.

And yet, like many of Kafka's premonitions, the snail's impossibility too, though not mentioned by him as such, would haunt the shadows of his unsettling, carnivalesque posterity.

Kafka's posterity extended the Jew's condition to many categories of nomads and exiles. Primo Levi saved himself in Auschwitz through the German language. After the Holocaust, Paul Celan wrote in the language of his mother's butchers. To the end, Mandelstam's motherland remained the Russian language, in which Stalin gave the order for his death.

It is hard to picture Kafka in our New World, and harder still to imagine him bearing the cap and bells of a telegenic promoter of his own Works, as is commanded by the computerized entertainments business of the Planetary Circus. Yet the way in which the solitary Franz Kafka went beyond these "impossibilities" without leaving them behind, surviving not only in the German language of his estrangement, may remind our memoryless society of that hope without hope contained in this unrepeatable and impossible model. We may wonder why and how Franz Kafka alone, the essential exile, and the word *kafkaesque*, essential for the language of estrangement and exile, became essential for our time. Some of us would probably like, childishly enough, to believe this a proof that writing, as secular prayer, may still accommodate parts of our daily life comedy.

I left the socialist "penal colony" much too late, because I was childish enough to believe that I did not live in a country, but in a language. Liberation, I knew, entailed a malignant curtailing of freedom itself. In December 1986, I boarded a flight to Berlin knowing full well that I may have traded my tongue for a passport. But I didn't feel, even in this extreme situation, that my language was "the usurpation of an alien property," as Kafka thought. It was, in fact, my only property, and the willingness to accept this loss speaks volumes about the "flaming brothel," as Cioran called the region he himself left behind, not suspecting the horrors the socialist combination of brothel, circus, and prison would bring.

For the writer, language is a placenta. Language is not only a sweet and glorious conquest, but legitimization, a home. Being driven out of this essential refuge, his creativity is burned to the core.

My second exile (this time at the age of fifty instead of five) gave expropriation and delegitimization new meaning. The honor of being expelled was inseparable from the course of being silenced as a writer. Nonetheless, I did take my nomadic language with me, like a snail its house.

—

The sacred text was, as we know, the instrument of exilic Jewish survival. In my case, it was not the old, sacred text of the Bible that accompanied me in exile. It was a secular language, my very inner language, the language of writing.

In Berlin, during my first year in the West, I pondered daily the question of estrangement. I thought not only about the internal exile from which I had just escaped but also about the concept of exile itself, overwhelmed as I was by doubts and questions from the past. And because it happened in Berlin, I also had to confront my ethnicity, as I already confronted the invective "alien" in my own country. Precisely because the need for a homeland is more acute in those belonging to one is questioned, losing it also pains them more. On the threshold of a capital decision, facing a new and possible dislocation, I had to ask myself once more who I was.

Is the Jew in exile "restored" to his nativity of dispersal, as George Steiner says? Does this "chosen foreignness" become "ontological," as Hegel argues? The house I was carrying was my language, and my language happened to be Romanian. Nazism and then communism robbed me of connections to a real Jewish tradition, yet I always was and became again not only a Jew but "the Jew," housed not in place but in time, and, as usual, a not very hospitable time. I would have liked to believe that my case proves again that "truth is homeless," as Steiner kept repeating, that exile is the only realm of truth, but I wasn't yet sure about this.

At that time, I didn't know Steiner's essay "Our Homeland the Text." I only recently discovered that I was then putting to myself the same questions he was asking at precisely that period.

"Plato records the hunter's halloo when a truth is cornered—even if this hunt should lead to his own destruction or that of his community. It is here that the creed of Spinoza and of Kafka meets with the conduct of Socrates," Steiner says. "A true thinker, a truth-thinker . . . must know that no nation, no body politic, no creed, no moral ideal and necessity, be it that of human survival, is worth falsehood, a willed self-deception or the manipulation of a text. This knowledge and observance *are* his homeland. It is the false reading, the erratum that make him homeless. . . . The man or woman at home in the text is, by definition, a conscientious objector: to the vulgar mystique of the flag and the anthem, to the sleep of reason which proclaims 'my country, right or wrong,' to the pathos and eloquence of collective mendacities on which the nation-state—be it a mass-consumer mercantile technocracy or a totalitarian oligarchy—build its power and aggressions. The locus of truth is always extraterritorial; its diffusion is made clandestine by the barbed wire and watch-towers of national dogma."[1]

Paradoxically, German was soon to become my first linguistic asylum in the West. In 1987, during my fellowship in West Berlin, my first translated book, *Composite Biography*, was published by Steidl Verlag. My familiarity with the German language eased the trauma of uprooting, fraught with discouragement and confusion. German, spoken by my friends and my parents' friends, had survived the decades of socialism in Bukovina, once part of the Habsburg realm. In 1987, I was overjoyed to discover that the German language, so long dormant in me, was ready to be resurrected.

When I arrived in Göttingen for the final editing of my German book, my editor and I knocked our heads together over the manuscript until midnight. He tried to console me. "I assure you, we can translate anything. In Goethe's language there are equivalents for everything! Absolutely everything! Even the most unusual, astonishing turns of phrase. All you need is talent, dedication, and work. Hard work and then more work. And, of course, money."

Yes, translation is badly paid in the capitalist markets. Unlike Günter Grass, not every author can offer his translators extended working visits that can help circumvent the semantic obstacles that arise in moving from one language to another.

My first public appearance in New York in the fall of 1989, when the East's implosion gripped the world's attention, was with a panel on Romanian literature sponsored by the American chapter of PEN on "The Word as Weapon." Suspicious of the topic's belligerence, I chose to speak about "The Word as Miracle." Naturally I evoked that July afternoon in 1945 when I discovered the marvelous Romanian folktale by Ion Creanga. A few days later I received a letter from a distinguished writer and translator of Romanian descent who had attended the event. She mentioned the author's (Ion Creanga) anti-Semitic writings and comments.

I knew that German was not only the language of Schiller and Goethe but of Hitler and the SS as well; that the Romanian of Caragiale and Bacovia was also that of Zelea Codreanu, "Captain" of the anti-Semitic Iron Guard. It is unfortunate and very disturbing when great writers and intellectuals become accomplices of the ideology and language of hatred; but, again, Romanian was for me also the language of love and friendship and literary apprenticeship, the language my parents and grandparents speak to me even after their deaths.

Jewish authors have often been reproached for writing in the "executioner's language," African writers for serving the "colonialists' language." Language cultivates and preserves the poison of hatred just as it gives rise to love or innovative art. It encompasses both indolence of mind and lashes of brilliant creativity, majesty and monstrosity. Baudelaire's French *Les Fleurs du Mal* (Flowers of Evil) and Tudor Arghezi's Romanian *Flori de mucegai* (Flowers of Decay [or Mould Flowers?]) broach this ambivalence even in their titles.

When I spoke of the wonder of the word in New York in 1989, I referred to my native, nomadic language and not to the language to which I had emigrated. Its wonders were not accessible to this shipwrecked latecomer. Could it have been? Could I have relived in English the enchantment I had first encountered as a nine-year-old and then my subsequent adventure of self-discovery through Romanian words?

During a stay at the Ledig House writer's colony in Switzerland some years ago, I asked a renowned German translator of Russian until what age could one learn another language well enough to become a writer in it. Nabokov had learned foreign languages as a child. Conrad had sailed between ports and languages when still young enough to adapt. I knew that the usual examples did not fit. "Twelve," the expert announced. "Too bad," I said, "I'm already thirteen." By then I had more than doubled the double of that age.

The uprooting and dispossession of exile are a trauma with positive aspects that only become apparent once one understands the advantage in relinquishing the idea of one's own importance. Impermanence and insecurity can be liberating. Exile is also a challenging pedagogical experience. There is much to learn when one is forced to begin again at an advanced age, to enter into the world anew and to prove one's abilities again like a child whose past has been wiped out but has been offered a "second chance" to rebuild his life from scratch, even if without one's former energy and vigor.

At the age of twenty-six, the Romanian writer E. M. Cioran began appropriating the wealth of the French language like a greedy
pirate. He called this metamorphosis of linguistic identity "the
greatest, most dramatic event that can befall a writer." "Historical catastrophes are nothing compared to this," he later claimed.
"When I wrote in Romanian, words were not *independent* of me.
As soon as I began to write in French, I consciously chose each
word. I had them before me, outside of me, each in its place. And
I chose them: now I'll take you, then you." The break to which
Cioran had aspired in leaving Romania was not solely linguistic.
"When I changed my language, I annihilated my past. I changed
my entire life." Is this true? As a famous French author and
brilliant stylist in his adopted language, Cioran was constantly
haunted by ghosts of the past, which he found oppressive and hu-
miliating. "My country! I wanted to hang on to it at any cost—but
there was nothing to hang on," he wrote in the 1950s. Cioran's
glorious linguistic transmutation, however, was not completely
triumphant after all. "Today again it seems that I am writing in a
language that does not fit me at all, that has no roots: a hot-house
language. French does not suit any temperament. I need a *savage*,
drunken language," he told Fernando Savater in 1977. On his
deathbed, the expatriate Cioran lapsed back into the language he
had refused to speak for decades! He rediscovered Romanian, but
not himself. He experienced the ecstasy of Alzheimer amnesia.
The greatest joy, the highest penalty. The End.

My reasons for severing my ties were perhaps stronger than
Cioran's, but still I hung on to my native tongue, and, since I
could not turn back the clock, I could not aspire to the transfiguration and profound, radical change toward which Cioran
struggled during his decades in exile.

Ultimately the question concerning writers is related not only to their linguistic identity but also to their individual drive and destiny. Compared to collective historical disasters, their worries seem childish. Many artists and writers collapse in exile or at home before the problem of a change in their linguistic identity arises. And yet, historical catastrophes can pale beside the dark forces that destroy their language.

⟋

I was almost completely at sea in English. To my fright, I found myself to be like Nabokov's Professor Pnin, who thought *Hamlet* sounded better in his native Russian than in English. In my first decade here, I became terribly anxious when invited to speak at conferences. Not only because of my accent, but also because I constantly feared I would lose or forget my script. I still remember arriving in Turin in 1991 and finding that my bags were missing. I was to give my lecture in English the next morning and, in despair, I tried to convince the conference's organizers to move it to the afternoon. In the meantime, my suitcases arrived and my luck increased: several Italian–Romanian interpreters were attending so that I could speak off the cuff. This epilogue was much happier than the story of the poor Pnin, who not only misses his train to the conference but also brings the wrong lecture.

⟋

The legitimization that translation confers when one lives in one's own country changes when one has left. "At home," translations are welcome gifts from the unknown. An author who is translated into several languages cannot evaluate all these translations. He lives in his own language, in which he has found his voice and character. The foreign travesties do not disturb his essential creativity; the alien codes in which his writing has been encrypted and which he himself often cannot decipher are nothing but flattering gifts.

For an author who has been uprooted, translation becomes a sort of entry visa into the land where he now resides (as well as into other lands and realms). It ensures him, along with citizenship, a literary ID, an entry into a new and fully ambivalent sense of belonging to a community he has joined as an "alien." Translated, he is better expressed than in his daily speech, and it may open opportunities for more communication with his fellow citizens and with his fellow writers.

Yet it all remains hopelessly indefinite for an exiled writer, who, although translated into another linguistic territory, still writes in his native and now nomadic language. Such a frustrating working hypothesis merely spreads uncertainty. The heteronymous, as Fernando Pessoa called his contradictory and complementary creative valences, are replaced by one and the same orthonym that appears wearing the masks of different languages.

⁓

A writer's integrity and his inner self are inseparable from his language. They become variable and indefinably foggy when he is robbed of his native tongue. The doubts he has always had to hem in can gain the upper hand in the ambiguity and uncertainty of his new situation.

"My infallible method of determining whether a sentence is good or bad is to imagine I am in the middle of the Sahara without any books. In my pocket I find a note with one sentence. If it suddenly illuminates the desert's meaning and I no longer wish to leave, then I know the sentence is a good one." A Romanian writer and friend wrote this. In the Sahara of exile, in the desert that Levinas believed to be the root of the spirit, able to replace the ground with the letter, I have often had to repeat these words. For a moment they lent this desert meaning and offered the refuge I had sought for so long. And yet . . . in New York, a "good" Romanian sentence would have to be channeled through contortions and convolutions, metamorphoses and mutilations in order to be translated into the language in which my identity was now clothed.

—

The years had flowed by like water and I knew quite well how unreceptive I was to the illusion of imperviousness, but I also knew how much I depended on that illusion. My dilemma became much clearer in the summer of 1991 than it had been in Germany in 1987 during my apprenticeship in Göttingen. My New York publisher, Grove Press, planned a collection of short stories and a collection of essays for my American debut. Various translators had taken on the short stories, and, together with my editor, I tried to improve their English versions. The Romanian text lay on the table next to the French and Italian translations. Fortunately for me, the American editor spoke both those languages. Together, we jumped from one language to the next and reworked the English version. *How* each sentence tried to express something became less important than *what* it tried to say. It was a logical, "Aristotelian" reduction to erasure, a kind of Darwinian struggle for existence in which originality could prove the greatest disadvantage. As Walter Benjamin said, "any translation which intends to perform a transmitting function cannot transmit anything but information—hence, something inessential."

My book finally appeared in a version that had been cobbled together from many sources but sounded reasonable in English. Despite my three months in purgatory, I was delighted to hold the book in my hand. Seeing it displayed in the bookstore's windows and reading the flattering reviews, I was forced to remind myself that the ordeal of translation is a privilege many gifted authors, at home or in exile, never receive.

Was I accepting a surrogate, an impostor, a shallow impersonator? I reminded myself that I had read Spanish, French, Russian,

Italian, German literature mostly in translation and how important it proved to be in such an encounter with great masters. In translation, of course, always so or mostly so.

—

The first sentence of my 1984 collection of essays, *On the Outline*, goes like this: "The unity of a people is, above all, one of language." I truly believed that language was the matrix, the fundamental, formative factor of communication between the individual and community. During that period, I was attacked in the socialist press as "extraterritorial." That is, foreign, cosmopolitan, antinationalist, antiparty.

In the end, as we can see, I could not avoid becoming a true extraterritorial, expatriate, exile. Yet, as Wittgenstein says, "The boundaries of my language are the boundaries of my world." Common sense, or the not quite tender age in which my exile occurred, should have been cause enough to disabuse myself of the chimera of writing. Still, I have continued the adventure begun in the difficult political conditions of my own country and language.

An author's exile is a terrible trauma for the writer, skinned and unsouled, forced to replace the internal organs of his linguistic being. It has proven, more than once, to be his suicide.

The simulacrum offered by translation, although just a substitute, a surrogate, a double, can provide some unexpected relief. It has similarities with exile itself; it's a textual migration, a process of migrating from a place (a language) of *departure* to a place (a language) of *destination*. In the same way, it is a process of rebirth and adaptation of the nomadic text to a new context.

Assimilation entails the translation of the ego into another language and culture, where it tries to find its place and its expression. Aggressive "distortions" (to recall, again, dispossession and dependence) bring with them incentives of uncertainty. Conscious or unconscious mimeticism often marks the childishness inherent in the spectacle of assimilation.

The exile has new, particular themes for reflection. He is, in the end, a hybrid, a compromise between what he brought with him and what he acquires later.

Translation provides a new linguistic form for the old content. We find, in the process of linguistic relocation, many of the modulations that the exile experiences himself. The text is a living body, a being. The final product must belong entirely to the new language, to the target language, as they say, and not to the old language. The transformation takes a defined period of time and the result is already beached on the new shore, in the new linguistic territory, the new textual residence. In contrast, the exile often swings, for a long time, if not forever between the past and the present. Between formation–deformation–reformation, between different possible egos until, gradually, *the double* appears to represent him on the new social stage. It is an osmosis: loss and gain, wound and revitalization, the fracture of the old and the nutrition of the new, an intense exchange of energies.

Exile also is an extraordinary process of education and reeducation, especially for those who come to the new land as adults. Where one begins and where one ends are poles of a privileged existential adventure, with intense suffering and exaltation. The great school of pointlessness, of dispossession, and in the end, of death, the ultimate dispossession, does not exclude scenes of extraordinary jubilation. Feelings of rebirth are gifts of inestimable worth to our ephemerality.

As with everything human, the extreme condition of exile contains both loss and gain, hopelessness and hope. The trauma of translation has also positive effects. It has happened more than once that in checking even an imperfect translation, I have discovered certain word choices I like better than in the original. I have then changed the original Romanian to a word translated from English. Translation may sometimes be, as the Romantics said, the best literary criticism. You are forced to see where the text is clumsy.

We should remind ourselves that Proust only found himself through Ruskin's translations. In translation, in writing as translation, he found a model and a voice. "I have two more Ruskins to finish," he wrote in 1904, "and after that I will try to translate my poor heart, if I haven't died by then." We can never emphasize the importance of translations enough, for the expansion of knowledge, for dialogue among nations. Especially, though, for the individual discovery of unforeseen, great friends. More important friends than those we meet in the morning for a coffee.

—

I am connected to Paul Celan not only through Bukovina and the camps of Transnistria, which marked our fates in different ways. Celan's German, from the beginning a language of exile, came to the Habsburgian province of Bukovina from Vienna and not from Berlin. He called his brief, carefree youth in Bucharest a time of word games and puns. He believed his German gave him an unfair advantage over his friends who wrote in Romanian. Eugene Ionesco claimed that he himself would probably have been a better writer in Romania rather than the more important one he became in France. My Romanian biography and language were not just episodes in my youth. My "word games" have lasted throughout the greater part of my life, as an alternation between horror and joy, danger and rebirth, apathy and creativity, back to drama, humiliation, uprooting.

It was in Paris, and not in Vienna or Berlin or Zurich, that Celan settled and continued to write in his exiled, nomadic German. No wonder he considered language to be the poet's homeland, even when the language is German and the poet a Jew.

Even when the language is Romanian and the writer a Jew, I would add . . .

Had Paul Celan won his well-deserved Nobel Prize, which country could have claimed him? The prize is explicitly awarded to an individual and not a country. I was not surprised when V. S. Naipaul responded to the news from Stockholm by saying that he did not belong to any particular country. He should have added, I think, that he does indeed belong to a language. And so should have Elias Canetti, Isaac Bashevis Singer, and Kafka, too, for that matter, had his marvelous, nocturnal cryptograms managed to reach that dubious committee of world glory.

One of the most interesting debates at the 1998 Conference of Jewish writers in San Francisco concerned the hypothesis that the greatest Israeli writer in Hebrew in the twenty-first century may not be Jewish. In recent decades, as world events have followed their bloody course, Israel took in immigrants from Vietnam and Chile. Their children have been Israelis for more than twenty years and are "grounded" in the Hebrew language. Today many Romanian workers and cleaning ladies from the Philippines and Thailand are living in Israel. What if the next inspired bard of Hebrew is a Chilean-Israeli, or the child of a Romanian worker, or a Philippino, and not a Jew? Most of the conference participants, including the Israeli delegation, composed of Jews from Iraq, Morocco, Romania, and Germany, responded enthusiastically. Quite a paradox for a state that believes itself the solution to the insoluble question of Jewish exile. It is not impossible that this new century will also see a great German poet of Turkish descent, or French-Algerian or Japanese-Australian.

In New York I still live in the Romanian language, as in Paris Paul Celan lived in German. Despite the fact that I also publish now in Romania, my literary message is no longer sent in a bottle to someone on a distant shore but in an ephemeral capsule that floats through a dream in which—and only in this dream, under lucky circumstances—it will have to invent its own legitimization, its own recipient.

The structural differences between Romanian and English are more difficult to bridge than those between Romanian and the Latin languages. Romanian is, in fact, a mix of Latin and oriental languages. My volume *Compulsory Happiness* came into English through a French translation; some other stories and essays were translated into English from German translations. It seems difficult for a not too experienced translator to find English equivalents for vagueness, metaphors, wordplay, lacunae, equivocal allusions, ironies, intertextual blurrings, as they are practiced in Romanian literature. To embrace the American idiom, the text has often to be retailored, incompatibilities eliminated, and altered from all that is too obscure or specific. Naturally, a great translator, with the necessary time and dedication, can find brilliant equivalents for anything. Intermediaries of genius, unfortunately, are not found on every corner. As my first German editor pointed out, some twenty years ago, translations require persistence and talent, effort and money. And he was not even considering today's ever decreasing literary standards, the increasingly rushed tempo of reading and editing, the growing aversion to any oddities or eccentricities within other literary traditions in favor of what easily can be understood and sold. Books have become simple products that should be readily bought and used as any other market product.

Should one simplify one's thinking or expression in order to ease the task of the translator before easing the task of the publisher and the reader? I sometimes tried this compulsive distortion in order to avoid being caught in a dead end. The result didn't resemble Kafka's "white" style but a vacant account of absence with no digression, enchantment, or mystery. Avoiding stylistic risks, difficulty, or subtlety, picturesque or idiomatic expression, I myself became simpler, so pale as to disappear completely into the blank page.

The writer's block underscores the insanity necessary to pursue this venture, an absurdity that exile only heightens. It was difficult to weather this crisis, if I have indeed done so. When I am occasionally asked in New York in which language I write, I answer, only half in jest, in the language of the birds.

—

Hannah Arendt, herself an exile, once said: "What remains? The mother tongue remains." No one can take away the language in which one has been formed and deformed. The Romanian I hear in my thoughts or that I speak with my wife, and the English of the newspapers, television, and banking forms, of my American friends, of the college where I teach, or of my doctor are not easily divided into public and private realms. Their interaction cannot be compared merely to that between an individual entity and social identity. The tension is not simply linguistic but also geographic, historic, and psychological in origin.

My English is a rented tongue, borrowed by this Robinson Crusoe for the social interaction needed to fit with those harboring him. Far from its natural sphere, my "old" language now exists only for me; I alone reign over its nomadic magic.

The language of life after exile accosts me from all sides. Those nearby who speak to each other or even to me started, gradually, even if timidly, to reach corners of my inner language. The tension between my two languages of today eventually creates fruitful synergies and interferences. Misunderstandings and misrepresentations are only the unavoidable negative side of an exchange that also brings insights when the languages mirror and enrich each other. Time and again, I rediscover the original meaning of a Romanian word through its English equivalent or find I must reformulate a sentence in Romanian after reading its English counterpart. Just as often, I am rewarded with sudden inspiration when I return to a chapter in the original Romanian text after the simplifications of the English version. A therapeutic spirit helps me recover the way back into myself, heals the cramping undergone in the foreign text that is mine but, strictly speaking, also not my own. Marvelous, untranslatable Romanian words and expressions I had never thoroughly examined before suddenly reveal their uniqueness, incisiveness, and originality.

If separated from the land and the people who rejuvenate it every day, one's mother tongue, one's language "with roots," risks petrifying into an artifact. When transmuted into another linguistic medium, however, it may reveal beauties buried by routine. Yet, the relationship between one's native and now nomadic tongue and its homeland, left ever further behind, does not become any simpler.

The fact that one belongs to a language in no way heals the wounds that the homeland has inflicted in one's life; and however incurable the wounds, they do not lessen the priceless gift, language, which we inhabit.

—

When my first translated stories were published in 1970 in Israel in a Hebrew anthology called *Jewish Writers in Romanian*, I was annoyed by the title. I considered myself, quite simply, a Romanian writer. My "ethnicity" was my burden and my wealth and my history, but it was no one else's business. I didn't consider the language a "tormenting usurpation of an alien property," as Kafka said.

Since then, I learned that writers are often classified by other categories than the "essential" one of language: black writers, gay writers, Catholic writers, women writers, and, of course, Jewish

writers. They are all claimed by subgroups according to particular identities and not according to their intrinsic "entity," their
language.

My own biography reminds that history and personal history
cannot be ignored. A biography marked by holocaust, communism, and exile points to a certain identity, independent of the
language of its owner.

Do we eventually grow into the identities that are repeatedly
assigned to us? Do we finally become what we're always told we
are? Am I an American writer in the Romanian nomadic language
or an American Jewish/Jewish American writer in the Romanian
language? Or am I, simply, a Romanian writer in America? An
exiled writer, as I was even before exile? Or a Jewish writer in the
Romanian language, as I was labeled by fellow sympathizers and
by many enemies?

These seemingly futile questions became more confusing
since the once exiled alien was forced to become again an exile
and his language became, again, a nomadic one. I couldn't avoid,
in the last twenty years, wondering if the annoying title of that
Israeli anthology wasn't—despite my irritation at that time—a
right premonition, therefore the right assessment of my destiny.

⁓

In one of the dreams Antonio Tabucchi describes in his picaresque novel *Requiem: A Hallucination,* a dream expedition
in search of Fernando Pessoa, the narrator meets his dead father.
The father is young and, surprisingly, does not speak Italian, the
only language he knew, but Portuguese. Is that because the hallucination takes place in Portugal or because the Italian writer
did not write his book in his native tongue but in his second
language, Portuguese? "What are you doing in a sailor's uniform
here in the Pension Pensao?" the son asks. "It's 1932," the father
answers. "I'm doing my military service, and our ship, a frigate,

dropped anchor in Lisbon." He wants to know from his son, who is older than he and knows more, how he will die. The son tells his father of the cancer which has, in reality, already killed him.

Not only in the beginning was the word. Before the final silence, we often end our existence with the Word. Chekhov spoke his last words, "Ich sterbe" ("I'm dying") not in the language of his life and works but in that of the land where he ended his earthly adventure. In the rare dreams in which I see my parents, they speak Romanian. And yet, I cannot foresee in which language I will take my leave of this world. Death's language sometimes differs from that of the life to which it is putting an end.

Note

1. George Steiner, *No Passion Spent* (New Haven: Yale University Press, 1996), 321.

On Norman Manea's
The Hooligan's Return

— *Matei Calinescu*

The three major, interwoven, and recurrent themes of Norman Manea's oeuvre (both fiction and nonfiction) are the experience of the Holocaust as a child during World War II; living and writing under a totalitarian system—namely, the Romanian version of communism; and exile. These themes are fully developed in the writer's most directly autobiographical book, *The Hooligan's Return* (2003), which is also his most wide-ranging and complex work to date. It is a memoir, as the subtitle makes clear, but not a memoir in the usual sense: for throughout are interspersed pages of fiction as well as numerous reflective digressions that are characteristic of the genre of the moral essay. The presence of fictional elements (describing dreams, imaginings, counterfactual scenarios) is always unambiguously marked as such and the "autobiographical pact" (namely, the implicit promise made by the author to the reader that the *facts* of his life, as recounted, are in the fullest sense true) is scrupulously respected.[1] Manea sees the careful separation between fact and fiction as an ethical obligation and, in this sense, his memoir is both historically and internally verifiable, in the strictest sense. Moreover, the reader feels that even when the author opens fictional "windows" on possibility or dramatizes meditative passages, the end is always the truth, including, to be sure, the personal truth, with its more complicated and ambivalent zones. The memoirist conveys the sense that he feels under a double obligation: to tell the truth, however painful, and not to simplify it, not to resort to formulas or clichés, not to trivialize it. The task of the genuine writer, as Manea knows well, is not to simplify but to *desimplify*. For the truth is never simple.

—

"My exile," Manea writes at the beginning of *The Hooligan's Return*, "which had begun at the age of five because of a dictator and his ideology, came full circle at the age of fifty, because of another dictator and an ideology that claimed to be the opposite of its predecessor." Born in 1936, the future writer was barely five years old in 1941, when the Jewish population of his native Bukovina was deported to concentration camps in Ukraine, in the territory known as Transnistria, by the regime of Marshal Ion Antonescu, the Romanian military dictator and ally of Nazi Germany in World War II. The traumatic episode ended four years later, in 1945, when, together with the survivors in his family, he returned to Romania, only to witness, as he grew up, the transformation of the country into a Stalinist satellite of the Soviet Union under Gheorghiu-Dej and then, after 1965, into a national-communist dictatorship under the ferocious and grotesque rule of Nicolae Ceauşescu, which came to an abrupt and bloody end in 1989. Three years before that, in 1986, Manea, who at the time had been on a fellowship in (then) West Germany, decided not to return to Romania and to live in self-exile in the West—eventually in the United States, where he became a writer-in-residence at Bard College in New York and won a MacArthur Foundation Award and a Guggenheim Fellowship. In 1986, at the age of fifty, he was already a well-known writer in Romania, although barely tolerated by the regime. He had written six books of fiction and two volumes of essays in Romanian, and once the first transla- tions of his prose and essays (in German, French, Dutch, Italian, English, Spanish, and other languages) started appearing after his exile, he was rapidly recognized as one of the outstanding con- temporary writers from Eastern Europe, comparable to a Danilo Kiš, an Ivan Klima, or an Imre Kertész, the recipient of the Nobel Prize for literature in 2005.

In his characteristic style of manifold symbolic allusion, pre- cisely recalled historical detail, and implicit irony and self-irony, Manea explains the origin of *The Hooligan's Return*, his memoir written in America during the last years of the old and the first years of the new century, and published almost simultaneously in its original Romanian version and in English translation.[2] The passage occurs just past the midpoint of his narrative (one notices the narrator's shift between "he" and "I" in his alternate move- ment away and then back to his subjective remembering self): on a rainy day, at an elegant dinner party in New York, while "playing his refugee role in the comedy of the present," as he puts it, the writer, bearer of "the biblical code-name of Noah, not for public use," speaks of himself as a "shipwrecked exile" who, in the course of the conversation, "finds himself telling the company about Transnistria, about the Initiation, about the war, and about Maria, the young peasant woman who was determined to join the Jews on their journey to death. Responding to their interest, he went on to talk about communism and its ambiguities, and about the ambiguities of exile" (p. 224). The next day, he received a letter from the publisher who had hosted the party, urging him to write his life story, which had fascinated the audience: "because you lived and acted at the center of the worst time in history." (As a friend of the author, I can confirm the power of Manea's oral story-telling, the engaging quality of his voice, warm and thought- ful, the mixture of lucid melancholy and brooding humor that transpires from his reminiscences.) Reading the letter, the writer feels at once challenged and obliged—the ethical obligation of testimony—to take up again an enormously difficult task, a task of memory that in fact he had set up for himself a long time before, from the very beginning of his literary career in Romania, in the 1970s, and that he had always tried to fulfill, mostly under the guise of fiction, in his earlier works:[3] to speak about what it means to have been "at the center of the worst time in history," to bear witness. This time he will speak freely in his own name, no longer having to evade the censor by resorting to codes and recondite allusions, and will be addressing an English-speaking reader, even though he can do so only in his "nomadic language," that is, in Romanian, the only language he masters as a writer, a language now in exile that will have to be translated (more about this specific linguistic predicament and its implications later). He is expected to give an account of his life, including his Initiation, to uninitiated readers.

Recounting the circumstances in which the idea of his new book came about, Manea remembers: "Little Noah was initiated into life, as well as its opposite, in Transnistria. First death claimed my beloved grandfather, Avram, then my maternal grandmother, striking twice within three weeks. The sudden magic of lifelessness: the afterlife, in a dead grave without a name. . . . I was alive, thinking about my own death, but what I understood then was that crying and hunger, cold and fear belonged to life, not to death. Nothing was more important than survival, Mother kept saying, as she sought to sustain her husband and son. Death was extinction, which had to be fought at any cost. This was the only way in which we could be worthy of survival, she kept repeating" (p. 227). Of course, the dark theme of the Initiation (a theme with numerous variations, to be taken also in a musical sense) had appeared and reappeared earlier in the chronological zigzag of the memoir, in the apparently haphazard, but in fact carefully thought-out, narrative back-and-forth between the present and various layers of the past. It had been intimated early on, in the chapter "The Beginning before the Beginning," as "the long night of the Initiation. Only there and then (in October 1941) was the comedy about to begin. Transnistria, beyond the Dniestr. Transtristia, beyond sadness" (p. 65). The word "comedy" is used here both ironically and seriously, recalling the sense it was given by a Dante (whose *Comedia* starts with a descent into the Inferno) or by a Balzac, in the famous title of his *Comédie humaine.*

The background historical information, in its brutal factuality, is interspersed throughout the book. It is clearly summarized in the chapter from which I quoted before, "Anamnesis": the order given by Marshal Antonescu for the Jewish population of Bukovina and Bessarabia to be deported and the human tragedy that followed, as seen from the perspective of a five-year old, and then from the perspective of the mature writer. It is interesting and significant to note here that one could not speak straightforwardly about anti-Semitism in Communist Romania: the official line was that the responsibility for the persecution, for the pogroms (of 1941, in Bucharest and in Iaşi), and for the deportations of Jews during World War II was strictly limited to the German Nazis and their Romanian emulators, the members of the notorious Iron Guard, and that once they had been defeated, there was no point in bringing up the issue. The confrontation of the Jew with other forms of anti-Semitism (unofficial and official, more indirect, more hypocritical, less violent overall but no less poisonous) under communism's "compulsory happiness" was of course a taboo subject. It was, for Manea, what he calls "the Initiation after the Initiation" (p. 238) or "a new Initiation" (p. 241) in the same chapter, "Anamnesis." This second Initiation followed an all-too-brief period that started in the spring of 1945, when the nine-year-old child was, as Manea puts it, "restored to fairy-tale normality" (p. 201). The notion of normality as a "fairy tale" is not accidental here. It is recurrent throughout the memoir in reference to the immediate postwar years, and it signifies that, from the perspective of both the first and the second Initiation, normality in the most common and modest sense could appear as indeed unreal, as a state that could only be imagined.

—

The somber theme of life in the "penal colony" of communism had appeared before in the memoir, as well as in previous works, such as *On Clowns* or *Compulsory Happiness*,[4] but it reappears with particular poignancy in "Anamnesis," right after that of the first, indelible Initiation: it is now introduced by the revelation that a close friend, Alin, had been blackmailed by the Romanian communist secret police, or Securitate, to become an informer with the specific task of informing on Manea himself. The friend, amazingly, remains candid in his duplicity: for he confesses that very duplicity to the man he is supposed to inform on: "His usual double-triple life as a socialist citizen was now augmented by a precise, secret, unpaid mission: to report on the double-triple life of his best friend. . . . He continued to provide his reports and keep me informed of their trivial contents until, at last, he decided that he had had enough of the socialist paradise and opted for emigration." But the departure of the informer-friend makes Manea's own situation psychologically much worse: "Alin's replacement was less quick to reveal himself, and I never discovered his identity. The powers above must have refined their criteria for recruitment. I kept an eye on my close contacts, one never knew who the informer might be, every face wore a mask. This apprehension, verging on paranoia, had become so generalized as to be considered the ordinary condition. Anxiety was now a collective possession" (p. 236).

One can only be impressed by Manea's subtle, penetrating, and cogent analysis of the phenomenon of suspicion—the anxiety of imposed suspicion, the particular terror induced by suspicion, against the background of totalitarian terror pure and simple—not only in the chapter from which I have quoted but in the whole book. The main reason for my own emigration from Ceauşescu's Romania, some fourteen years earlier than Manea, was the same sick atmosphere of generalized mistrust that penetrated ever more deeply the everyday life in our native country and that Manea describes with all its painful ambiguities, not ignoring its often ridiculous—humiliatingly ridiculous—aspects. "Compulsory happiness" was of course doubled by compulsory mendacity and, for a writer, whose natural inclination is to be true to himself and to his vision of the world, the consequences of the ever vigilant and ever unpredictable censorship were hugely complex. One can get a sense of this complexity by perusing the essay "Censor's Report" (with regard to Manea's novel *The Black Envelope*,[5] which appeared in a censored version in Romania in 1986 and in an uncensored one, first in English translation, in 1995, and then again in Romanian in 1996). This text, included in the volume *On Clowns: The Dictator and the Artist* (1992), is one of the most detailed and revealing accounts of the functioning of Communist censorship, not only as an institution (which Ceauşescu had officially abolished, although officially it had never existed, and although it could produce confidential "reports" like the one analyzed by the author!), but also as an oppressive ambience of literary day-to-day life. The long fight with the censor, which resulted in the eventual publication of the novel (in an incredibly large print run!) played a major role in Manea's decision to leave Romania for good. I quote from the essay: "The book came out in 1986. The publisher, strangled by the pressure from the censor's office, had to make a profit on every book it put out. Thus he printed twenty-six thousand copies. In twenty years as a published writer, I had never aspired to such an unusually large run. Most probably public interest was aroused by the rumors that flew around any time a book was held up and chopped up by the censor's office. The novel sold out in Bucharest in a few days. My friends assured me that even in the 'substitute version' it had retained its critical acuity and literary originality. The first reviews, highly favorable, appeared in the country's main literary journals in the fall of 1986. In December 1986 I left Romania" (p. 85). In July of the same year the author had celebrated, in Bucharest, his fiftieth birthday.

—

Why did the writer wait so long before emigrating? Emigration for Romanian Jews was possible and, in spite of the hypocrisies of the regime, was even encouraged, secretly and cynically, in exchange for "ransom" in hard currency.[6] What kept Manea in Romania, as he explains, was "language and all the chimeras that it offered—and not only language and its chimeras, but my whole life, of course, with its good and bad, a life of which language and its chimeras were the essence" (p. 191). It took the humiliating experience of wrestling with censorship in order to publish his most ambitious work up to that point in his career, and the disgust with the transformation of the regime along increasingly nationalist, xenophobic, and anti-Semitic lines, during the 1980s, that made him choose exile. (A painstakingly detailed account of this transformation is found in "The History of an Interview" included in On Clowns.) Language, it turned out, did not tie him to a place.

Manea has lived and written in exile for two decades now. Perhaps the most difficult part of this new exile—itself inscribed in the larger historical exile experienced by his people and in the even larger metaphysical exile of human existence—has been linguistic: for he continues to write in Romanian. In The Hooligan's Return, the question of language comes up again and again. One of the memorable metaphors for his language-in-exile (the language of the books he wrote and keeps writing) is that of the "snail's shell"—the title of a chapter and, independently, the title of an earlier book of interviews published in Romania in 1999 (*Casa melcului*).[7] "What if I do not inhabit a country but a language?" is a question by which Manea answered, somewhat evasively, somewhat petulantly, the relatives who urged him not to return to Romania on the occasion of his first trip to the "free world," some ten years before his decision on self-exile (p. 291). At that time, language still seemed to tie him to the country. In his life in Romania, becoming a writer was fulfilling a need for "something else," for "the home that only books can promise. The double exile of the divided ego—was that a redeeming disease? . . . . I had finally found my true home. Language promised not only a rebirth but also a form of legitimization, real citizenship, and real belonging" (p. 208). But if it is the case that "exile begins as soon as we leave the womb," as Manea notes with ambiguous irony at one point, one's home cannot be a specific territory. One's true home—which is also one's "Promised Land"—must always be constructed; how else than by language? When at long last he decides to leave the (geographic) motherland, "all that was left for me to do was to take language, my home, with me. I would be carrying the snail's shell on my back" (ibid.).

The Romanian thinker Emil Cioran, who became a French author of elegantly pessimistic aphorisms after World War II (not only to make a name for himself in a great culture, but also in order to separate himself from an unsavory political past), spoke in his youth, in his flamboyantly nationalistic manifesto *The Transfiguration of Romania* (1936), of "the tragedy of small cultures."[8] He lamented the fact that Romania did not have the political destiny of France and the population of China, but feverishly hoped that it could at least develop an "intermediate culture" and exert, ruthlessly, it goes without saying, hegemony in the less than glamorous region of the Balkans—a vain and, in retrospect, ridiculous hope. However, if we choose to see the cultural world in competitive terms, the notion of "the tragedy of small cultures" is not without a grain of truth. Recently, a French researcher of an orientation totally opposed to that of the young Cioran spoke with perhaps greater (still metaphorical) appropriateness of "the tragedy of translated men."[9] Needless to say, such "tragedies" are symbolic and less overwhelming than the notion of tragedy, even as a cliché, would suggest. It is to Manea's credit that he deals with the problem of his "nomadic language," or, as he sometimes calls it, his "nocturnal language," more subtly and, on occasion, with a playful touch of irony.

A good example of the latter can be found in the chapter entitled "The Home of Being" in *The Hooligan's Return*. Language as "the Home of Being" is a scoffing allusion to Heidegger, to the philosopher's ponderous meditations on ancient Greek and German as the only languages capable of giving expression to true Being. The reader is invited to participate in an imaginative game triggered by a witty postcard the author received from an American friend: "I wish for you, that one morning we will all wake up speaking, reading, and writing Romanian; and that Romanian will be declared the American national language (with the world doing the strange things it is doing today, there is *no reason* for this NOT to happen)" (p. 324). The tone is one of warm friendly teasing, and we must read the whole chapter, which is an extension of the quoted message, in this key, as a semi-serious, semi-self-mocking, semi-poetic, gracefully absurdist personal essay, a genre for which Manea has a genuine knack. It helps him make light of the endless frustrations of finding a good enough English translator for the texts he writes in his "nomadic language," in the language that he carries about as his snail's shell. Being a Romanian writer in exile is not without its irony—one more of "life's little ironies," to use Thomas Hardy's phrase—and Manea deals with this predicament in a variety of ways and tones, ranging from self-questioning exasperation to poetic acceptance. His linguistic identity—as distinct from his other identities, the Jewish one in the first place—is at once the most comprehensive and the most constraining. But constraint, as Manea knows well, can be a source of creativity.

———

Why is Manea's memoir entitled *The Hooligan's Return*? More precisely, what is the meaning of the word *hooligan* in it? In what way are its metaphorical suggestions (always present, however faintly, in a literary title) related to the dictionary meaning of *hooligan* as "ruffian" or "hoodlum" or "thug"? In English, the word has existed since about the turn of the twentieth century, as a derivation from an apparently Irish surname, and has carried unmistakably negative connotations. More recently, *hooligan* and *hooliganism* have referred to the senseless acts of violence perpetrated by frustrated sports (mostly soccer) fans when they are disappointed with a referee decision or with a loss of their team. Obviously, this is not the direction in which to look for an answer to the foregoing questions. *Hooligan* has a particular history in Romania—both in the language of interwar political name-calling and in communism—which is certainly more relevant to the significance of Manea's title. A *hooligan* was, in a general sense, a rebellious, anarchic, violent person, a troublemaker. After the formation of the mystical-terrorist Legionnaire movement (in 1927), the word was often employed by its opponents to designate, derogatorily, a member of the Legion and later, by extension, a fascist thug. But, as happens with such fraught notions, the term developed more ambiguous, sometimes even positive connotations. It could thus be used to characterize the interwar "young generation," or its more active part, attracted to the mystique of revolution and death, as in Mircea Eliade's novel *The Hooligans*, which created a stir when it appeared in 1935. (No mention by name of the Legionnaires or Iron Guards can be found in Eliade's novel, although the allusion, deliberately vague, pointed also in their direction, suggesting that their choice was existential rather than political.) But it is another text, dating also from 1935, namely, Mihail Sebastian's *Cum am devenit huligan* (*How I Became a Hooligan*) that Manea cites and that can help us get a better understanding of his memoir's title.

Sebastian was the pen name of the Jewish Romanian writer Iosif Hechter (1907–1945), a close friend of Eliade until the latter veered to the extreme right in the late 1930s. *How I Became a Hooligan* is a polemical memoir that Sebastian wrote in response to the scandal created in Romania by the appearance, a year before, of his thinly disguised autobiographical novel *De două mii de ani* (For Two Thousand Years). The reason for the scandal was not the novel itself, but its unexpectedly anti-Semitic preface by Nae Ionescu, a charismatic philosophy professor for whom Sebastian had had an ambivalent admiration.[10] (Interestingly, as it results from his posthumous *Journal*,[11] Sebastian continued to visit with Nae Ionescu even after this episode and was shaken by his death in 1940, on which occasion he noted: "Nervous, uncontrollable sobbing as I entered Nae Ionescu's house yesterday morning, two hours after his death.") *De două mii de ani* (For Two Thousand Years) is a novel in the form of a diary about anti-Semitism in Romania, as experienced by the unnamed narrator, an assimilated Jew, a student at the beginning of the book, an accomplished architect at end, when he describes, with pride, the beautiful house he has designed for his intellectual hero, Ghiță Blidaru, who is an easily recognizable portrayal of Nae Ionescu himself in this roman à clef. Sebastian had no way of predicting the transformation undergone by Ionescu between the moment, in 1933, when he had been asked and had accepted the task of writing the preface, and the moment, in 1934, when he completed it. Even though he profoundly disagreed with it, Sebastian decided to publish the book with the preface—hence the scandal and, a year later, *How I Became a Hooligan*. Referring to the latter, Manea writes, clarifying the title of his own book and at the same time hinting at its complexity: "Attacked from all sides, Christians, Jews, liberals, and extremists alike, Sebastian had responded with a sparkling essay, *How I Became a Hooligan*. In a sober and precise tone, he candidly reaffirmed the 'spiritual autonomy' of Jewish suffering, its 'tragic nerve,' the dispute between a 'tumultuous sensibility' and a 'merciless critical spirit,' 'between intelligence at its coolest and passion at its most unbridled.' A hooligan? Did that mean marginal, nonaligned, excluded? 'A Jew from the Danube,' as he called himself with some delight. He defined himself clearly: 'I am not a partisan, I am always a dissident. I can trust only the individual man, but my trust in him is complete.' What does a 'dissident' mean? Someone dissenting even from dissent?" (p. 17).

As for the word *hooligan*, it continued to be used in a new accusatory sense during the years of communism: it meant broadly, in official parlance, an open, vocal opponent of the regime. Hooliganism was a criminal offence in the penal code of communist countries, and the law was often used against political dissidents involved in public protest or what might be construed as public protest. In fact, anyone who voiced disagreement with the policies of the party-state could be accused of this crime. There was no clear borderline between *hooliganism* and *social parasitism*, another serious crime in Soviet Russia, for which a poet who did not belong to the Writers' Union could be judged and sentenced to years of hard labor. I have mentioned the latter, thinking of the great Russian poet Joseph Brodsky who, before becoming an exile in the United States, had been accused precisely of *social parasitism* in the early 1960s. But the main reference intended by Manea's title is without doubt Mihail Sebastian, as Manea himself explained in a recent interview in Romanian with Gabriela Adameşteanu: "Assaulted from all sides for his novel *For Two Thousand Years*, Sebastian was the object of a hooligan attack, being at the same time defined himself as a hooligan, a definition he turned on its head. . . . The questions that obsessed the 'hooligan' Sebastian have a special resonance for those who have lived under dictatorships of the right or the left. . . . My *Hooligan* sees himself as an eternal outsider, as a misfit, a suspect, a marginal, a clown and a loser, an Augustus the Fool forced to experience the traumas of a demented century, a history of bloody convulsions. The eternal exile, exiled again and again, wherever he happens to be."[12]

I remember that after first reading Manea's book in Romanian, but thinking of its intended reader who was not likely to grasp the tangled web of allusions implied in the title, I felt it was not the most felicitous choice. But, at least, "it had punch," as Manea told me. He was right—and doubly so. For, on second thought, I realized that *The Hooligan's Return* was indeed a very good title also because, leaving aside its initial "punch," it reveals its full, complex meaning after one has read the book. The title synthesizes the spirit of the whole memoir, memorably. For a Romanian "competent" and sympathetic reader it has, of course, a different and more immediately graspable significance, which will be confirmed and enriched in the course of the process of reading. The ironic, on occasion polemical (polemical without bitterness, much as in the case of Sebastian), on occasion melancholy, serene, or simply amused self-representation of the author as a "hooligan" is not only a way of internalizing and reacting to the gaze of the Other—the alien gaze that, according to Sartre's famous definition, constitutes the Jew—but also a technique that allows him to convey the ambiguities and paradoxes of his situation in both his native Romania and in the last two decades of exile. As a literary technique—related to what the Russian formalists of the 1920s called the device of *de-familiarization* or *es-*

trangement—the "hooliganism" of this obviously very sensitive, introspective, reflective authorial figure, not seldom defensive to the point of withdrawal and shyness, is a challenge to the non-Romanian reader: a challenge to attention, in the first place. The close attention required to go through this book, sentence by sentence and page by page (this is by no means "an easy read") is always rewarded with uncommon insights into the psychological and human implications of the three major experiences that the author recounts: that of surviving, as a child, the trauma of the Initiation (the Holocaust), that of surviving intellectually and morally the Second Initiation (coming of age and becoming a writer in an ideologically occupied society and language), and that of exile.

When I first read *The Hooligan's Return*, in its original Romanian version, I was impressed not only by the literary qualities of Manea's reflective prose, but also, on a subjective level, by the special evocative power it had for me as a doubly privileged reader: one with a Romanian linguistic identity and, more important, one who has known personally a good number of the people portrayed in the book. The second "privilege" may be actually a disadvantage insofar as the critical reception of a literary work is concerned. But it certainly is an advantage insofar as the act of reading is also always, unavoidably, as Proust insists in his *Remembrance of Things Past*, an act of self-reading: while perusing the text I had the nostalgic opportunity of recalling old friends or close acquaintances from the Bucharest literary life who make fugitive appearances in the memoir, such as the Flying Elephant (Paul Georgescu) and his wife, Donna Alba, the poet nick-named after a character in an old Romanian folktale, Half-Man-Riding, Half-One-Legged-Hare (Florin Mugur), and others.[13] I won't expand on this aspect of my reading. Another aspect deserves to be singled out here: as a linguistic compatriot of the author, in exile myself, I could not ignore the fact that the memoir was primarily addressed to an American reader, although what literary theorists call the "inscribed" or "implied reader" could only be a speaker of Romanian, to be taken in a broad, "extraterritorial" sense. A few years earlier I had published my book *Rereading*, in which I discussed the diverse interpretive demands issued by the diverse figures of the "reader-in-the text," and now I was confronted with an interesting tension between the intended reader and the linguistically implied reader. The intended reader, who was likely to have at best an extremely vague knowledge of the history of Romania between the 1930s and the 1990s, including the fate of the Jewish community in that country, had to be instructed by the text in order to be able to grasp the personal and collective drama the author tries to present, with its human complexities and nuances. The Romanian-speaking reader was challenged in a different way: his or her likely gaps in the knowledge of the real history of the period covered by the memoir were the result of Communist and National-Communist falsifications of the historical record for its changing ideological purposes (one must take into account the fact that the regime lasted for more than four decades). For the latter, the real challenge was that of coming to terms with a painful truth.

A few words about the way Manea's memoir is constructed are in order here. The narrative, which does not follow a chronological order, is divided into three large sections, the first two being separated from the last by the chapter, "Anamnesis," from which I have quoted. The first part, "Preliminaries," refers to the present and recent past and starts with the anxieties of the author, residing now in New York City, before he decided to undertake a short trip to Romania, after almost a decade in exile. The second part, entitled "The First Return (The Past as Fiction)," is a descent into the past, both personal and historical, and it contains, alongside evocations of family and friends (there stand out the portraits of his "strict and authoritarian" father who, thirteen years after returning from Transnistria, was to become an inmate in the Communist Gulag, at Periprava; and that of his "anxious, enterprising, passionate, fatalistic" mother, pages of self-analysis and meditations on the writer's craft). The third major part, bearing the title "The Second Return (Posterity)," is a day-by-day description of Manea's trip to Romania between April 20 and May 2, 1997, interrupted by numerous flashbacks that maintain the narrative tension, the constant if always unpredictable alternation between present and past.

Since his leaving Romania in 1986, many things had changed in that country, but under different appearances many had stayed almost the same: communism had collapsed and Ceauşescu had been executed (in December of 1989), but former high-level party apparatchiks, converted overnight into "democrats," continued to rule the country, directly or from the wings. The still powerful Securitate, dominated by Nationalist Communists, was ready to co-opt older extreme nationalists. A secret police Communist–Fascist alliance was rumored to have been concluded, and it seemed to be confirmed by a mysterious assassination that had occurred—of all places—in the United States of America: Professor Ioan Petru Culianu was shot in the Divinity School building of the University of Chicago, on May 21, 1991. Culianu's is the first Romanian name occurring in Manea's book, in the very first chapter, and his murder is important for understanding the author's hesitations before the trip to his native country: "The unsolved mystery of the assassination," Manea writes, "had, naturally, encouraged speculation—the relations between the young Culianu and his mentor, the noted scholar of religion, Mircea Eliade, with whose help he had been brought to America; his relations with the Romanian community in Chicago, with Romania's exiled king, his interest in parapsychology. There was, in addition, the Iron Guard connection, that movement of extreme right-wing nationalists whose members were known as *legionari*, the Legionnaires. The Iron Guard, which Mircea Eliade had supported in the 1930s, still had adherents among Romanian expatriates of Chicago. It was said that Culianu was on the verge of a major reassessment of his mentor's political past. The Chicago murder, it was true, coincided with the publication of my own article about Eliade's Legionnaire past, in *The New Republic*, in 1991. I had been warned by the FBI to be cautious in my dealings with my compatriots, and not only with them" (pp. 9–10).

Manea's apprehensions before he eventually went to Romania in April of 1997 were justified, as he explains, by some vicious attacks in the Romanian press, in response to his 1991 review of Eliade's memoirs. Mircea Eliade (1907–1986), one of the internationally best-known Romanian intellectuals of the last century, an exile after World War II, author of many books translated into many languages, respected in American academic circles as one of the founders of the discipline of the history of religions, had in the 1970s published substantial fragments from his personal diaries and memoirs,[14] in which he never addressed his embarrassing association with the Iron Guard. Only in the posthumously published second volume of his autobiography did he mention it, briefly and misleadingly.[15] Manea's article in *The New Republic* (included later in *On Clowns*, under the title "Felix Culpa") focused on Eliade's evasions and provided the historical information necessary for an understanding of such evasions, attempting to initiate a broader ethical debate about the responsibility not only of Eliade but also of a highly gifted generation of Romanian intellectuals in the period preceding the outbreak of World War II, a generation of which Eliade was the acknowledged leader.

Why had most of them (with the important exception of Eugen Ionescu/Eugène Ionesco and Mihail Sebastian) supported an extreme right-wing ideology? What had been the consequences of such a wrong-headed commitment? How could Romanian culture, now freed from the dogmas of communism, come to terms with its own history? By 1991, Eliade's public support for the Iron Guard in the late 1930s (forgotten for a long time with the help of Communist censorship!) had been partially documented, among others, by a careful American researcher, a former student of Eliade himself.[16] However, it was Manea's article, which was also published in Romania's liberal post-1989 periodical 22, that triggered a controversy in Romania. The recently reborn extreme right-wing Bucharest press (now openly espousing both fascist and Communist ideas) described Manea as a Jewish detractor of a great Romanian scholar and writer. Even more moderate voices reproached Manea for exaggerating the "youthful sins" of a towering cultural figure like Eliade at a time when the more urgent task was to consider the cases of major Romanian writers who had opportunistically collaborated with the Communist regime. Manea's few defenders understood, however, that he had, beyond the case study of Eliade's selective amnesia, attempted to call attention to a larger problem: the tragic failures of a highly gifted generation (a new version of what Julien Benda had called "la trahison des clercs" or "the betrayal of the intellectuals") and the implications of its refusal to confront and assume their past mistakes.[17] Essentially, what Manea would have expected from a great intellectual like Eliade, whose work he respects, and even more so from someone almost obsessively preoccupied with autobiography, would have been a candid and reflexive self-examination. Subsequent research has come to a similar conclusion: for instance, the young historian Florin Turcanu, in his massive biography of Eliade in French, devotes one full and well-documented chapter to "The Impossible Avowal."[18] Manea's article has the merit of having opened a necessary ethical debate, a debate that continues still today, fifteen years after its publication, and not only in Romania. Read in light of what has been said by both apologists and critics on the questions it raised, "Felix Culpa" strikes one by its balanced thoughtfulness.[19]

———

The last part of the memoir, "The Second Return (Posterity)"—which, in the musical-like composition of the book, can be seen as a distant variation on "The First Return (The Past as Fiction)"—relates in detail the author's visit to Romania, in the spring of 1997. The trip was undertaken at the friendly insistence of Leon Botstein, the President of Bard College, a musician who had been invited to conduct the Bucharest Philharmonic Orchestra and who also had a special interest in the work of the Romanian composer, George Enescu—he wanted to get acquainted with the Enescu archive kept in Bucharest. Interestingly, as we learn at the very end of the book, the abundant notes Manea took during the trip were forgotten on the plane (on the author's return flight), and attempts to retrieve them had been fruitless. Thus, all the extensive notations in what the first-time reader of the book normally would have considered transcriptions from a travel diary turn out to be reconstructions from memory—an amazingly precise memory. As for the accidental loss of the original diary, it clearly falls within the category of the Freudian slip, or parapraxis. Such accidents, as Freud explains in *The Psychopathology of Everyday Life*, are the equivalent of symptoms insofar as they express a compromise between the conscious intention of the subject and his unconscious desire. Commenting on Freud's insight, Jacques Lacan notes that any instance of parapraxis is at the same time a *discours réussi*, a "successful discourse," a felicitous expression of an inner conflict. In Manea's case, we can metaphorically expand Lacan's observation to the whole of the "The Second Return" and say that the accidental loss of his notebook (pointing to his profound ambivalence with regard to the country of his birth and its culture) has become the occasion of a second "successful discourse": the text itself, its writing from memory being at once a literary act and a sustained, lengthy self-analysis and self-therapy. The whole book, in fact, may convey an indirect, subtle sense of the therapeutic virtues of writing. At any rate, a close perusal of "The Second Return"—which, I repeat, may be difficult, even taxing for someone unfamiliar with the history of East European Jewry in the twentieth century—will enable the reader to understand the symbolic significance of the loss of a notebook on the seat of an airplane and of the loser's creative response not only to this particular loss but also to loss in general. It throws a retrospective and retroactive light on the memoir in its entirety. In this light, its overarching theme is none other than that of loss: loss regained in the act of remembering and of writing.

Notes

1. For the notion of "autobiographical pact," see Philippe Lejeune, *On Autobiography*, ed. Paul John Eakin, trans. Katherine Leary (Minneapolis: University of Minnesota Press, 1989).

2. Norman Manea, *Intoarcerea huliganului* (Iaşi: Polirom, 2003) and *The Hooligan's Return: A Memoir*, trans. Angela Jianu (New York: Farrar Straus and Giroux, 2003). Subsequent page references are to this translation. By now, the book has been translated into German, Italian, and Spanish, and a French version is due out soon. The Spanish translation, by Joaquin Garrigos, was selected by the cultural supplement of the newspaper *La Vanguardia* as the best foreign book published

in Spain in 2005 (among the contenders were books by Ian McEwan, Kazuo Ishiguro, and Haruki Murakami).

3. See, among others, the stories included in *October, Eight O'Clock* (New York: Grove Weidenfeld, 1992). Particularly powerful are "The Sweater" and "Proust's Tea." The latter is the title story of the French volume *Le Thé de Proust et autres nouvelles* (Paris: Albin Michel, 1990).

4. See Norman Manea, *On Clowns: The Dictator and the Artist* (New York: Grove Weidenfeld, 1992) and *Compulsory Happiness* (Evanston, Ill.: Northwestern University Press, 1994). See also my review of *On Clowns* in *World Literature Today* (Winter 1994): 111–112.

5. For the English translation, see Norman Manea, *The Black Envelope*, translated from the Romanian by Patrick Camiller (New York: Farrar, Straus and Giroux, 1995). I reviewed this book when it came out. See Matei Calinescu, "Totalitarianism's Mad Mysteries," in *The Boston Sunday Globe* of June 11, 1995.

6. See Radu Ioanid, *The Ransom of the Jews: The Story of Extraordinary Secret Bargain between Romania and Israel* (Chicago: Ivan R. Dee, 2005).

7. Norman Manea, *Casa melcului* (Bucureşti: Editura Hasefer, 1999).

8. For an enlightening discussion of this book, and more broadly of Cioran's Romanian writings, see Marta Petreu, *An Infamous Past: E. M. Cioran and the Rise of Fascism in Romania*, with a foreword by Norman Manea (Chicago: Ivan R. Dee, 2005). See also my article "'How Can One Be What One Is?' Reading the Romanian and the French Cioran" in *Salmagundi* 112 (Fall 1996): 192–215.

9. See the chapter thus titled in Pascale Casanova's *The World Republic of Letters*, trans. M. B. DeBevoise (Cambridge.: Harvard University Press, 2004), 254–302.

10. For a discussion of Sebastian's novel in its historical context, see my article "Romania's 1930s Revisited" in *Salmagundi* 97 (Winter 1993): 133–151.

11. See Mihail Sebastian, *Jurnal, 1935–1944*, text îngrijit de Gabri-

ela Omăt, prefaţă şi note de L. Volovici (Bucureşti: Humanitas, 1996). For the English version, see Mihail Sebastian, *Journal, 1935–1944, The Fascist Years,* trans. Patrick Camiller, introduction and notes by Radu Ioanid (Chicago: Ivan R. Dee, 2000). Manea published an article on Sebastian's *Journal* in *The New Republic,* on April 28, 1998, which also appeared in Romanian, in *22* (June 9–15, 1998) and was reprinted in the second edition of *Despre clovni: Dictatorul şi artistul* (Iaşi: Polirom, 2005).

12. "'Cum suportă individul şocurile istoriei': Norman Manea în dialog cu Gabriela Adameşteanu," in *Observator cultural,* 19–25 ianuarie 2006.

13. These and other Romanian friends are also portrayed in a more recent book in Romanian, one of Manea's best, *Plicuri şi portrete* (Envelopes and Portraits) (Iaşi: Polirom, 2004).

14. See Mircea Eliade, *Fragments d'un journal* (Paris: Gallimard, 1973); *No Souvenirs: Journal, 1957–1969,* translated from the French by Fred H. Johnson, Jr. (New York: Harper & Row, 1977); *Autobiography, Volume I, 1907–1937, Journey East, Journey West,* translated from the Romanian by Mac Linscott Ricketts (San Francisco: Harper & Row, 1981).

15. Mircea Eliade, *Autobiography,* Volume II, *Exile's Odyssey: 1937–1960,* translated from the Romanian by Mac Linscott Ricketts (Chicago: University of Chicago Press, 1988).

16. Mac Linscott Ricketts, *Mircea Eliade: The Romanian Roots, 1907–1945* (Boulder, Colo.: East European Monographs, 1988), 2 vols.

17. One of the few members of this generation who resisted the pull of the Legionnaire ideology was Eugen Ionescu who, twenty years later, as the French playwright Eugène Ionesco, used his painful personal experience of the late 1930s in his allegorical play *Rhinoceros* (1959). However, the collective hysteria described in the play (involving the grotesque metamorphosis of people into rhinoceroses) symbolizes more broadly any form of regimentation in the name of an extremist ideology, right or left, fascist or Communist. For a detailed discussion of this play, see my "Ionesco and *Rhinoceros*: Personal and Political Back-

grounds" in *East European Politics and Societies* 9, no. 3 (Fall 1995): 393–432; also, the chapter devoted to it in my book, in French, *Ionesco: Recherches identitiaires* (Paris: Oxus, 2006), 223–246.

18. Forin Turcanu, *Mircea Eliade, le prisonnier de l'histoire* (Paris: La Découverte, 2003), "L'impossible aveu," pp. 477–498.

19. On the broad theme of Eliade's intellectual generation, see also my article "The 1927 Generation in Romania: Friendships and Ideological Choices (Mihail Sebastian, Mircea Eliade, Nae Ionescu, Eugène Ionesco, E. M. Cioran)" in *East European Politics and Societies* 15, no. 3 (Fall 2001): 649–677.

Writing about Uprootedness

— *Henryk Grynberg*

I had been uprooted a long time before coming to America. First, when I became homeless at the age of six, I had to hide like an animal or criminal, forget I had ever been a Jew, and assume a gentile Christian identity. A couple of years later, among orphaned and semi-orphaned Jewish children, I was taught to shed that assumed identity and return to a Jewish world that was barely there. As soon as I managed to do so, my school changed its direction and instructed me to become an atheist and internationalist, to assimilate into an imaginary world where there were no such divisions as gentile and Jew. A few years later, however, after another evolutionary turn, those divisions became relevant again. Uprooted once more, I found a shelter in a semi-real Jewish theater and at the same time turned inward, into the world of writing. My first short story described a work crew charged with exhuming the victims of mass executions; a subsequent collection of my short stories carried that piece's title, "The Antigone Crew" (*Ekipa Antygona*, Warsaw 1963); and, ever since, critics have characterized my writing as exhumation in a literary sense.

I began to write and publish at about the same time that Truman Capote invented the "nonfiction novel," as he termed his

In Cold Blood. I didn't know the term, or the book, or even his name, but I have written nonfiction short stories and novellas and novels ever since. For personal and/or legal reasons, I sometimes used fictitious names, and for reasons of literary condensation, I developed the method of the composite, which I now regret because the reality of those true stories should have overruled (even at the expense of literary shape and form) their young author's ambition to become a fiction writer. It must have been a trend at that time. Similarly, Elie Wiesel's *Night*, which is treated now as a memoir, was upon its publication in English in 1960 often regarded as a novel. Jerzy Kosinski's *Painted Bird* underwent an even more complicated evolution: a third-person narrative about the horrific ordeals of a displaced child, it was originally presented as a universal parable (with an appropriately grotesque scene from Bosch on the cover); later it was "authenticated" as an autobiographical Holocaust story; and eventually it was proven to be entirely a work of fiction.

My subject was Jewish, but my language was Polish — which meant my work spanned a deep cultural divide. In the lifetime of Julian Tuwim, a Jew had to abandon his heritage if he wanted to become a Polish poet. I never acquiesced to this kind of uprooting, though I did hear remarks that "Grynberg should make up his mind whether he is a Polish writer or a Jewish writer." By the late 1950s, the Yiddish theater in Poland resembled a monument in an abandoned graveyard. For me that meant again a balancing act between the living and the dead, between cultures, between worlds — not necessarily a disadvantage from an artistic point of view. I took several trips to the West (in 1959, 1963, 1965), but always returned. I was often asked, "What do you have back there?" and replied: my Polish language and my Jewish theater.

But that special niche of mine didn't last long, either. An "anti-Zionist" campaign in the aftermath of the 1967 Arab–Israeli war turned into anti-Semitic hysteria, not unlike that in Germany of the 1930s, resulting in a mass emigration not much different from deportation. Those painful events, which peaked in March 1968, surprised the few Holocaust survivors who, for various personal reasons, tried to stay in Poland in spite of everything. I wrote about that stage of my uprooting on several occasions and have returned to it again in my latest autobiographical novel, *Refugees*: "It wasn't the first time, or the first homeland that had betrayed the Jews, yet I was taken by surprise. I thought that this ugliest of things was already in the past and could not repeat itself, particularly in a country soaked in Jewish blood. Yet again it turned out that logic had nothing to do with it, and I could see right through it, as in the joke about the Soviet x-ray: *Yah tiebia, blad', na skvoz' vizhu!* (I can see through you, you son of a bitch!). It was the same old *świństwo*, in German *Schweinerei*, both derived from swine, as something swine apparently do. English doesn't seem to have a word for it. All that Hemingway could find in his vocabulary was 'just a dirty trick,' but he never mentioned this one—the dirtiest trick of all and one that went on forever. After what I had remembered from childhood, I knew I could not endure anything like it a second time. I wasn't afraid. I felt anger. I would not let them do it to me again. I would not give the bastards the pleasure. I felt contempt."

At about the same time, the censors emasculated my novella, cutting out all the key Jewish elements. Uprooted not only as a Jew but also as a writer, I no longer would have been able to fulfill my duty, and so I followed the old Jewish dictum—though without knowing it at the time—that if you can't study the Torah at home, you should leave your home. On the other hand, where or what was my home? For Tuwim, home or homeland was his Polish language (*ojczyzna-polszczyzna*). In my case, this was only partly so, because—as a friend once pointed out to me—I "continue to imaginatively inhabit the small towns and villages of Poland whose Jewish populations were almost entirely destroyed."

A proof of that is in my collection of short stories, *Drohobycz, Drohobycz* (Warsaw 1997). Subtitled, in the English-language edition (Penguin Books, 2000), *"True Tales from the Holocaust and Life After,"* they are narrated by uprooted and dispersed child survivors from such towns and villages. We share a common fate, and I thoroughly identify with my narrators. Treating their stories as my own, I wrote most of them in the first person. I speak for them, but at the same time they speak for me and give me another opportunity to express my own thoughts and feelings. They felt the need to tell me their stories, and I felt compelled to retell them as variations of my own and as parts of our collective experience.

The *Drohobycz, Drohobycz* tales are different from Holocaust stories that tend to follow a pattern: idyll—disaster—flight or fight for survival—victory of good over evil—and a sort of happy ending. In the *Drohobycz, Drohobycz* collection, as in the real world, there was no such thing as an idyll, no true victory of good over evil, and no happy ending, nor even catharsis. An Oscar-winning documentary film tells about a young Jewish woman who survived deportation and slave-labor camps, married her liberator, who happened to be a Jewish officer in the American Army, had children with him and later grandchildren—a classic happy ending. But for most, the real story does not end there. As various studies show, the trauma and post-traumatic stress syndrome of Holocaust survivors is frequently transmitted to their children and grandchildren, often with devastating effect. A child survivor from Slovakia told her story to an audience at the United States Holocaust Memorial Museum. I have condensed it in verses:

> **I**
>
> When they were taking away our shul
> Grandpa carried out the Torah
> and we prayed at home

when they were pulling out his beard
he became speechless
and prayed in silence

when they were driving us out of our home
he took the scroll with him
because you can't live without the Torah

when they drove us off the train
and ordered us to drop our luggage he disobeyed
because you can't drop the Torah

they beat him yet he held on
although we begged him
Grandpa what are you doing

and so they beat him even more
reassured it was a treasure
—as it was

II
Mother firmly held our hands
and when they tore our youngest brother away
she ran after him

they pushed her away yet she wouldn't heed
they beat her but she ran
to the other side

and I have remained so that I could pass down
to children and grandchildren
what we are made of

It sounds like an epitome of another first-person narrative from *Drohobycz, Drohobycz,* but the ending, although not entirely happy, could be deemed cathartic. This pleased me, because, as we know, good poetry should pass on a glimmer of hope. I entitled the poem "Jewish Treasures" and wanted to dedicate it to the narrator using her original Jewish name, which I didn't know. But when I called her, she could barely speak, because she had just lost her grandson. She wouldn't tell me the cause of his death.

"The world had ended and I was supposed to go on living. I didn't know how," says a teenage girl in the conclusion of one of the *Drohobycz, Drohobycz* tales. Most of the other narrators also faced this existential question. Their trauma did not end when they returned to empty homes and hometowns. It followed them to America, Australia, even to Israel. In her collection of short stories entitled *Osmaleni* (in English, *Scorched*), Irit Amiel, originally from Częstochowa, depicts tragic endings of uprooted child survivors who, like herself, sought refuge in Israel, the country that, it was hoped, would put an end to all Jewish tragedies. The title, *Scorched*, refers to the flames of the Holocaust. One of the author's scorched protagonists tries to flee from his past by assuming the false identity of a native Israeli, a *sabra*. In vain, for his past catches up with him.

The extreme uprootedness of Holocaust survivors and the lasting post-traumatic stress that follows them everywhere keep looking for a writer. No wonder this leitmotif reappears in almost everything I have produced on paper. My cycle of autobiographical tales—*Żydowska wojna* (The Jewish War; Warsaw, 1965), *Zwycięstwo* (The Victory; Paris, 1969), *Życie ideologiczne* (Ideological Life; London, 1975), *Życie osobiste* (Personal Life; London, 1979), *Ojczyzna* (Fatherland; in *Kultura*, Paris, 2/1970–1/1971), *Kadisz* (Kaddish; Kraków, 1987), and *Uchodźcy* (Refugees; Warsaw, 2004)—depicts stages of that uprootedness from Holocaust-era Poland to the United States today. Although written in the first person, these tales do not concentrate on the author–narrator. The main heroes of *The Jewish War* (as indicated by the titles of its two parts) are the father and the mother; in *The Victory* they are the mother and stepfather; in *Ideological Life,* they are the young generation represented by the pronoun

we; in *Personal Life*, despite the title, an epic background domi-
nates; in *Kaddish* (also known as *California Kaddish*), the main
protagonists are again the mother and the stepfather; in *Refugees*, the main heroes are both the Jews and gentiles of a wrecked
generation, demoralized in childhood by their exposure to total
war and immediately after by a totalitarian system, and uprooted
even before they left their home country, like the protagonists of
my earlier autobiographical and biographical tales. My autobiographical novella, *Fatherland*, is aimed at describing the core of
uprootedness. In the middle of the story, the young narrator, who
for the first time in twenty years takes a bus to his native village, is
astounded to realize that in less than two hours he could return
to places he "once heard in distant conversations" and thought
they existed only in the past. He arrives at a bitter definition of
fatherland when he finds the site where his father was murdered
and buried purposely defiled by human feces; thereafter, the narrator decides to flee and join the refugees in faraway lands where
"no one will come and shit on our grave. For my son who will
bury me that may be very important. For that is just what is meant
by fatherland. . . ."

Bogdan Wojdowski—whom I have called "my brother" in my
foreword to the American edition of his masterpiece novel, *Chleb
rzucony umarłym* (*Bread for the Departed*, Northwestern University Press, 1997), never left his native Warsaw, yet uprootedness
was always his main subject. "Not a single house stands here in its
place, not even a tram stop; streets and squares carry new names,
bridges span new shores; soon there will be not a single stone
in the place where the bricklayer had put it." That's just a sam-
ple from his collection of short stories, *Mały człowieczek, nieme
ptaszę, klatka i świat* (A Little Man, a Mute Birdie, a Cage and
the World Warsaw; 1975). Wojdowski's acute case of uprootedness ended with his suicide in 1994 (three years after Kosinski's).
Hanna Krall, another Jewish child survivor who has remained

in her hometown of Warsaw, is a reporter for whom "the world that existed before the Shoah is like a lost civilization." Her short stories, or reports from the past, are desperate attempts at recovering and preserving the "archeological" remnants that Wojdowski had in mind.

I was born in a Warsaw hospital, but my home was the countryside some forty miles away, halfway between Warsaw and Treblinka. When my mother and I returned to her home shtetl after our two-year Holocaust odyssey, only a dozen Jews of the entire vicinity were still alive. After the war ended my hometown was Łódź, where I spent whatever remained of my childhood. Warsaw became my home in 1954, when I enrolled in the university there, and remained home until my 1967 escape to my mother and stepfather in Southern California, where they are now buried at a well-kept Jewish cemetery. I liked sunny California, my new home, but was unable to make a decent living there; subsequently, I accepted a federal job in gloomy, bureaucratic Washington, D.C., where I immediately felt like a real exile. And so where is my home? My writing proves that it is mainly in the past. "Only the past is faithful like a dog," I have concluded in a poem. An echo of that statement reverberates also in *Refugees:* "Polański made universal films, Komeda wrote universal music, Mrożek had his abstract theatre, I continued my Polish-Jewish story which wasn't that universal, but it followed me like a dog." This specific condition of mine is contrasted there with the situation of Marek Hłasko, a gentile refugee of my generation, who became helpless as a writer, because "everything [he] could write about had remained in Poland" and in the present, which—contrary to the past—you can't take with you; and so "he was constantly short of material, while I had it in abundance, even more than I could carry; he sought stories and worked hard to invent them, while my stories sought *me* and caught up with me wherever I went."

The *Drohobycz, Drohobycz* tales caught up with me at meet-

ings of Child Survivors of the Holocaust or at similar social en-
counters, in one case as far away as Australia. One narrator called
from Boston, because his former schoolmate from Drohobycz, a
historian, had sent him protocols from prewar debates of the Polish parliament over the "Jewish question" along with anti-Semitic
articles from the press of that time. An emotional note in my call-
er's voice told me that he carried a painful story in need of a writer. That is the genesis of the title tale in *Drohobycz, Drohobycz*,
which I illustrated by those excerpts from the Polish press of the
mid—and late—1930s. Titles of other stories, such as "A Family," "A Family Sketch," "A Brother in Volhynia," "Cousin Benito,"
indicate a common denominator: the family as the main root,
its destruction, and desperate attempts to restore it. My narrators
often didn't know the historical background of their experiences.
I searched Polish sources, Yad Vashem archives, and protocols
of German courts to verify their recollections and put them in
perspective. "Escape from Borysław" came to me from Israel in a
compilation of a young girl's songs and fragmentary notes. After
interviewing her in Haifa, I composed her story in the form of
an orphan's complaint, integrating the rhythm and some phrases
of her folkloric sing-song verses. My protagonist liked my job so
much that she had it translated into Hebrew and published in
Ha'aretz under her own name with mine mentioned in a foot-
note. I wrote my *Drohobycz, Drohobycz* stories like condensed,
emotionally charged poems. On the other hand, I see them as
nonfiction mini-novels, short and sketchy because that's all my
young narrators were able to take away and save in their minds
and hearts.

The protocols of prewar Polish parliamentary sessions came
in handy in *Memorbuch* (Warsaw, 2000), a biographical novel
upon which I stumbled in Stockholm. Invited by fellow refugees
to deliver a keynote address on the thirtieth anniversary of the
anti-Jewish campaign that forced us out of our homeland, I met

the daughters of the late Adam Bromberg. They offered me his taped and transcribed recollections. Born in 1912 in Lublin as the child of a wealthy Jewish family, Bromberg became a Communist activist in his school years and, subsequently, a political prisoner, a slave in a Soviet labor camp, a frontline political officer in the Communist Polish army, a Communist dignitary, and a major Polish publisher of international renown. Arrested during the anti-Semitic campaign of the late 1960s, he faced a show-trial on fabricated charges, but was released due to pressure from abroad and with significant help from his business partner, the tycoon British publisher Robert Maxwell. Bromberg ended up as a refugee in Sweden, where he managed to establish another successful publishing house. This story of self-uprooted, misguided Polish Jewish intelligentsia had epic proportions, but the material, chaotic and incomplete, needed a great deal of research, including consultations and interviews with my hero's relatives and acquaintances. I wrote it in the first person, as I did most of the *Drohobycz, Drohobycz* tales, and it reads like an autobiographical novel. However, I am not the late Bromberg's ghostwriter. The basic raw material was his, but the product with its vast background, interpretations, and conclusions, is mine. As in *Drohobycz, Drohobycz*, I often applied the protagonist's language and style, but I am the composer of the narrative and the painter of the portraits, including his, for which he served as a model. *Drohobycz, Drohobycz* and *Memorbuch* may be classified as memoir literature because both are strictly based on testimonies and documents; nothing is invented. The books are, respectively, a collection of nonfiction short stories and a nonfiction novel. The title *Memorbuch* is taken from the chronicles of medieval Jewish communities in the German-language lands. These books contain detailed accounts of persecution and destruction and often were carried by the exiles and refugees from one country to another. The main point of my modern *Memorbuch* is thus stress on the similarities between anti-Jewish persecutions in the Middle Ages and in the Nazi period, and even after that.

Łódź, the town of my school years, always catches my attention, and so after thoroughly reading *The Chronicle of the Łódź Ghetto* (Yale University Press, 1984), edited by the historian Lucjan Dobroszycki, a former inmate of the Łódź ghetto and fellow refugee, I called *Commentary*, where I had previously published an essay on attempts at dejudaizing the Holocaust ("Appropriating the Holocaust," *Commentary*, November 1982), and offered to write an article that would exonerate Chaim Rumkowski, the head of the Łódź ghetto's self-rule, whose innocence is apparent in selected documents of the Yale publication. Besides, I knew that the Jewish Children's Home near Łódź, where I had spent three very formative years of my post-Holocaust life, had been established by Rumkowski, and I remembered his portrait hanging in the main entrance hall until 1949, when it was replaced with Maxim Gorki's. "No, thanks," said *Commentary*, whose editors informed me that a reliable conference on Rumkowski has already arrived at different conclusions. I asked Doctor Dobroszycki for the unpublished parts of the chronicles. A true historian, he refused. But Shmuel Krakowski—also a historian, a former inmate of the Łódź ghetto, and a fellow refugee—sent me from Yad Vashem the microfilms that he had smuggled out of Poland in 1968.

The self-ruled Łódź ghetto was a self-organized slave labor camp. Its inmates included deportees from Prague, Berlin, Hamburg, and Cologne. The original ghetto chronicles, especially those written in German, detail the helplessness of the ill-adjusted foreign Jews. The complete chronicles reveal the inner mechanisms of the Holocaust, and Rumkowski appears in them as a much more ambiguous figure than in the Yale edition. Presumptuous, pretentious, and pompous, basking in the appearances of his power and capable of unscrupulous means to retain it, he yet believed he should do whatever he could to save at least part of the ghetto (even though at a very high cost). He almost succeeded. The Łódź ghetto lasted until late August 1944 and could have survived longer had Stalin not stopped the Soviet offensive, allowing the Germans to bleed the 1944 Warsaw insurrection to death and to deport the last seventy thousand Jewish inmates to Auschwitz. Thus, instead of writing Rumkowski's defense, I wrote an epic drama, *Kronika* (first published by a Polish émigré press in West Berlin in 1987, revived by the Marie Curie-Skłodowska University Press, Lublin 2005). It is composed of selected sentences or parts of sentences, skipping the redundancies of the bureaucratic style, and squeezing two thousand pages into two hundred. The chronicles were written by employees of the ghetto archives under the orders and supervision of Rumkowski himself but without the knowledge of the German authorities. While playing up to the boss and defending him in a potential court of posterity, the chroniclers used caution and circumspection just in case their writings were to fall into German hands. Even under these restraints, they managed to leave a precious documented picture of the behavior and mentality of a highly organized, terrorized, and corrupted society that is not necessarily a thing of the past. The Łódź ghetto chronicles convinced me once again that Holocaust literature could do without fiction. All I needed as a writer was to select from the mass and weight of the existing material and put it in a shape and form that could reach a lay audience.

I used the same method of sifting sentences and parts of sentences in *Pamiętnik Marii Koper* (Kraków, 1993), an emotional diary of a Jewish woman who hid for two years in a barn and wrote to maintain sanity. The original document, deposited at Yad Vashem among hundreds of first-person accounts, would have remained there in its wordy, often ungrammatical, unpublishable form, had it not been shown to me by the diarist's daughter. As in *Drohobycz, Drohobycz* and *Memorbuch*, I applied my personal writing skills while trying to preserve the language, style, and voice of the narrator.

A Polish researcher telephoned me from the Stanford Hoover Institute: she had come across the so-called *Palestinian Protocols* that included testimonies of 871 Jewish children who in 1939 got out of Nazi-occupied Poland only to be deported in 1940 with their families to Soviet slave labor camps. They lost many members of their families in Siberia; then, under pressure from Western Allies, they were released in 1941 and allowed to starve as homeless people in the overcrowded, typhus-infected cities of Soviet Central Asia, where they suffered even heavier losses; eventually, as orphans and semi-orphans, they were evacuated in 1942 by the Polish (Anders) Army to Iran and from there by the Jewish Agency to Palestine. Speaking of uprootedness! Eliminating the wooden, bureaucratic language of the protocols, I selected phrases and sentences from their testimonies and arranged them in an oratorio of voices entitled *Children of Zion*. The children came mostly from small towns and villages of the borderlands between the German and Soviet zones. Their stories start with the destruction of those little known or unknown Jewish communities that had begun as early as September–October 1939, well before the "final solution." They also testify to the fact that inhuman mass deportations by cargo trains and slave labor camps were not exclusively a Nazi practice, which raises some moral issues, including the question of why a country that has become a major exporter of increasingly lucrative oil, natural gas, and nuclear technology is not even asked to pay compensations for the slave labor and the death of hundreds of thousands of innocent foreign civilians?

To the same genre, which I call "documentary prose," belongs *Dziedzictwo*, or *Inheritance* (London, 1993; Warsaw, 2005), a composition of dialogues recorded before, during, and immediately after the filming of the documentary *Miejsce urodzenia,* or *Birthplace,* in 1992, when I first returned to Poland to exhume and rebury the remains of my father. The term *documentary prose* seems appropriate also for the first-person narrative *Szmuglerzy* (Smugglers; Warsaw, 2001), based on the wartime experiences of a teenage gentile, Janek Kostański. He had his recollections tape-recorded, transcribed, translated, and self-published under the title *Janek: A Gentile in the Warsaw Ghetto* (Melbourne, 1998), yet the story remained disorganized and lacked chronology, continuity, and clarity, not unlike Bromberg's raw material for the *Memorbuch.* But Kostański was still alive and, after some thirty hours of phone interviews, I managed to fill most of the gaps. The teenage protagonist and his immediate family had a close relationship with their Jewish neighbors, helping them to survive first in the Warsaw ghetto and later on the "Aryan side." Janek remained with them even after the August 1944 uprising, in the totally destroyed city—a condition portrayed in the story of the pianist from Roman Polanski's famous film, *The Pianist.* After liberation, both Kostański and his mother married into the family, and, in 1958, when revived anti-Semitism in Poland became unbearable, emigrated with them to Australia. His story is a unique gentile insider's eyewitness account of the destruction of the Warsaw ghetto. I had never before encountered a Polish gentile who so completely identified with the fate of the Jews in the Holocaust. At one point, he and his mother tried even to follow their Jewish friends to Treblinka in the hope of getting them released. "If an anti-Semite reads this," says Jan Kostański. "I want him to know that I have always been and remained a Pole and a Christian. But I am also an enemy of racism and dictatorship, and that's why I emigrated with my wife and children. I miss Warsaw and its Old Town, where I was born and grew up, and I have never stopped loving my homeland." This very special case of uprootedness was one more reason why I felt compelled to retell his story.

According to one school of thought, censorship and self-censorship unintentionally "help" the writer to become cleverer, deeper, more artistic. But the best Polish literature was written in exile, and the best Russian literature flourished before and outside of Communist censorship. I remember that strange sensation in my head, my chest, even in my fingers, when, settled in California, I started to write the sequel to *The Jewish War*. Previously unknown to me, it was a feeling of complete relaxation. For the first time in my life I could write whatever and however I wanted. It took me awhile to realize that the name of that feeling was freedom. A refugee yes, but I didn't feel like a victim. On the contrary, watching the anti-Semitic hysteria in my homeland from afar, I woke up each morning with a sigh of relief that I was no longer there and very glad that I had denied the bastards the opportunity to victimize me again, and so I entitled the first collection of my refugee poems *Anti-nostalgia* (London, 1971). A reviewer in the Russian émigré press made a reference to a statement by the Russian refugee poet Ivan Yelagin: *Mnie nieznakoma goriech nostalgii, mnie nravitsa chuzhaya strana* ("I do not know the bitterness of nostalgia, I like this foreign land"). But I went one step farther and declared in the title poem of the volume my gratitude to the anti-Semites who made it so easy for me not to feel nostalgic.

Yes, there was a downside to the freedom of being a refugee. Some writers cut by the censors in the East were published in the West by the "Index on Censorship" or in the Penguin series Writers of the Other Europe, but refugees did not qualify. Writers who remained in Poland were invited by the Iowa Writers Program—but refugees did not qualify for that either. Writers who lived in Poland were offered contracts from Western universities—true, they could be denied permission to go, but a refugee did not need to apply. Editors of an anthology, *The New Polish Poetry* (University of Pittsburgh Press, 1978), explained in the preface that they had not considered poets who "for whatever reasons, have lived abroad," because "their work has not, it seems, been shaped by the same kind of experience." Not true: most Polish exile poetry, both in the nineteenth and the twentieth centuries—including Mickiewicz, Słowacki, Norwid, Wittlin, Lechoń, or Miłosz, to name but the best-known—was concentrated on and clearly shaped by the Polish national experience and collective consciousness. The prosaic truth was that publishing nonkosher refugees hampered a Western publisher's access to very inexpensive authors in the Communist country, while cooperation with its censorship was rewarding, as indicated in the acknowledgements section of the above-mentioned Pittsburgh anthology by the editors, who "wish to thank the Authors' Agency of the Polish People's Republic." Besides, a writer in Poland could earn royalties both abroad and at home—where an advance of as little as one hundred dollars could feed him for a year—while a refugee couldn't survive without a full-time job, seldom saw any royalties at all, and felt successful each time his or her book was published free of charge. On the other hand, holding a "day job" to earn a living prevented refugee writers from diluting and polluting their talent by unnecessary production. Arthur Miller in his *Turns of Time* complained he had to make concessions to keep his head above water. He wouldn't need to do that, had he earned his living by other means. "Slaving from nine to five, I was buying my freedom to write without concessions to publishers, critics, or sponsors," as I explained in an essay ("Szkoła opowiadania" in *Prawda nieartystyczna*, Wołowiec, 2002). "The price was high, but I don't regret it. I would have written much more had I not sat for twenty years in a cage behind a federal desk, but at least I know I have written only what was necessary."

"Where, if anywhere, is home?" a friend asks of me. In 1981, at the World Gathering of Holocaust Survivors in Jerusalem, I was one of the very few who survived the murder of a million Jewish children in the middle of European civilization, and I felt astray between generations, between the living and the dead, "neither here nor there or both here and there," as I described it in an essay written soon after the gathering ("Obsesyjny temat," in *Prawda nieartystyczna*, 1984). The boundaries of time are vague for us survivors. In one of her short stories, Irit Amiel relates a conversation with a woman who as a child escaped from the gas chamber. The woman talks about her experience while cooking compote and interrupts time and again asking her interlocutor to taste the compote: "She had such ability to spring back and forth from one time to the other; she was simultaneously here and there . . ." ("Ostatnie rozmowy," or "Last Conversations" in *Podwójny krajobraz* or *Double Landscape*, forthcoming by Świat Literacki, Warsaw). I do feel at home in this country of refugees, by refugees, for refugees. I have accepted and adopted the culture and mentality (except the sexual immaturity), and I can't think of a better place for me. I also feel a strong spiritual affinity with Israel and more than once considered making my home there. But I can never again live in Poland or anywhere in what Aharon Appelfeld (in his address at the Hidden Children Gathering, Jerusalem, July 1992) called "the sphere of European culture of which we had been the victims."

I feel most at home with fellow child survivors. We meet once a month for a potluck lunch and a discussion of topics concerning our past, present, and future. We come from various countries, cultures, and walks of life, and so our discussions are often lively indeed, but we feel like brothers and sisters. We are somber and sorrowful when retelling or listening to our stories, but we also often joke and laugh, and I am probably the group's most active joker and clown. Most readers of my *Refugees* are surprised by the book's humor and light tone. But others, who remember epigrams and satires I wrote in my student years at Warsaw University (I was nicknamed "Fraszka," Polish for "epigram"), say I am myself at last. On the other hand, I recall that when back then I showed my satirical and humorous pieces to an editor of a literary radio program, she looked me in the eye and said, "Young people tend to hide their true feelings. I think you have something else to tell." Is this a case of split personality? Perhaps it is a defense mechanism, because even a superhuman as writer cannot live in the mode of tragedy 24/7. Samuel Sandler, my professor of Polish literature from Warsaw University, a survivor of the Łódź ghetto and a fellow refugee of the 1968 wave, told me that my previous books were written with a sense of duty, while this one conveyed pleasure—which is true. I remember that also as an actor in the Jewish theater, I was the happiest when I made the audience laugh. Had it not been for my biography, I would probably—and gladly—write comedies.

I write Polish as very few of today's Jews can, and I write "Jewish" as very few of today's Poles can. But I also believe that some of my poems, essays, short stories, and at least two autobiographical novels, *Refugees* and *Kaddish* (the latter depicting Holocaust survivors who try but fail to adjust to the normal American way of life and death), are products of my acquired American culture. My most intimate readers should be Jewish, yet due to my language (a very intimate relationship in itself) and its deepest cultural references, I first of all address the Poles. My ideal readers would be Jews whose mother tongue is Polish, but very few such people exist. And so I try to translate my Jewish culture for the Poles, and my Polish culture for the Jews, and both of my cultures for Americans—an unenviable task. My English language translators are some of the most frustrated people in the world.

A Jewish writer who writes Polish in America is a case study in isolation, to say the least. But isolation is a writer's natural state, and being in a no-man's land between cultures is a vantage point from where one can see more than is immediately visible to others. Beside that, from my survivor's outer space of time, I often see how the past overlaps the present and how the present grows out of the past, as in this short poem entitled "Tsunami":

> It also attacks unexpectedly
> murdering entire towns
>
> but everybody rushes to help
> no need to beg or pay for it
>
> and everybody gets help
> and compassion
>
> and tsunami is more fair
> because it doesn't choose

or in a poem entitled "Despair":

> Unfortunate town Beslan
> will never cease to despair
> contrary to Dobre Kałuszyn or Jadów
>
> where the more experienced Jewish God
> had seen to it that no one was left
> to despair

or in a poem entitled "We survived but":

> We survived but war
> never ends
>
> we survived but fate
> does not really change
>
> (. . . .)
> we survived but
> not for ever

> we survived
> but not the fear
> of what comes next

or in a poem entitled "Unforgivable":

> death does not forgive everything
> and rightly so
>
> if you survive do not forgive
> implored those who were murdered
>
> and it's time to recognize
> the unforgivable
>
> especially now
> when it's increasingly frequent

In May 2005 I landed for the first time in Spain, another land with a traumatic past. A local professor read to the public a translated scene from *The Victory*, where my Jewish child narrator and his mother watch the tanks of their Soviet liberators rolling in, yet are still afraid to reveal their identity. The eight-year-old boy pleads with his mother that he not be a Jew again. The audience listened intensely and applauded, and then the professor asked excitedly: "Why? Why? Why?" I didn't dismiss his words as a rhetorical question and replied by quoting my short poem entitled "The Myth":

> If this were a myth a legend a story
> —which whoever cares may believe—
> about a perfidious and cruel tribe
> that never existed or did but long ago
> then this would be a myth, a legend, a story—
> not a libel an insult
> and murder

There was no response, no more questions, not even a single word. No one approached me after the meeting was over, and I left alone. Apparently no one expected and no one liked such a simple and obvious answer to the allegedly complex and mystic "Jewish question."

My proverbial "Jewish arrogance" has earned me several titles, such as "controversial," "one-sided," "confrontational," "uncompromising," and "very Jewish." I admit, the Holocaust has taught me that anti-Semitism should be confronted rather than ignored or appeased. The history of the Jews has taught me that being Jewish has always been controversial. But "very Jewish" I am unfortunately not. My Jewish life was destroyed in childhood and never fully recovered. Not allowed to be a Jew in my early years, and then misguided by doctrinaire approaches afterwards, I was unable to return to a true Jewish way of life. I am a post-Holocaust Yom Kippur Jew, who easily fasts but is unable to pray, and in the race against time cannot abstain from writing on Saturday. "One-sided"? True, because I side with the wronged, and I can't even imagine myself on both sides of the fence. Adversaries who really want to hurt me try to classify me as a proponent of "right-wing views." I admit that after my experience with Communist schools and betrayals, I no longer trust left-wing teaching or that state of mind, but I have never shared any of the narrow-minded, nationalistic opinions of the right, unless suggesting some measure of justice for the crimes of the left-wing's holy cow known as the Soviet Union places me in the "right wing." An eyewitness to crimes committed by both "wings," I distrust all ideologies, doctrines, and political groups. As a German poet said: "Ich bin mein eigener Dalai-Lama, ich bin mein eigener Jesu Christ," which in my rough interpretation means: "I am my own Chairman Mao, I am my own Karl Marx," or "I am my own Ayatollah, I am my own Prophet X." To totalitarian minds, he who is not on the left has to be on the right—there is no third way. But to me, the main difference between anti-Semitism on the left and anti-Semitism on the right is that the latter is and has always been frank and sincere. I also admit that unlike most European "liberals," I do prefer civilized, democratic Israel to the savagely fanatic, anti-Semitic, authoritarian, or outright fascist states of the Middle East. The demagogic dictum of anti-Israeli propaganda stating that "hatred begets hatred" and "violence begets violence" does not apply to the Jewish experience. Hatred and violence against us—as in domestic violence—were begotten, inspired, and intensified by our weakness and appeasement. The pacifism of the 1930s did not restrain Hitler—on the contrary, it encouraged him. But his violence, thank God, did beget violence, which, for the time being, has saved the world.

A chance survivor of the greatest crime of civilization, I see that the eternal crime against the Jewish people has not ended. A democratically elected leader incites a nation against "descendants of those who crucified Christ [and] became the owners of the riches of the world." European public opinion names Israel, the shelter of Holocaust survivors, as "the greatest threat to world peace"—which is a carbon copy of Hitler's war cry, except his obsessive *Judentum* has now been replaced by the current codeword. The Holocaust shows what humanity is capable of, and so does denying the Holocaust. A fanatic head of state declares it a myth and the fanatic mob screams, "The Holocaust is a lie." An even worse nightmare for a Holocaust survivor concerns jokes about Jews in the ovens and Jews in the chimneys—with clever puns based on the linguistic proficiency of educated, intelligent people. When I expressed my indignation over these obscenities during a panel discussion in Warsaw, a sociologist slighted the phenomenon as mere "ethnic jokes" and countered my complaint with a statement about the "superficiality" of American Holocaust studies, while the moderator (one of the so-called new Polish Jews also known as "professional Jews") tried to mediate a "compromise." All of the above proves once more that there was no victory over evil, as I am certain there never will be. Am I disgusted? Yes. Am I frightened? No, because I know that evil cannot win, either. Facing it throughout my surprisingly long life, I have learned to accept evil as an integral part of the human condition. That does not mean I welcome it or agree with the Tolstoyan nonresistance to evil. On the contrary, I resist it at every step and stage. In compensation for my helplessness as a child, I have made resistance to evil the main purpose of my "uncompromising" writing.

The most "uncompromising" to my detractors is my insistence that I had been sentenced to death at the age of five for being a child of Jewish parents, and not just a member of humanity. This fact, obvious to me as both an eyewitness and a victim of the crime, is still strongly denied in my previous homeland. To some opponents, my views on anti-Semitism and the Holocaust are "radical" and even "scandalous." To them, it is not the Holocaust and not anti-Semitism after the Holocaust that is "scandalous" but the protests of a Jew. Even in an otherwise respectful doctoral thesis published as a monograph (Dorota Krawczyńska, *Własna historia Holokaustu: o pisarstwie Henryka Grynberga* or *His Own History of the Holocaust: on the Writings of Henryk Grynberg*, Warsaw, 2005) my statements are repeatedly characterized as "uncompromising" or "increasingly radical"; and a subchapter on my polemics entitled "The Scandalist" presents the arguments of my critics without my responses—a tactic resembling the national "discussion" on Zionism in Poland in the late 1960s. It also reminds me of my physical scuffle with an anti-Semite at a New Year's Eve party back in 1965 in Warsaw's hotel "Europejski" (nomen-omen). As I depicted it in the novella *Fatherland*, several peacemakers grabbed my arms, but not his, so that he could rush up and give me a black eye and more.

My older and more experienced brother Bogdan Wojdowski,

in his testament known as "Open Letter to the Writers of the Shoah Generation" (published in the quarterly *Masada* [Fall 1991]), warned that "cholera in a delitescent endemic state lingers on in Naples until this day, and similar is the state of anti-Semitism. We have survived the big epidemic that had swept over Europe taking millions of Jewish lives, yet time and again we notice convulsive relapses of the plague." Therefore, he urges writers of the Shoah generation to "much more closely watch what is going on at the universities, in the culture, in the high places of politics, and theology." I try to do that. As the Holocaust was the most defining experience of my life, my writing can certainly be classified as Holocaust and post-Holocaust literature. Yet no matter how vast and deep the tragedy, the Holocaust is for me only part of the universal Jewish experience called anti-Semitism—a subject that triggers the brainstorms that wake me up at night, urging me to take notes and spend the best hours of my days fighting back with all my fingers on the keyboard and all the anger of my scorched soul.

In conclusion, I feel much less uprooted as a refugee in America than I did while living on my native continent. This is the best shelter I have ever had. Despite my foreign language, I feel much more at home here as a writer, a human being, and certainly as a Jew. I am not entirely isolated. I have my "scorched" brothers and sisters of the child survivors' group, and the spiritual company of a few, but close literary siblings, such as Bogdan Wojdowski, Irit Amiel, Hanna Krall, or Aharon Appelfeld. I share Appelfeld's opinion that we children of the Holocaust have invented a straightforward form for our story, "a new kind of melody" for our song. Testifying to the lowest downfall of civilization, I cannot imagine a more important subject or more important lessons than the ones that can be learned from our true tales, especially after September 11, 2001 and that day's truly universal crime against humanity.

Exile as Life after Death in the Writings of Henryk Grynberg and Norman Manea

—— *Katarzyna Jerzak*

It is a delicate task to write about a living author and even harder
to speak about his work to his face. When several years ago I gave
a lecture at the United States Holocaust Memorial Museum,
my subject was living authors[1]—W. Sebald, Stefan Chwin, and
Pawel Huelle—but all were comfortably far away. And yet my
talk was interrupted by a lady of a certain age in the audience.
"Tell me," she said, "is this Sebald a tall, lanky fellow? I think my
mother's people knew his people." "Shsh," the representative of
the museum said; "this is a lecture, and there will be a question
and answer period at the end." But the woman would not be put
off. "I think my family knew his family. Did he have blond hair?"
she persisted. After the lecture I apologized to her, embarrassed
because she, who had survived the war near Drohobycz, and had
known Bruno Schulz if not Sebald, was hushed on my account.
After all, I was only talking about what I had read, while she was
speaking about what she had lived. Hers was a living voice next
to which Sebald's, Huelle's, Chwin's, and mine most of all, were
only echoes.

If I dare write about Henryk Grynberg and Norman Manea today, it is because I must make up for the silence and the amnesia that plague Grynberg's Polish neighbors. Writing in *The New York Times* about Jan Gross's book *Neighbors*, Adam Michnik admitted that as a Pole he was ashamed because of what had happened in Jedwabne, and yet he knew that as a Jew he would have been burned there.[2] Henryk Grynberg's neighbors were my father's people. My father was born in 1931 in Stanisławów, just a few kilometers from Mińsk Mazowiecki, Radoszyna, Dobre — Grynberg country. Neither my father nor any of his older brothers remembers anything about the sudden disappearance of several hundred Jewish families from their town. My mother, on the other hand, who was born in Kalisz in 1936, the same year as Grynberg and Manea, remembers clearly the hands begging for water through the cracks in the cattle cars she saw passing through her town. She still screams when she dreams about them. As I read Grynberg's and Manea's works, I remember my mother's memories and my father's amnesia, and with every word I take in, I become more Jewish. I, too, am on the side of the Jews of Dobre.

When one hears *exile*, one thinks lamentation, loss, nostalgia. But Jewish exile is also a kind of celebration: of survival against the odds, of the power of the word, of the persistence of the Jewish soul. It is thanks to my American exile that I could, openly, name my younger son Dawid-Emmanuel. In 1967 my mother was advised against naming my brother Dawid. "Do you want him to come home from school crying?" her Jewish friends asked. In my twenty-one years of life in Poland I never met a Dawid. Our way of being Jewish was to know that my brother's name was supposed to be Dawid.

In Polish *wizja lokalna* means a visit to the scene of a crime. My original untranslatable title for this paper was "Rewizja lo-

kalna" because both Grynberg and Manea return to the scene
of one of the greatest crimes in history. Grynberg's essay "Blue
Wannsee" is also a visit to the scene of the crime. So this is where
it took place, in this villa. This is where they sat, made the decision, planned, and volunteered who would implement the final
solution first. The speaker—Grynberg—is in two times at once:
the time of the crime and the time of his visit. The past overtakes
the present, swallows it up, spills over. The *now* is pale and phan-
tasmatic, the *then* is full-blooded and real:

> They gathered on January 20th and the winter of 1942 was harsh.
> The frozen lake was pale like an Aryan eye. The swans danced in
> the wind, a ravishing, breathtaking ballet. That was our last winter
> in Radoszyna. I wore a heavy coat, long to the ground, with room
> to grow—the optimism of Jewish parents—and a fur hat with ear
> flaps. Little Buciek spent the entire winter indoors. This was his
> first winter and he never saw the next one because the participants
> of the Conference did not allow him to see it.[3]

Unlike his little brother, Grynberg himself survived, but only because he was "overlooked." The photograph that accompanies
the essay in the *Journal of Modern Jewish Studies* shows Grynberg looking back with the backward glance of Orpheus. Looking
back is burdensome; looking back at the scene of the crime is
even heavier.

An exile, however, is someone who necessarily looks back.
Someone who still has ties. Ties of blood—usually spilled blood.
An exile has unfinished business. He lives in two places at once:
in one as a body, in the other as a phantom. He lacks peace because the other place, the other time, lives on, beckons, tugs at
him. An exile is someone who has two centers, as Czesław Miłosz
once said. But also someone who is pursued by the Erynies, he
added. When Grynberg revisits Poland in 1991, he does it against

his better judgment, as it were. In his essay "A Duty," he ascribes his decision to set foot in his homeland as a call of conscience: "In addition to my father, the bones of my little brother, who was one and a half year old then, were lying about somewhere there."[4] It is the blood and the bones that beckon, and Grynberg comes back as their avenger. Much of the opening pages of the essay are taken up by the details of Grynberg's actual journey: the plane, the flight attendants, the fellow travelers—everything is accounted for. These are, however, no mere preliminaries. Everything about the journey itself announces the life-after-death motif: when he gets on the plane, his seat is already taken, as if he no longer existed. The flight attendant offers him another seat, but in a row without a window, as if he didn't need to see. Then, to top it off, his seatbelt doesn't work. All this could be a commentary on the sorry state of affairs in the newly capitalist Poland ("Something is rotten in the state of Denmark"), but it is more than that: Grynberg consistently portrays himself as lacking in existence and his trip as the return of a phantom. There are also hints of another kind of nonbeing, echoes of other deaths, because Grynberg describes the return as an asphyxiating experience: "There is less and less air in the box, and my throat is so dried out it hurts."[5]

This is not, then, an ordinary transatlantic flight. Instead it is a journey to the netherworld, or, conversely, a painful return of the dead to the living, an ironic reminder of Adam Mickiewicz's *The Forefather's Eve,* in which as part of a pagan custom the dead are briefly conjured up. But it is Mickiewicz's *Sonety krymskie* that Grynberg quotes as an equally ironic backdrop to his misadventures on the airship carrying him home. That patriotic intertext, ringing a bell familiar to every Pole, underscores the theme of the exile's return, as it was Mickiewicz's Romantic poem *Pan Tadeusz,* written in exile in Paris, that became the epitome of Polishness itself and of the exiled writer's desire to come home. Grynberg's revisit is the opposite of romantic: he deflates the Bard's pathos by evoking him while he shaves in the plane's bathroom. He is interrupted by a vigorous knocking: "I try to shave faster. Someone knocks again. The knocking becomes stronger and then turns to banging. That's right, I'm in Poland."[6] This scene reinforces what already has been established: Grynberg feels unwelcome on that plane, he is nearly *a persona non grata*, there is no room for him here, and he will not be able to make himself comfortable even briefly. The attempt to shave invokes both a sense of home (it is a domestic, intimate image of a man grooming himself in front of a mirror) and of loss: the reader familiar with Gryberg's work will hear a distant echo of the forcible beard shaving that Grynberg's forefathers and hundreds of thousands of other Orthodox Jews underwent in the first days of the war, as well as of the beards shaved off to pose for the photographs for the fake, "Aryan," papers. "I gather everything into my bag and open the door. The ladies waiting outside look away, they don't see me."[7] In two brief, prosaic sentences that ostensibly do nothing more than report soberly the uneventful events of one flight, Grynberg masterfully encodes the whole pathos of repeatable Jewish exile—the readiness to pack up and leave on short notice and the quasi-invisibility of the ever-exiting Jew. For an exiled writer everything becomes allegory, and thus a seemingly minuscule incident stands in for a story or even a history.[8]

The journey back to Poland is then at best a metaphor for the Jewish fate and at worst a personal nightmare. "In February of 1992 the Okęcie Airport was a dark, cramped hole, like the Koluszki transfer railroad station of my youth. Even the stench was the same. All of a sudden I recognize my dream. 'Are you sure I'll be able to leave?' I ask the young men who are aiming their camera at me."[9] The exile returns not to Ithaca so much as to a kind of prison. It doesn't matter that he himself unlocks "the cell," as he calls the little hotel room where he is staying; what counts is that the keys are "heavy," the bolts "clanging," and "the water of a nondescript color smells as if it's been used before."[10] This uncanny feeling of a *déjà vu* or, rather, of a *déjà vécu* is strengthened by explicit comparisons to Grynberg's past life in Poland as an actor in the Jewish theater, another kind of ghost: "The mirror is discreetly placed where there is the least light, just like in the small hotels where I used to stay while on tour with the theater, and just like then I shave in front of a pocket mirror placed on the window sill."[11] That which should be home but isn't: as in Freud's original definition of the *Unheimlich*, the familiarity is what makes the "unhomely" truly horrorful.

When Grynberg sums up the anonymity of his impromptu visit—"No one knows who I am or what I'm doing here"—he by the same token belies the topos of the exile's return. No nanny, no dog, and no old father wait for him in Warsaw. Even his—figurative—scars are anonymous and mark him only as a son of a nation: "I stop by to get water and the shopkeeper pulls out a bottle that says 'Kosher' from beneath the counter:

'I've kept it just for you . . .'

Here nobody asks because everyone knows."[12] It is no wonder then that, unable to feel at home in the Polish reality (despite the unmistakably homey taste of Polish bread and farmer's cheese), and as if cast in the predictable role of the Jew, Grynberg goes to the theater. Theater, an illusion of reality, offers an illusion of home because that's where Grynberg performed his Jewishness in the past. Explicit in his insistence on the return as a kind of life after death, he writes: "In my previous incarnation here I used to spend most of my evenings at the theater."[13] But even though he now attends a play by a non-Jewish author (Gombrowicz), "the house is empty like in our Jewish theater."[14] The nearly empty theater—"a class of high school students and I"—is a feeble sub-stitute for home; it fails even as a shelter. "I'm wearing an ordi-nary grey sweater so as not to attract attention but everyone stares at me wherever I go. Have they recognized me, like in my dream? Only at home, when I take the sweater off, I see pieces of the tape with which the microphone cable was attached to my back dur-ing the filming."[15] The involuntary reenactment of being chased, pursued, and identified intertwines here with the momentary sense of refuge that his Warsaw hotel "cell" offers—*nolens volens* Grynberg calls it home, but all he means by that is a place where one can take one's sweater off in private, little more than the changing room the actor uses after the play.

Grynberg's "A Duty" is also a meditation on the difference between the old and the new world, their contrasting chrono-topes that momentarily fool the exile into believing that indeed nothing has changed: "In America everything changes from one year to the next but here the same florist's is still at the corner of Jerozolimskie and Krucza Street."[16] Is the place the same or is it only the set that has remained? In what in a Greek tragedy would have been a recognition scene, Grynberg at last runs into one person who did know his previous self: "Even the same birch hair tonic is sold at the same drugstore where behind the counter once stood a good friend of the beautiful girl whom I did not always call after returning from a tour; the friend had a sharp eye and my phone would ring right away. I go in, she's standing behind the counter but doesn't see me, even up close: I am no longer visible. I go back to my place, no one calls."[17] Grynberg's tragedy, though of ancient origin, is not Greek; it is Jewish, and hence there is no recognition here. His theater—the play that his life becomes in the essay—is therefore closer to that of Beckett or Ionesco because the painful element of the absurd permeates the script. "A Duty" ends with the recognition of the fact that the father Grynberg was looking for is gone, the time is gone, and the last witness, the ladybug preserved in the bottle that the father took to his grave, is now gone as well. The writer remains.

Norman Manea's memoir *The Hooligan's Return* opens with the ostensible antithesis to exile: Paradise regained, otherwise known as Manhattan. The narrator stands in front of his apartment building that reminds him of Stalinist architecture. He is performing, willy-nilly, the quintessential mental operation of an exile: "This," he thinks, "is like that." This thing I'm seeing is like the thing I used to know, back home. Except . . . not quite: "No Stalinist building ever reached such heights."[18] This is *almost* like what I used to know back home. "Stalinist nonetheless," persists the narrator, asserting the role of memory in perception, and "defying the stage set of his afterlife."[19] An exile never ceases to compare. Therefore, the immigrant who has not stopped comparing after twenty years is also an exile, permanently accompanied by the cognitive dissonance of double vision.

"Afterlife" or "life after death" is what Manea calls this phenomenon. Life in exile is unreal: not only is it *after*, but it is fake, theatrical (hence his frequent use of the term *stage set*). Even though— or because—everything here exists in abundance—fruits, coffee shops, styles, people of various color and shape—nothing "seems irreplaceable." The passers-by, the shops, the flowers are all part of the set. They lack reality. Like the flowers that Proust's narrator in *Remembrance of Things Past* did not know in his childhood and which therefore seem less real to him in adulthood, Manea's narrator, too, refuses or is unable to accept the new reality as real. This may be a Paradise, but it is as utopian as the advertisement with the palm trees that made Poles daydream in gray, Communist Poland. It is a world without a past, where "what really matters is the present moment." Milan Kundera says that America is the country of forgetting. Manea doesn't forget anything, but he walks along Amsterdam Avenue as if it were the Elysian Fields.

So when he refers to himself as "the survivor,"[20] it is not only because he physically survived the concentration camp in Transnistria or the Ceauşescu regime. He's a survivor in the etymological sense: to survive comes from the Latin *supervivere*. There is life and then there is survival, being above or on the surface of life, as if real life were elsewhere. To survive is to be beyond life, next to life, but not in it. This may not be an ideal situation for a human being, but it offers a writer, if he can harness it, an extra vision, a supplemental perspective. Such a writer is an inner outsider. He is, to all appearances, a participant in life, but he is also elsewhere. As a writer he imports that elsewhere—landscapes, languages, people, events—and they intersperse with his here and now. Another contemporary Jewish writer in exile, André Aciman, in his "Shadow Cities" sees Paris, the Italian Riviera, Rome, and, above all, his native Alexandria when he looks around the Upper East Side: "My repeated returns to Straus Park make of New York not only the shadow city of so many other cities I've known but a shadow city of itself, reminding me of an earlier New York in my own life, and before that of a New York which existed before I was born and which has nothing to do with me but which I need to see . . . because, as an exile without a past [here], I like to peek at others' foundations to imagine what mine might look like had I been born here, where mine might fit if I were to build here."[21] This sense of simultaneous dispossession and extension of one's estate is one of the characteristics of Jewish exile.

It is not a coincidence that Manea carries to the Upper West Side the memory of Suceava next to the memory of Rosa Stein, who, demented, asked at the crossing point on the Dniester whether someone could kindly show her the way to her house "in the same building as the Weiner bookstore."[22] "The Weiner bookstore still survives in the memory of the exile now being lulled to sleep in his New York refuge."[23] This is the bounty of exile. But there is also the curse: I am not from here, I am not even altogether here. I write in a minor tongue that is certainly my own and yet is begrudged me (Manea continues to write in Romanian, Grynberg in Polish). This sense of belonging elsewhere is of course as real as it is illusory: both writers return to Poland and Romania only to discover that they can feel as ill at ease "back home" as anywhere else.

On the first day of his return to Romania—April 21, 1997— Manea experiences the obverse of his feelings abroad. There, in America, certain things, places, tastes were almost like the ones back home. Here, everything is the same as it used to be but not quite. "The facades look dirty, the pedestrians rigid, diminished, ghostlike. The atmosphere is alien, I am alien, the pedestrians alien."[24] The return does not return the exile to life. Gombrowicz writes in his *Diary* that he never returned to Poland; he did not feel like digging up the dead body of his younger self. Manea returns not only as a foreigner and a stranger, because he returns as a phantom. He, like Grynberg before him, experiences the otherness of the erstwhile home as an *Unheimlichkeit*, as the uncanny, which he puts once more in theatrical terms: "Everything is the same and yet not the same. Something indefinable but essential has skewed the stage set, something akin to an invisible cataclysm, a magnetic anomaly, the aftermath of an internal hemorrhage."[25] The wording is unmistakable, this is the chronotope of afterlife: life after paralysis, life after catastrophe, life after death.

The patient goes to the doctor, the vital signs are checked, the reflexes tested—the doctor proclaims him to be well. "But I'm not the same," insists the patient. The exile is not the same because the place is not the same. They have diverged, and each has gone on separately, but the place remains lodged in the exile while only an empty space remains in the place. When the two are reunited, time has intervened and prohibits their complete fusion. Even language, the medium of life, is not the same. Time has deformed and killed, and therefore a return in space does not resuscitate the former self: "Death has passed this way, in the footsteps of the dead man now revisiting the landscape of his life in which he can no longer find a place or a sign of himself."[26]

"Postmortem tourism should never be underestimated"[27] quips the exile on his temporary visit to the former home. Tourism after death is the opposite of nostalgia: it is not a return, it's only a visit, it does not bear life, it dissects the dead self. It's an autopsy (the one Gombrowicz wanted to avoid, could not bear to face).

"To survive" is to remain alive after the death of someone. Proust claims that we are our own cemeteries, layers upon layers of our selves, the selves we have survived. As Arnold Weinstein argues in his book *A Scream Goes through the House*, Proust's narrator's survival of his grandmother's death and of Albertine's death is only possible at the price of the death of his old self.[28] Manea and Grynberg have experienced this kind of survival a thousandfold: they each lost not just one grandmother and a beloved, but more kin than they could enumerate at the age when it happened. After his grandfather Avram and his maternal grandmother die in the camp, Manea graphically describes his own death: "In his mind, the boy saw himself lying, mummylike, in an eternal stupor. He could see the grave, the snow-covered earth, the frozen blades of grass, the wriggling worms. The wind was howling, the bearded men were swaying to the cadences of the ancient Kaddish prayer."[29]

The wisdom of *The Hooligan's Return* is contained in the moment of epiphany that follows these real and imaginary deaths: "I was alive, thinking about my own death, but what I understood then was that crying and hunger, cold and fear, belonged to life, not to death."[30] This is the wisdom that young Americans born and bred in artificial Paradise need so badly.

Grynberg returning to Poland would be Odysseus returning to Ithaca, except that Penelope is not there. As he says in one of his poems, "My wife died before I married her / before I fell in love with her / before I saw her / I don't even know her name."[31] He would be Antigone, returning to bury his brother, but the brother was so small when he was killed, only eighteen months old, so there is nothing left to bury. He is Hamlet, returning to avenge his father's death, but the murderer is not a royal scoundrel, just an ordinary pair of scoundrels. He is the soldier coming home after twenty-five years of serving the tsar—and everybody at home is dead. It is no accident that when I taught Grynberg's *The Jewish War*, *The Victory*, and *Birthplace* in the fall of 2005, among the students who chose to do their oral presentations on Grynberg was an Iraq war veteran who had been shot over Baghdad (he had been the pilot of an Apache helicopter) and who spent a month as a POW before the Marines rescued him, and a criminal justice major who could not eat for three days after he had watched the documentary film *Birthplace*.

Grynberg would also be Rip Van Winkle returning to his village, except he has not slept for fifty years. The villagers have. As the film *Birthplace* makes clear, for him it has been a sleepless night while they aren't only well-slept: they are still there, the same families, the same houses, the same dogs, cats, cows, the same mud, the same snow. . . . The war came and went, communism came and went, and these people survived. He did not: "None of the Jews of Dobre survived, not even I. Because one cannot survive it."[32]

That is why he is also the dybbuk, one returning as if from the dead. People don't like ghosts. They try to exorcise them. Is that why his voice is not welcome? When I submitted his translated essays, they were rejected—not because they were bad or badly translated, the editors argued, but because the publishers were concerned that they would not sell like hotcakes. Well, they are not hotcakes. But they are burning. No one can hold them for a long time; no one can stand it. They pass them on, to the next

person or they drop them. "We are not well liked because witnesses are not well liked. They say no one knows what truth is.
But it is known where it is or at least where it should be: in a tale,
under the text. Between the lines, between the words. Sometimes
truth hides like a Jew. There is an obvious connection between
the witness, the writer, and the Jew. And the exile."[33]

But what does Jewish exile mean to a southern boy or girl
in Athens, Georgia, in the twenty-first century? To someone for
whom "the war" means not the Second World War, not even
the Gulf war, but only the war in Iraq? As it turns out it is meaningful because some of them stop eating, start reading Martin
Buber, and remember a friend who had totalitarian parents or
another friend who committed suicide. Why do my students react to Grynberg and to Manea as vehemently as they do? Not
because they recognize a resemblance to Hamlet, Antigone, or
Orpheus. They do not because most do not read—not even the
daily paper. Cereal boxes, road signs, price tags—yes. Maybe
Harry Potter. Certainly not literature. So when they react to the
Polish or the Romanian writer's works, it's not because of implicit
intertextuality. Rather, they react as if hit in the stomach. They
react because they cannot do otherwise. They, who have not traveled, who, in many cases, have never left Georgia, are suddenly
elsewhere. They feel trapped, threatened, on the verge of death.
They, who have no experience of Jews (in the fall of 2005 I did
not have a single Jewish student in that class of thirty-five, except
for one so-called Messianic Jew), felt Jewish. In another class
we read a love poem by Szymborska called a "Thank-you Note."
Nothing. No reaction. "What is love?" I ask. Nothing, a silence.
One student hesitantly raises his hand. "Yes?" I ask. "Peace," he
answers. "Love is peace." "No, that's death," I say, just to provoke
them. Nothing. They couldn't be provoked. But Grynberg and
Manea did provoke them, made them react. They reacted to the

fear, to the lack of fear, to the death, to the survival, to the supposed victory and to the real one. They were speechless after the film *Birthplace,* but not numb. Some cried, others clenched their fists. Years ago I used to show a different film: Alain Resnais's *Hiroshima Mon Amour* with Marguerite Duras's script. But I had to give up because the most tragic scene in the film, when the heroine speaks to her Japanese lover as if he were her first love killed in the war, and the man slaps her face to make her come to her senses because she is descending into anguish beyond return, that scene made my students laugh out loud, heartily. Once I had 250 students in that class. I showed the film and during that scene watched their faces instead of the screen. Of that total, 249 laughed, and one did not. I asked her later why she didn't. She said she couldn't laugh because at that moment she felt she was the woman in the film. The others felt nothing but they saw: a man slapped a woman. Hence the slapstick. So how did they manage not to laugh during the film about Grynberg's return? They felt. Not all of them felt right away. The criminal justice major said it left him indifferent the first time. But the second time he began to feel, and the third time made him sick to his stomach. By the time I showed it to the whole class, he asked for permission to leave the room. As Grynberg writes in "A Duty": "I cannot watch the film at all."

It turned out that while I thought I had no exiles and no Jews in the class—only one immigrant from Nigeria and one Iraq war veteran—by the end of the semester they were slowly *becoming Jewish* and feeling exile if not in exile. When time came to write their final papers, it was as if Pandora's box opened again. All manner of plagues came out. Everybody had a wound that was still bleeding or barely scarred over, so they could feel pain. One young woman could understand Grynberg because her father had been in Vietnam. Another identified with Manea because her grandmother had nearly died in the Philippines from grief.

Yet another compared exile to clinical depression, to feeling disconnected. A black student whose parents emigrated from Ja-
maica compared the Holocaust to slavery. But none of it was à la
Sylvia Plath. None of them identified with the victims in order
to take center stage. Rather, they recognized Martin Buber's You
in the other. When I say they were "becoming Jewish," I mean
more than the sense of solidarity, of commonality that they developed through reading. The sense of heightened empathy was
certainly there: "Dear Mr. Grynberg, I am not Jewish but I hear
what you're saying" wrote one student, the one who could not eat
for three days after watching Birthplace.[34] But even more striking
was the fact that these young people, in times of general illiteracy and of Jewish cultural illiteracy described by Rabbi Byron
Sherwin in his Sparks amidst the Ashes, turned to reading Martin
Buber, Janusz Korczak, Theodor Adorno. . . . If the metaphor of
exile as life after death holds true, it is because both Grynberg
and Manea manage the feat of turning ink to blood again. Their
works compel a revival.

Duality is the chronotope of exile, its peculiar time-space that
resists simplification. An exile is never wholly here or of here.
Ovid, exiled from Rome to what is now Romania, defined the
modern poetic topos of cultural exile. Baudelaire in "Le cygne"
and Proust in Remembrance of Things Past codified the meaning
of exile in time. Grynberg and Manea define the nature of post-
Holocaust exile: it is not merely a displacement in time, natural enough, or a displacement in space, equally common. It is
a dislodgement from life. Miraculously, this apparent loss of life
is not deadly; rather, both authors perform a transfusion of sorts,
awakening the posthuman subjects to their nearly lost humanity,
proving to them that no man is indeed an island and that the
loss of countless lives in a distant land long ago is also their own.
And they cry. Being less—having lost a part of yourself—becomes
more through writing, so much more that it can fit the maimed

young Americans with what they need most: a soul, a feeling, and a thought at once, as if they, too, were phylacteried Jews. So if there is a true homecoming, this may be it: two nonreligious Jewish writers come home not so much to language—already Adorno warned that one cannot inhabit language[35]—but to their readers, who, willy-nilly, become Jewish.

Notes

1. "Second Generation Holocaust Literature: Phantom Pains in Three Contemporary European Novels (Sebald, Huelle, De Luca)." United States Holocaust Memorial Museum, August 2, 2001.

2. Adam Michnik, "Poles and the Jews: How Deep the Guilt?," *New York Times*, March 17, 2001.

3. Henryk Grynberg, "The Blue Wannsee," trans. Katarzyna Jerzak in *The Journal of Modern Jewish Studies* 4, no. 1 (March 2005): 59.

4. I quote here from my unpublished translation of Henryk Grynberg's essay "Obowiązek" from the collection *Monolog polsko-żydowski* (Wolowiec, Poland: Wydawnictwo Czarne, 2003).

5. Ibid.

6. Ibid.

7. Ibid.

8. It is consciously that I evoke here Baudelaire's line from "Le cygne" ("tout pour moi devient allégorie") because it is that poem and that very line that the German Jewish exile Walter Benjamin adopts as the quintessential mark of Baudelaire's exilic consciousness in the *Arcades Project*.

9. My unpublished translation of Henryk Grynberg's essay "Obowiązek" from the collection *Monolog polsko-żydowski* (2003).

10. Ibid.

11. Ibid.

12. Ibid.

13. Ibid.

14. Ibid.

15. Ibid.

16. Ibid.

17. Ibid.

18. Norman Manea, *The Hooligan's Return: A Memoir*, trans. Angela Jianu (New York: Farrar Straus and Giroux, 2003), 4.

19. Ibid.

20. Manea, *The Hooligan's Return*, 5.

21. André Aciman, "Shadow Cities" in *Letters of Transit*, 32–33.

22. Manea, *The Hooligan's Return*, 227.

23. Ibid.

24. Manea, *The Hooligan's Return*, 263.

25. Ibid.

26. Ibid., 264.

27. Ibid., 277.

28. "My interest here is in the way Proust rewrites our notions of mourning, expands the picture of what it actually means when we 'lose' a loved one, shows us how the final acceptance of another's death must be understood as a form of our own dying." Arnold Weinstein, *A Scream Goes through the House* (New York: Random House, 2003), 320.

29. Ibid., 228.

30. Ibid.

31. Henryk Grynberg, "Orpheus II," http://www.zwoje-scrolls.com/shoah/grynberg.html (accessed February 5, 2008).

32. Henryk Grynberg, "We, the Jews of Dobre," trans. Katarzyna Jerzak in *Judaism* 53, no. 1–2 (Winter/Spring 2004): 133.

33. Ibid., 134.

34. Brian Vessels, "Dear Mr. Grynberg," unpublished final paper for CMLT 4400, December 2005.

35. "In the end, the writer is not even allowed to live in his writing." Theodor Adorno, *Minima Moralia*, trans. E. F. N. Jephcott (London: Verso, 1978), 87.

The Writer as Tour Guide

— *Lara Vapnyar*

About a year ago I received a letter from a recent Russian immigrant who had read my work in the *New Yorker*. He wrote that my stories made him uncomfortable because of the overpowering figure of the presumed reader, who, as he felt, was influencing the narrative. The reader in question was a "normal, nice, educated American," to whom the author constantly tried to explain things about Russians and Russian immigrants, to make him understand, to make him form a certain opinion, that the author would want him to make, and more importantly to persuade him to accept the author. "You are a writer, Lara, not a tour guide," he wrote. "As long as you continue to write on these stupid immigrant topics, the 'reader' (that nice, educated, American one) would continue to loom above, hinder you, make you pause to consider him."

As much as I am used to the fact that Russian immigrants are my sternest critics, I was particularly affected by this comment. At first, I attempted to shrug his words off. What nonsense, I tried to tell myself. I'm not influenced by any reader, no matter how nice, normal, educated, or American he might be. I'm just writing my stories the way they form in my head; I'm writing about life the way I see it, the way I've experienced it. And I decided to look at my stories again just to prove to myself how wrong that man was. To my great surprise, I found the proof to be the opposite, not with big screaming evidence, but little things here and there. Why would I, for example, refer to a famous Soviet newspaper as *The Young Muscovite*, when the correct translation of its name would be *The Member of the Moscow Branch of the Youth Communist Organization*? Clearly, my intent was to make it easier for the American reader. Or why would I put the words "a typical Moscow preschool" after the description of a room in another of my stories? Another proof of my touching care for American readers. Yes, that Russian man was right, I was a tour guide, and possibly a suck-up at that.

Most writers don't need much to sink into a state of deep self-disgust, and this would be just enough for me, if I hadn't thought of Mary Antin's *The Promised Land*. Now, this was a great immigrant book, whose author didn't shy away from serving as a tour guide for her reader, and doing so explicitly and unapologetically, to the extent that there is even a glossary of Russian and Yiddish terms appended at the volume's end.

Antin has a forceful and bold author's persona. One doesn't have to search for traces of the hidden dialogue with the reader in her work because she addresses the reader openly. She appears to have taken his hand and not let it go until she has led him through all the places she deems necessary for him to visit. In the first part of her book, the reader is taken on a thorough tour of a Jewish settlement in tsarist Russia, led through its streets, inside the houses, schools, and shops, and is introduced to all kinds of quirky but very real characters populating the place. In the second half of the book, the reader is led on a similar journey, this time into the anxious, overcrowded world of recently arrived

Jewish immigrants in the United States. But there are no pleas for acceptance in Antin's book; rather, one finds a resolve to explain, to make a reader understand what it was like to be a Jew in tsarist Russia and to feel what it was like to be a poor immigrant in the United States. This zealous resolve, along with a stubborn lack of objectivity, is what makes *The Promised Land* so fascinating. Antin doesn't just serve as a tour guide; she takes on the role of advocate for her people, a passionate and at times violent defender of their character. She says, for example, that even if Jewish residents of Russia were often engaged in some unsavory business practices, this was because they were forced to do so, and, most importantly, they would never behave in such a way to fellow Jews:

> Yes, I say, we cheated the Gentiles whenever we dared, because it was the only thing to do. Remember how the Czar was always sending us commands,—you shall not do this and you shall not do that, until there was little left that we might honestly do, except pay tribute and die. There he had us cooped up, thousands of us where only hundreds could live, and every means of living taxed to the utmost. When there are too many wolves in the prairie, they begin to prey upon each other. We starving captives of the Pale—we did as do the hungry brutes. But our humanity showed in our discrimination between our victims. Whenever we could, we spared our own kind, directing against our racial foes the cunning wiles which our bitter need invented.

Antin's approach to portraying the non-Jewish population is strikingly different. Even in the glossary, where she displays the most restraint and detachment, she couldn't help but express her negative attitude to the people she thought of as foes.

> *Vodka* (vod'-ka), *Russ.* A kind of whiskey distilled from barley or from potatoes, *constantly* (emphasis added—L.V.) indulged in by the lower classes in Russia, especially by the peasants.

If the presumed reader, the so-called "American friend," wouldn't share in Antin's sentiments, he is subjected to her wrath, as happens in this famous passage, where she shames the reader for despising Jewish immigrants and even threatens him.

> Dozens of these men pass under your eyes every day, my American friend, too absorbed in their honest affairs to notice the looks of suspicion which you cast at them, the repugnance with which you shrink from their touch. You see them shuffle from door to door with a basket of spools and buttons, or bending over the sizzling irons in a basement tailor shop, or rummaging in your ash can, or moving a pushcart from curb to curb, at the command of the burly policeman. "The Jew peddler!" you say, and dismiss him from your premises and from your thoughts, never dreaming that the sordid drama of his days may have a moral that concerns you. What if the creature with the untidy beard carries in his bosom his citizenship papers? What if the cross-legged tailor is supporting a boy in college who is one day going to mend your state constitution for you? What if the ragpicker's daughters are hastening over the ocean to teach your children in the public schools?

Antin's memoir was published in 1912. It is hard to imagine that there were many writers like her at the time, who worked in English and possessed the deep knowledge of Jewish life in Russia and immigrant life in the United States. She must have felt like a sole representative of these two worlds, responsible for properly introducing them to the third world, that of progressive, educated, gentile Americans, which she claims as her own as well. But does she really feel at home in this new world? Despite the title (by no means ironic), despite all the praise Antin heaps on the United States as the country of opportunity, and despite all the enthusiasm of the second, American, part of the book, *The Promised Land* never becomes a straightforward memoir of one person's tremendous success. There is, of course, a story of success here, the story of a Jewish girl who struggled and suffered through the oppressive tsarist regime in Russia, then came to America and managed to make something big out of her life. But there is also a story of tremendous trauma:

> Emigration became of the most vital importance to me personally. All the processes of uprooting, transportation, replanting, acclimatization, and development took place in my own soul. I felt the pang, the fear, the wonder, and the joy of it. I can never forget, for I bear the scars. But I want to forget—sometimes I long to forget. I think I have thoroughly assimilated my past—I have done its bidding—I want now to be of to-day. It is painful to be consciously of two worlds.

While serving as a tour guide to her reader, Antin tries to patch up her world divided in two and connect with her new culture. "I was born," she writes; "I have lived, and I have been made over." It doesn't look as if she had been completely made over by the time she worked on *The Promised Land,* but, perhaps, such a radical transformation was what she was trying to accomplish through writing.

I understand Antin's feeling of being "of two worlds," yet despite the similarities in our immigration stories, I've never experienced it myself. I'm not consciously of two worlds, and I am not even sure if I might be of more than two worlds or of no world at all. For one thing, when I lived in Russia, I didn't feel that the world of Soviet Moscow belonged to me, the way Antin could claim the world of tsarist Polotzk as her own. As awful and inhumane the idea of the Pale was, it created a close-knit Jewish community. There were some class differences, but, by and large, people with diverse personalities had similar educations, similar professions, similar opportunities. They had to deal with the same set of problems, the main one being anti-Semitism and govern-ment-induced regulations against Jews, and they had developed well-tried mechanisms of dealing with those problems. For the Jews of the tsarist ghettos, one of the most important means of emotional survival was to have an unwavering belief in the supe-riority of the Jewish way of life, Jewish religious beliefs, and even personal character.

In the Moscow of the 1970s and 1980s there wasn't anything like the close-knit Jewish community that Mary Antin describes. All nationalities in the Soviet Union were proclaimed to be equal; more than that, it was considered a crime to openly doubt that they were. Soviet Jews didn't have to go through a painful and hu-miliating process of assimilation by renouncing their religion and heritage; rather, assimilation was proclaimed to be unnecessary. Yet everybody knew that the Russian majority was, in the words of George Orwell, "more equal" than the others. If everybody was equal, why would Soviet authorities require that each person's nationality be clearly printed on all his documents? There were some Jews whose connections enabled them to have their first names changed from Moses to Mikhail, their last names from Grossman to Ivanov, and the word *Jewish* replaced in their inter-nal passports for the word *Russian*. They believed that this way they would have a better chance at success. Other Jews, who wished to do the same, but couldn't, joked that it was their Jewish faces that mattered, not their Russian passports. "When a pogrom comes, you'll be punched in your Jewish mug, not in your Rus-sian passport," they said.

I was aware of the inequality ever since I was a small child, but I didn't see anything wrong with it as long as I believed that I belonged to the majority. I remember looking at the map of fifteen Soviet republics in my preschool classroom and feeling overcome with pride at being a Russian. On the map, each repub-lic was represented by a man and woman in a colorful national costume. I admired the Georgian woman in her beautiful white dress, but I knew that Russia was the most important republic. Who were they kidding when they said that all the republics were equal! Moscow, the capital of the entire Soviet Union, was in Russia; everybody in the other republics spoke Russian; and just look at the size of Russia on the map! I was sure that I was a Russian: I lived in Moscow, spoke the language, and never wore any kinds of national costumes. I thought of the other nationalities with great generosity: let that Georgian woman on the map wear her pretty dress, let that Uzbek girl have her multitude of pretty braids, let those Armenians hold the basket bursting with fruit (so expensive and so hard to get in Moscow); we, the Russians, were the superior ones, and everybody knew it.

My happy arrogance was shattered at the age of six. A classmate led me by the hand into the dark preschool bathroom and said in an ominous whisper: "I know something about you. You're a Jewess." I had never heard the word before, not in family conversations, not in my school, not spoken from the television screen, but somehow I instantly knew that it had to do with my nationality and that it was something horrible. My reaction quickly went from shock to denial, and I protested to my classmate that it couldn't be true. "But it *is* true," she said, proceeding to demonstrate the most apparent attributes of my Jewishness. I had a wrong (long and rounded) nose, wrong (black and thick) eyebrows, and wrong (thin) ankles and forearms. Not having the right nose, brows, legs, and forearms, I was not Russian. And since a colorful picture of a Jew and Jewess didn't grace the map of the Soviet Union in my preschool classroom, I didn't even belong to one of those inferior but still legitimate nationalities. I was something infinitely worse. Denial quickly evolved into anger after my mother confirmed that yes, we were Jewish, had always been Jewish, and no, there was no hope that we would somehow change into Russians, or at least Uzbeks. "This is unfair! This is simply unfair!" I shouted, sobbing and choking with tears. My anger wasn't directed at the Soviet state, or at the Russian majority, or at the Jews, but rather at fate in general.

Over the years many more attributes of my Jewishness accumulated, adding to the collection of things that were different and wrong about me. Some were acquired from non-Jewish neighbors' and classmates' remarks, others from the words of my Jewish relatives, and still others from my own observations.

Being Jewish meant eating different food: pale and bland, easy on fats and meats, especially designed for digestion in weaker Jewish stomachs. "I don't want this Jewish soupchik," my half-Russian cousin often said. "I don't cook swine food," my grandmother retorted.

It meant getting sick a lot, or being expected to get sick by your mother. It meant being laughed at for wearing your winter coat in the middle of spring. It meant hiding in the bushes behind the school to remove your woolen leggings that your mother forced on you. It meant not being able to swim in the lake if the temperature was below 100. It meant hearing your mother reply to your protests like this: "But other children are Goyim, they're stronger than you, they won't get sick."

Being Jewish meant constantly failing in physical education. It meant falling off the climbing rope, not being able to throw a ball farther than five feet forward, catching the plank with your feet when trying to jump over, listening to the whole class laugh at you as you tried to force your body to do one more pathetic push-up.

Being Jewish also meant getting top grades in all the unpopular subjects like math or Russian. That was not much of a consolation, though, especially when, after the math teacher announced the quiz results, I heard somebody say: "But she is a Jew, they know how to wiggle their way through." (I was overjoyed when a music teacher said I was one of the worst in class. At least, I'd been spared something Jewish!)

I soon learned to blame everything that I didn't like about

myself on being Jewish. I had crooked teeth because I was Jewish. Cavities, too. Jews must have more cavities. My breasts were maddeningly slow to emerge because I was Jewish. Hair grew on my legs because I was Jewish. I slouched because I was Jewish. I was ignored by boys at school dances. I didn't blame the boys.

But the worst thing of all was that being Jewish meant being disgustingly timid, practical, and cautious. It meant lacking the generosity and wideness of the Russian nature, the mysteriousness of the Russian soul, the courage, the nobility, all the admirable qualities that were assigned to Russian characters from the folktales we studied in school and the real-life heroes from the pages of our history and literature textbooks. None of the remarkable people we studied was Jewish, and none of the remarkable deeds that were lauded was done by a Jew.

Being Jewish, in sum, meant not being able to be proud of your heritage.

There were some Jewish families in which parents tried to maintain a hushed-up pride about being Jewish. But in most families, mine included, the parents were too scared to talk about things Jewish, lest the child discuss any of that in public and get the family in trouble. While growing up, I experienced shame, resentment, and anger, but not pride. I longed to get rid of my Jewish nationality, to forget that I'd ever had it, but this too wasn't allowed. Along with my Jewish nose and hair, I had the word "Jewish" clearly printed in all of my important documents, from my passport to the class roster in school. The first thing every teacher saw while taking attendance in the morning was our nationality printed next to our names. How I wished to come to class one morning and find that the word "Jewish" disappeared from the school roster! But I knew that it wouldn't. I felt like an outsider in my school, a guilty intruder, somebody different and infinitely inferior. I used to be very proficient in my studies of the Russian language, but when a teacher asked a question in class,

I never raised my hand, feeling that it was somehow wrong to be proficient in a language that didn't really belong to me. I was embarrassed to get high marks for my Russian essays because I felt that I didn't have a right to them.

As I was growing up, I had one more reason to be ashamed of my nationality, and that was precisely the lack of national pride. I had been ashamed of my nationality ever since I realized that I was Jewish, and now I became deeply ashamed of being ashamed. There were stories in our schoolbooks about religious and ethnic minorities (never Jews though; usually Chechens) who were actually proud of their heritage and who fought against the Russian majority, even though their cause was clearly hopeless. Those people were enemies of the Russians, yet their struggle was described with admiration. I was deeply ashamed of having quietly accepted a deep sense of Jewish inferiority. I didn't understand that my lack of Jewish pride was the fault of my Soviet education; instead, I blamed it on my disgusting and treacherous personality. I came very close to hating myself, but I was simply too young to know how to do so, and thus I made my anger change its direction. Slowly, gradually, I was learning to hate and resent people who hated and resented Jews. They were stupid. They were swine, as my grandmother said. They ate fat greasy food, they failed their math tests, they couldn't spell in their own dear Russian language, they drank, they squandered their money on the first day of the month. They whispered "dirty Jew" behind my back because they were stupid. I hated them and, therefore, I could learn to live with their hatred and repulsiveness.

The trouble came if you happened to fall in love with one of them. I couldn't say if I first fell in love with Chekhov's stories or his portrait on the opening page of the book. Both were perfect. The stories were tender and light, serious and sad, yet comical—comical in a respectful way. There were no cheap laughs; Chekhov had to rely on the reader to get the humor. The face on the portrait was beautiful in a way I hadn't ever before seen. He looked at me through his pince-nez with understanding, he was serious with me, he knew me, he saw right through me, he knew that I loved him. I read story after story, and I identified with every character. I was Gurov, I was Anna Sergeevna, I was the circus dog Kashtanka.

It was a perfect untroubled romance until I happened to read "Rothschild's Fiddle." Despite its name the story wasn't about Rothschild, but about Yakov, a Russian undertaker, a tragic and complex character, destined to stay with you forever. Rothschild was just a minor figure in the story—just a little Jew, not a bad man, but a ridiculous, pathetic man who spoke in funny Russian and made odd movements.

> "Why are you pestering me, garlic?" shouted Yakov. "Don't persist!"
> The Jew got angry and shouted too:
> "Not so noisy, please, or I'll send you flying over the fence!"
> "Get out of my sight!" roared Yakov, and rushed at him with his fists. "One can't live for you scabby Jews!"
> Rothschild, half dead with terror, crouched down and waved his hands over his head, as though to ward off a blow; then he leapt up and ran away as fast as his legs could carry him: as he ran he gave little skips and kept clasping his hands, and Yakov could see how his long thin spine wriggled. Some boys, delighted at the incident, ran after him shouting "Jew! Jew!" Some dogs joined in the chase barking. Someone burst into a roar of laughter, then gave a whistle; the dogs barked with even more noise and unanimity. Then a dog must have bitten Rothschild, as a desperate, sickly scream was heard.

Now here was a Chekhov character with whom I wouldn't want to identify. A small and disgusting character, with whom nobody would want to identify. Yet I couldn't help but identify with him. Rothschild was a Jew, just as I was. I looked just as ridiculous and pathetic in my physical education class. And they laughed at me, too.

I discovered many other Jews in Chekhov's stories. They were never evil, but unfailingly little, dirty, smelly, devious people incapable of beauty and grandeur. I came to see that that was how Chekhov saw Jews, how Chekhov saw me. With disgust, with repulsion, with condescension. I wished I could hate or disregard Chekhov the way I hated and disregarded my neighbors and classmates. I wished I could just say that he was stupid, stupid, stupid! I couldn't. Chekhov didn't fail his math tests, Chekhov didn't squander his money on vodka, Chekhov was smart, wonderful, talented. Chekhov had a special deep and compassionate knowledge of people. He simply disliked Jews.

I couldn't stop reading Chekhov. I was hooked. Again and again I would pick a book and lose myself in his story, then invariably cringe in pain at another mention of Jews. I behaved just like a scorned lover who couldn't help but try to be near the object of her love, no matter how painful it was for her. I read while harboring violent fantasies of hurting somebody like Chekhov.

By the time I entered adolescence I was very far from developing a sense of Jewish pride, but I learned to find solace in the art of violent hatred, in wishing to get back at people who hated Jews. The most striking difference between my situation and that of the Jewish person from Mary Antin's times was the emotional isolation I suffered. Jewish problems were never discussed. I had to keep my shame, my revulsion, and my hatred private, and I believed that those feelings were perfectly unique, that nobody else shared them. I had a couple of Jewish friends, but it never occurred to me to ask them if they were ashamed of being Jewish as much as I was or if they hated anti-Semites as much as I did.

My first awareness of belonging to something like a Jewish community coincided with the mass Jewish emigration from the Soviet Union. This was something that most Soviet Jews were concerned with, and it was the first time that I witnessed Jews doing something as a group. This was also the first instance in which the Jews had an advantage over Russians. A lot of people were eager to discard their national pride and patriotism and leave a dreary and unstable Russia for a better, more promising place, but only Jews were granted coveted visas to Israel and the United States. With a feeling of glee we witnessed how the Mikhail Ivanovs were looking for ways to change back into Moisey Grossmans, how the most proud and patriotic of our Russian neighbors were desperately digging up their Jewish connections.

In 1994 my family made the decision to immigrate to the United States. I hardly knew what to expect from my new life, but I believed that I was finally coming to the place where Jews were free of the self-hatred, inferiority complex, and shame that were characteristic of Russian Jews, where Jews were at peace with their identity, well-assimilated but also proud of their heritage, and had all the opportunities for success. I believed that as an American Jew, I would become just as readily adapted, successful, and guilt-free.

The ironic thing was that when I finally arrived in the United States, I saw that I couldn't be considered either Jewish or American. What exactly was it that was Jewish about me? What made my Russian compatriots identify me as such and loath me as such? My nose? My hair? The nationality stated in my abandoned Soviet passport? Suddenly such designations seemed too small, too insignificant, too ridiculous even in light of my perfect lack of knowledge of Jewish history and my ignorance of most Jewish writers, philosophers, and artists. I knew that with my atheist upbringing, I would never be able to accept any kind of religion, including Judaism. I once walked up the steps to the heavy door of a Brooklyn synagogue, but I froze with my hand on the knob, unable to go further. I felt like an impostor.

I wasn't an American either. For one thing I didn't speak the language with the needed degree of fluidity. More than that, I knew that I would never speak the language without sounding like a foreigner. I didn't know American history or understand American culture. I didn't get American jokes. Worse than that, all the Americans I met in New York seemed so different that I couldn't find unifying features to define them, and couldn't determine what it was that made them Americans.

The Americans, on the other hand, defined me easily: I was a Russian. In the United States, I was finally granted the identity I had been denied my whole life. Here I became a Russian. And regardless of whether I liked it or not, I realized that I probably was Russian. I was definitely more Russian than anything else. I had an academic degree in Russian. Russian was the only language I spoke fluently, and Russian literature and history were the only two fields for which I had a passable knowledge. I had a strong liking for familiar Russian food, Russian customs, and Russian scenery. Of course, I was a perfect Russian in the eyes of others, but not in my own eyes. I couldn't possibly accept the identity of a people who had called me a dirty Jew. I would rather be a nobody, a rootless immigrant adrift in a foreign land.

Then, miraculously, I gained all three seemingly unattainable identities — Russian, Jewish, American — through acquiring a new and most unexpected identity — that of a writer. My book of short stories, *There Are Jews in My House*, is listed in each of the three categories: American — first novelists; Russian — social customs; and Jews — history. In reviews I'm now called a Russian-American, a Jewish-American, a Russian-Jewish, or — if a reviewer is not afraid of excess — a Russian Jewish American writer.

Nobody really knows how and why one becomes a writer. I don't know either. There are many reasons, or possibly no reason at all. I was lost, I was lonely, so perhaps writing became a desperate attempt to connect to the outside world, to the American culture that made up the outside world for me. Mary Antin wrote:

"Had I no better excuse for writing, I still might be driven to it by my private needs. It is in one sense a matter of my personal salvation."

I didn't have a better excuse.

The process of writing intervened with the process of finding a place in my new life, or looking for pieces of my different identities, trying to pick out those that weren't shuttered, those that made sense, those that connected me to the world. The first stories I've written fall into three groups. There are stories that take place in Russia, a lot of them based on my childhood memories; there are stories that take place in the United States and concern problems of immigration; and there is a novella, "There Are Jews in My House," that takes places during World War II and draws on the tragic consequences of anti-Semitism. I think I've had this story in me for a very long time, even before I knew that I would become a writer.

I've always found it unfair that most Holocaust stories are written about survivors or from the point of view of survivors or the people who helped Jews. It's understandable, of course, since only survivors can tell their stories. People who died are forever silent, and the people who killed or helped in killing Jews have preferred to hold their tongues. Since that is the case, the general picture of the Holocaust as painted in literature and cinema (excluding documentaries) is unjustly optimistic. Most of the characters we care about survive, and there are always those nice Germans, Poles, and Russians who help them survive while risking their own lives. I won't argue that these precedents didn't take place. There were people who tried to save Jews during the war, and we can only admire their heroism. But there were relatively few cases of gentile "neighbors" helping Jews during the Holocaust. Most people either closed their eyes to the persecutions and killings happening right before them or eagerly helped in harassing and exterminating the Jews. The decision to write *There*

Are Jews in My House came to me in one of the dark rooms of the Holocaust Museum in Washington, D.C. I was gazing at a picture of a crowd of people on some train station on the threshold of a concentration camp. They were all so different—city-dwellers and peasants, educated and uneducated, rich and poor, believers and unbelievers. Yet, there was something unifying about them that allowed Nazis to identify them as Jews and annihilate them as one pile of bodies. I would have been in that pile. It wouldn't have mattered whether I'd ever been to synagogue, whether I knew anything about Jewish culture or history, whether I spoke Hebrew, Yiddish, Russian, or English, with an accent or without, regardless of my upbringing, regardless of whether other Jews accepted me or not. That moment I knew with the utmost certainty that I was Jewish, whatever that meant. And as I looked back at my life I saw that I managed to go through all the quintessentially Jewish experiences. I've felt different, I've felt myself to be an outsider, I've been humiliated because of being different. I had to leave my land, to pack up my things with the knowledge that what I brought with me might be the only witnesses and reminders of my old life. I had to pack for my new life without having the faintest idea what it would be like and what I would need in it. I arrived in a new place, where I had to make sense of a new language, new rules, new ways of life. I embarked on a journey that took me from being an outsider in Russia to being a different kind of outsider in America. It required me to be "made over." This was the kind of journey that Jews have been making for centuries. And it was this idea that made me realize that I belonged to the larger Jewish community, that my small particular experience was in fact a part of the great narrative of Jewish history.

Before attempting to write *There Are Jews in My House* I studied many documents of the German occupation in Russia, and talked to a number of witnesses to gather accurate information on exactly how it happened. The most important question for me was "why?" Why did the gentile "neighbors" behave the way they did to their Jewish "neighbors" during the war? I thought that the only way to do it fairly was to try to look at Jews through the eyes of a gentile person. My protagonist is a gentile woman who gives shelter to her Jewish friend while harboring increasing resentment of her. In order to write the story I had to transport myself into the mind of this woman, and this became a self-guided journey into the private depths of anti-Semitism.

The second group of my stories is set in the Soviet Union, the country of my childhood, the country that I left by growing up, the country that I physically left for the United States, and the country that since then has ceased to exist. It sank like Atlantis, and the Russia of the present is an entirely other country. So when describing the Soviet Union, I become a tour guide into a lost world. The fact that it doesn't exist anymore makes me feel that it is at the same time more real and less real. On one hand, I have a responsibility to portray it exactly as it was with utmost realism; on the other hand, I'm conscious that there is no other reality for the Soviet Union than the flickering memories or changing fantasies of the people who used to call it home.

The third group of my stories, the ones that portray Russian immigrants in the United States, present an especially touchy subject. I take myself along with the reader on a journey into a world that is there, is very real, and actually fills my writing with questions and complaints. The thing that strikes me as most bizarre is that I probably am a part of this world, am one of those people who constitute it, am one of my characters. In order to portray all of that, I need to make a journey out of the place rather than into the place as I did in my other work. I need to achieve a certain degree of detachment, to become a tour guide who leaves his group and runs away to look at people in it from a distance.

Still, the most important reason for my Russian readers to see me as a tour guide is my choice of the language of my writing.

I write in English, which might seem a conscious decision to write with an American audience in mind. But the choice of the language wasn't that simple or that conscious. By the time I approached writing, I had been reading in English a lot, and whenever I thought about creating something of my own, I caught myself putting my images into words of the English language. I felt most comfortable when writing in English, even though I had to struggle with grammar and vocabulary. I would even say that I wrote in American, which for me was the language of immigrants. Russia remained the beloved and faintly hostile language of my past, and English was to be my only way to connect with the present and future. Boldly, I started writing in English, not the English of Shakespeare and Jane Austen, but in American English, which I came to see as the language of those who come from all over the world bringing their stories, their cultures, and their pain.

Recently, *There Are Jews in My House* was published in Hebrew. I am always overjoyed when my book gets translated into one or another language. But only its appearance in Hebrew made me cry. Somehow, it felt like my book full of Jewish emotions, conceived through the lens of Russian culture, and realized in American English, had come full circle.

So, am I a tour guide writer? Perhaps I am, but not in the first place a tour guide into Russian or immigrant culture for the general (normal, educated, nice) American audience. Or, rather, not only for those readers, but primarily a tour guide for myself, trying still to feel the new place, to explain it to myself, sometimes to explain it through comparison with the old world. Such a writer does not beg to be accepted but grapples with accepting the new life through her work.

Questions of Identity
The New World of the Immigrant Writer

— *Morris Dickstein*

When I was growing up in the 1950s there was no such thing as immigrant literature, though brilliant émigré intellectuals like Hannah Arendt played an important part in the cultural debates of the time. We certainly didn't know that we were living through the golden age of Jewish American writing, but these works could hardly be called immigrant writing, as immigration had been closed off at least thirty years earlier. Some of the best writers of that period, such as Bellow and Malamud or Ellison and Baldwin, were grappling with their own ethnic identity in relation to the wider forces of American life, but the travail of previous generations, with its experience of slavery, pogroms, and the Holocaust, remained in the distant background. We knew little or nothing of the writers who had dealt directly with the migration of Jews earlier in the century. Once-famous authors like Abraham Cahan, Anzia Yezierska, Mary Antin, Michael Gold, and Henry Roth were either unfairly forgotten (as in Roth's case) or dismissed as crude naturalists, unsophisticated in literary technique, whose work was merely of historical interest. The postwar world was unusually homogeneous, and yet New York, at least, still had large numbers of immigrants: Puerto Ricans for whom there was no immigrant quota, German refugees or survivors who managed to get out before or after the war, and even Eastern Europeans such as my older aunts and uncles, who had arrived decades earlier, whose country was still Yiddish and whose folkways belonged to the rural towns of Poland, the Baltic States, and Ukraine.

These quaint, old-world characters, strong in personality yet hobbled by immigrant fears, did figure in the works of writers who were young in the 1950s. But other subjects interested them more than the ancient history of immigration and accultura-tion. Some focused on the war we had just fought, not to rescue the Jews but to save the country, ultimately ensuring its postwar power and prosperity. Other writers like Philip Roth found their subjects in the material success of second-generation Jews or in the drama of growing up inside the Jewish family. Their charac-ters were busy trying to integrate into a nation that, despite the horrors of the Holocaust, still harbored strong prejudices against Jews. Or they portrayed Jews as exemplary victims or dark sym-bols of man's inhumanity to man, or delved into problems of as-similation and the barriers to full acceptance, which also spoke to their own needs as writers—not so much to live out the American dream as to gain a foothold in American literature. Where their predecessors had been written into the story as ethnic subtexts, they themselves demanded recognition as American writers, very much the way ordinary Jews struggled for inclusion as full-fledged Americans.

Yet when immigrants *did* appear in their work, as in the tragi-comic stories of Bernard Malamud, they were neither social be-ings defined by their historical community nor fully individu-alized characters pursuing a personal destiny. In tune with the existential mood of the moment, they were transformed into liv-ing metaphors, bearing the whole form of the human condition. Books including Malamud's *The Assistant* and *The Magic Barrel* or Bellow's *The Victim* and *Seize the Day* told grim, sometimes tormented stories. We hardly understood how much their ambiance was inflected by modernism, which equated dark with serious, pessimism with integrity, or by the Holocaust, which went largely unmentioned but seeped into every line, or by their own family histories, which were right up front in the autobiographical work of earlier Jewish writers but camouflaged in Malamud's and Bellow's more finely crafted tales. Later I was surprised at how autobiographical Malamud's work proved to be, since he set great store by his privacy and could be highly critical of confessional writing for its defects of craft or imagination.[1]

Within two decades after the war, America's relation to the world would shift again. Immigration laws were relaxed and the United States gradually reopened its borders, partly for reasons of justice—our country had long been a place of refuge—but also out of national need. The spirit of detente had eroded the barriers of the Cold War and we became more actively concerned about people imprisoned in totalitarian states. American Jews, abetted by Israel, were determined to do for Soviet Jews what Jews in the United Sates had failed to do, as a much weaker community, for Jews trapped in Hitler's Europe. But the expanding economies of the United States and Western Europe also required new immigrants if they were to continue growing, and the levels of education of Soviet Jews, especially in science and technology, were much higher than in the pool of immigrants from the Third World.

So something remarkable happened. The Jews of the Soviet Union, so long locked into a closed society, became a bargaining chip in trade negotiations between the US, which began using human rights as a weapon, and Soviet leaders, whose economy was faltering and who were perhaps not unhappy to see their Jews go. And since Jews were the only ones who could get out, it became fashionable to be Jewish, which swelled the ranks of those who claimed Jewish ancestry and caused consternation within the Orthodox rabbinate in Israel. Those were heady days, with some Russian Jews losing their jobs and even going to prison for demanding the right to emigrate, while American Jews, with growing confidence, marched in the streets for Soviet Jewry and made their influence felt in Congress. "This was 1983," as David Bezmozgis writes in one of his stories, "and as Russian Jews, recent immigrants, and political refugees, we were still a cause. We had good PR. We could trade on our history."[2]

As Bezmozgis's story goes on, the young hero's parents seek the patronage of a local rabbi sympathetic to these recent émigrés, so that the father, who works at a chocolate bar factory, can reestablish himself as a massage therapist, as he was in their native Latvia. They have been in Canada for two years and, typically, their nine-year-old son is negotiating the culture and language better than they do. "Seated across the table from the rabbi, my father wrestled language and dignity to express need. I sat quietly beside him, looking appropriately forlorn" (25). The rabbi, affecting a "posture of liturgical gravity," urges the boy's father to advertise, and the ads lead them to be invited to Friday night dinner by a local doctor. Slightly comical supplicants, dressed in their best clothes and bearing a home-baked apple cake, the Bermans meet another Russian couple, Genady and Freda, also overdressed, whose claims to persecution turn out to be greater than theirs.

Their curious host, Dr. Kornblum, inquires about how bad things had been. "My mother said it was bad, that the anti-Semitism was very bad. Jerry [a friend of the doctor] said that Genady and Freda had been refuseniks, he wanted to know if we had also been refuseniks. My mother hesitated for a moment and admitted we had not been refuseniks. She knew some refuseniks, and we were almost refuseniks, but we were not refuseniks" (33). The former refuseniks then tell about being evicted from their apartment, and Genady lifts his shirt to show where he had been stabbed by drunken coworkers, who called him a filthy Jew traitor. "My parents had to agree it was horrible." They are completely outclassed. The hapless Bermans not only lose out in the sweepstakes of competitive misery but their apple cake, made according to his grandmother's cherished recipe, is rejected because its kashrut, like their persecution, cannot be definitively established. Their offering is turned down along with the meager tale they have to tell. Their well-meaning hosts, social tourists with a hearty appetite for suffering, detached in their detached home, cannot quite conceal the huge condescension in their gestures of patronage, which predictably leads nowhere.

Or rather, they lead to the subtly toned story that Bezmozgis makes of his embarrassed recollections. His gentle irony draws attention not only to the humiliation of the Bermans by their would-be benefactors—and their grown-up son's smarting memories of that ordeal—but also to the uncertainties of their status in their new homeland. Ambitious but quietly desperate, they are unsure of how to behave if they are to restore even the modest standing they once had. In another story, "The Second Strongest Man," the father, Roman, is asked to judge a weightlifting competition in Toronto that involves a champion he discovered and trained in Riga and a coach who was one of his closest friends there—along with a comically thuggish KGB agent, suffering from a bad toothache, who is there to make sure that neither of them has a chance to defect. Roman grows exuberant, "energized by the proximity to his former life" (54). As he waxes nostalgic for the communal ties and camaraderie of the old world, his former comrades, now well past their prime, envy the Spartan but unfettered life he has managed to create for himself. "Don't be fooled, Grisha," Roman tells his friend. "I often think of going back. . . . Every day is a struggle." But Grisha in *not* fooled, for he sees things through the prism of his own condition: "Look, I'm not blind. I see your car. I see your apartment. I see how you struggle. Believe me, your worst day is better than my best" (60). The comedy of the story yields a Chekhovian pathos. The road of the immigrant is marked with pitfalls along with possibilities. The Bermans are still outsiders, lonely, needy, and uprooted. These friends will never see each other again, and both of them, for the moment, are at just this side of despair.

The other effect of the author's irony is to span the distance between the adult who narrates and the boy who barely understood these events as they were taking place. As a child visiting the rabbi, the young Berman "was sufficiently aware of our predicament to feel the various permutations of shame: shame for my father, shame for my shame, and even shame for the rabbi, who seemed to be a decent guy" (25). Subsuming the consciousness of the child in the reflections of the man, Bezmozgis makes us feel the profound awkwardness of the immigrant situation, the difficulty of knowing exactly how to behave. The most acclaimed of the new Russian Jewish immigrant writers, including Bezmozgis, Gary Shteyngart, and Lara Vapnyar, were born in the early 1970s and published their first books in English thirty years later. Bezmozgis and Shteyngart came here with their families when they were seven. They grew up here. Their home life was European, their street life and school life Canadian or American, though both also attended Jewish schools, less for religious reasons than to cushion their entry into a new world. Vapnyar, on the other hand, came here in 1994 at the age of 23 bearing a master's degree in Russian literature but not knowing much English. The stories in her first collection, *There Are Jews in My House* (2003), like theirs, unfold chronologically, like chapters in a bildungsroman. At each stage they try to recapture the child's or young person's angle of vision, and all but one of them are set in Russia. In her later work the locale shifts to the United States.

In short, while earlier Jewish immigrant literature was largely written by the children of poverty, reflecting on their parents' hardscrabble lives and their own struggles to live on different terms,

the new immigrant literature comes from the children of educated professionals; their own formation is as much North American
as European, since they came here so young. The global reach
of mass culture and the English language introduced them to
America even before they arrived. They feel little nostalgia for
a country that oppressed their parents and never fully absorbed
them. These are growing-up stories in which the embarrassments
of an adolescent's coming-of-age meld with the immigrant family's awkwardness at adapting to a new culture, a new language, a
somewhat alien way of life. The same themes, the same dilemma,
can be found in work by Eastern European writers who are not
Jewish, as in the Bosnian Aleksander Hemon's first novel *Nowhere
Man* (2002). The growing-up part of the book is set in the multi-
ethnic city of Sarajevo, with an interlude in Kiev (Hemon's father
was Ukrainian). The rest takes place in Chicago where Hemon
landed in 1992 as a visiting journalist, having planned to stay but
a month, only to be stranded by the outbreak of the Bosnian war.

Most young writers write autobiographically, immigrant writers especially so. But there is a sense in which every immigrant
story, like every adolescent's story, resembles every other. Hemon
is acutely conscious of this. Approaching his young protagonist's
love life, still largely imaginary, he stands back: "It might strike
the reader that the life of this hero is not particularly exceptional,
for many a boy indulged in fantasies in which the readiness of
unknown women to make passionate, yet educational love to a
gangly youngster was directly proportional to the impossibility of
such a scenario ever occurring."[3] Hemon's not quite idiomatic
English mirrors the sense of strangeness and detachment central to his experience. He is a particularly self-conscious writer,
acutely aware of the roles his characters play, but all four writers
stress the insecurity of their youthful surrogates, their loneliness,
their self-consciousness about their clothes, their accents, their

parents—above all, their desperate desire to fit in, a feeling nearly all immigrants share with nearly all adolescents.

Vladimir Girshkin, Shteyngart's alter ego in his first novel, *The Russian Debutante's Handbook* (2002), sees himself just as much the outsider at twenty-five as in his school days, when even among Jews he felt awkward and ostracized. His doting grandmother buys him a windbreaker, for she is "the only grown-up to realize that his trendy Hebrew school chums were making fun of his ill-fitting overcoat with its inherent East Bloc smell; the only one to understand the pain in being called a Stinky Russian Bear."[4] Besides its propulsive, caffeinated prose, the best thing about Shteyngart's novel, like Hemon's, is not its story, which is loose and picaresque, but its nice grasp of the stresses and paradoxes of the immigrant condition. In the work of these writers, virtually everything about daily life can be a challenge, a hurdle to be surmounted. Shteyngart's protagonist never lets his guard down; he is always careful to avoid "those slips of the amateur assimilationist" (186) that might expose or undo him. When a woman questions his calculated behavior and lack of spontaneity, Girshkin says, "I'm a foreigner. I speak slowly and choose my words with care, lest I embarrass myself" (30), a sentence so deliberate it displays the very caution he's describing. He *is* calculating, an operator, at once a schlemiel who doesn't fit in and a con artist fitting other people to his purposes. With another woman, we are told, "the immigrant, the Russian, the stinky Russian Bear to be precise, was already taking notes." He spies not only the prospect of sex but "a chance to steal something native, to score some insider knowledge, from an unsuspecting *Americanka* like this woman" (85). Like Alex Portnoy, *shtupping* girls whose ancestors came over on the Mayflower, Girshkin treats sex as a form of social mobility, a way of "gaining swift entrée into her classy little world" (89). But with such *shikse* goddesses he also loses confidence: "How did one go about changing one's warbling tongue, one's half-destroyed parents, the very stink of one's body? . . . [H]e was touched by the sight of a body more plausible than his, the body of a woman who approached the earth on equal terms" (316).

Girshkin gains the acceptance he craves, but not on American soil. "Assimilate or leave, those were his options" (85); he chooses to leave, reversing the usual trajectory of the immigrant novel. He departs New York for "the other side, the low-rent side of the planet" (179–180), to a somewhat fantastic version of Prague, called Prava ("a better place to be unhappy," [198]), in a lightly fictionalized state called the Republika Stolovaya. There, in the crossroads of Central Europe, in volleys of prose so forceful that they seem shot from a cannon, Shteyngart indulges his gift for combining local color with picaresque fabulation, mordant self-analysis with over-the-top satire, much of it centered on the cross-cultural condition of immigrants themselves. The circumstances of the novel's publication are something of a legend. After his own time in Prague, a contemporary East Village for many young Americans in the early 1990s, Shteyngart wrote the book rapidly as an undergraduate project at Oberlin College, with no thought of publication until his graduate writing teacher at Hunter College in New York, the Korean-American novelist Chang-Rae Lee, read the first thirty pages and passed the book on to his agent. It became a critical and commercial success, and Shteyngart's meteoric career was launched. (Bezmozgis's path to publication was also smoothed by a well-connected mentor, the late Leonard Michaels.)

The Russian Debutante's Handbook is not one but two books, first a sardonic, semi-autobiographical novel about growing up in Queens as the son of recent Russian immigrants, going off to a liberal arts college in the Midwest, feeling sandwiched between two worlds. What follows is a baroquely plotted tale, not even half serious: the protagonist is caught up with Russian mafiosi in a Ponzi scheme to swindle young American expatriates who made Prague a cheap bohemian enclave in the 1990s, as Paris had been from the twenties to the fifties. The first part has rightly been seen as an inversion of "the classic immigrant narrative — starring a sarcastic slacker instead of a grateful striver," and "an ingeniously crafted update of earlier sagas of upward-struggling American newcomers."[5] The second part, set on neutral ground halfway between West and East — the "Wild East," as David Fishman has called it[6] — can be taken for the fantasies through which the young immigrant loner, still angling for acceptance, compensates yet also takes revenge for his humiliations, the nagging sense of difference he has felt since childhood. Shteyngart has written an autobiographical essay that recalls how unhappy he was in his Hebrew day school in Queens, until he began writing fantastic stories that were eventually read aloud, gaining for him a measure of recognition among his peers.[7] Like Scheherazade, who spun out stories as a way of keeping alive, Shteyngart's novel exfoliates a plot whose weightlessness and whimsicality reflect the hero's doubtful identity — his need to find a locale and a narrative, however improbable, in which he can shine. Fearing he is nobody, a caesura between two cultures, the resourceful young immigrant turns his skill at role-playing to his advantage.

The question of identity is central to the immigrant narrative, but it also highlights the differences between earlier and more recent immigrant writers. This issue is often expressed through the metaphor of the journey. In Mary Antin's classic 1912 autobiography *The Promised Land* (in a chapter called "Exodus"), she describes her literal journey from Polotzk, in the Russian Pale, through Germany to Berlin and Hamburg, and then, in the course of sixteen days at sea, to New York and Boston. But her whole book is a journey from one identity to another, a "second birth," as she calls it, that will precisely close the book on her "earlier self." "My life," she says, "I have still to live; her life ended when mine began." At the close of her introduction she writes:

> It is painful to be consciously of two worlds. The Wandering Jew in me seeks forgetfulness. I am not afraid to live on and on, if only I do not have to remember too much. A long past vividly remembered is like a heavy garment that clings to your limbs when you would run. And I have thought of a charm that should release me from the folds of my clinging past. I take the hint from the Ancient Mariner, who told his tale in order to be rid of it. I, too, will tell my tale, for once, and never hark back any more. I will write a bold "Finis" at the end, and shut the book with a bang!"[8]

This long passage is full of Romantic tropes—the Wandering Jew, the Ancient Mariner, even Prospero and his book—all consciously deployed with anti-Romantic intent. These mythical figures were all haunted by the past, but (unlike Antin) they did not seek a radical break that would cast memory aside. Especially since the destruction of the Second Temple, Jews have survived in part through memory, as crystallized in oral tradition, writing, and ritual. Like the peoples of the Balkan States, they have obsessively commemorated the catastrophes that befell them. It's an American gesture, not a Jewish one, to put the old world, the old self, completely behind us to start from a clean slate—to run, to sprint away from one's past rather than to keep it in mind. The opening of Antin's book ("I was born, I have lived, and I have been made over") is Emersonian, not Hebraic. Philip Rahv once remarked that America should be nicknamed Amnesia.

The other oddity of Antin's outlook, also very American, is the sense of having two wholly distinct selves, one of which can simply take the place of the other. Yet Emerson, the great philosopher of American selfhood, did not project a transition between two fixed identities but rather an endless process of self-invention, a mobile coming-into-being. All immigrant writers sometimes feel that their complexity of identity can be a burden, that it can be painful to be "consciously of two worlds." Yet even before the current interest among scholars in "hybridity," highlighting the multiple sources of identity, few writers tried as vigorously as Antin to suppress the influences that made them who they are. For earlier immigrants, the physical journey itself—long, arduous, and usually irreversible—resonated with the inner transformation they hoped to achieve. Behind them lay rural poverty, medieval superstition, and a long history of persecution in lands where they never felt welcome. Ahead were not just fantasies of a promised land, its streets paved with gold, but a horizon that seemed open—if not for the immigrants themselves, then for their children, even in crowded ghettos that mimicked the old culture and reminded them of the poverty they had fled.

Many new immigrants from the Third World come from places as poor as the ones Russian and Polish Jews had left behind in 1882 or 1905. For recent Jewish immigrants from Eastern Europe this is no longer true. Their well-educated parents grew up in a fiercely secular society. Their surviving grandparents gave them a taste, but only a taste, of the old world of Russian Jews. Even the so-called ghettos they created here, as in New York's Brighton Beach, are little more than ethnic neighborhoods that offer a flavor, more like a caricature, of the old country. In a recent story by Lara Vapnyar, "Borscht," one of a series she is writing around food, a young Russian in New York, not formally an immigrant but a recently married man who is here on his own to earn money to buy an apartment back home, takes the train to Brighton Beach Avenue to call on a part-time hooker. She is also married, also here temporarily to earn some money. The visit is not a success. The neighborhood revolts him as a poor imitation of the world he comes from. "Normally he hated this street. . . . Sergey never felt at home there. . . . This was the fake Russia, the parody of Russia, that made the real Russia seem further away and hopelessly unobtainable." The woman, eager to please but no longer young or attractive, turns him off. In phone conversations with his young wife, he senses that she's less than eager to have him back. Her living presence for him has faded into the picture he has of her, a woman with a tight smile. "Lenka was far away, and getting farther every day." The woman in Brighton Beach has gotten the same message from her family at home. But feeling bad about this man whose money she has already taken, she insists on preparing a steaming bowl of borscht for him and even making a toast over a glass of vodka.

> "We have to make a toast," Alla said and looked into her glass. "For going home. No matter if they want us or not."
> "For going home," Sergey said, and they clinked their glasses.
> He felt a chill on the tongue followed immediately by a great warmth spreading down his throat and chest. He took a big heavy spoonful of borscht and brought it to his mouth, holding a piece of bread beneath the spoon.[9]

So the story ends.

For these characters, unlike Mary Antin, home has become a malleable concept, both portable and potable. They still envision going back, but meanwhile the borscht, the vodka, and the bread create a momentary community of two, providing a warmth they can no longer get from their spouses, or even from having sex with each other. The relations between the old world and the new, like their own identities, have grown more complex since Antin's time. These are immigrants who can always go back, who go back and forth all the time. The new immigrants belong to what Donald Weber has described as "a postcolonial world shaped by constant movement and upheaval, of orbiting families (to borrow the title of a Bharati Mukherjee story), unsettling their 'host' nations' fixed identities."[10] And also, one might add, unsettling their own. It is precisely this fluid, "postmodern" sense of identity that makes the current crop of immigrants—and immigrant writers—so different.

Just as their journeys are different from the steamer travel of old, and much less definitive, so are their identities labile in ways Antin could not have imagined. They've come here as young people, still unformed. The dark side of their mobility is the perpetual sense of dislocation conveyed by the titles of Edward Said's memoir *Out of Place* or Hemon's novel *Nowhere Man*, named after a Beatles song ("He's a real nowhere man, / Sitting in his Nowhere Land, / Making all his nowhere plans / for no-body"). Hemon's novel grew out of a surreal autobiographical novella, "Blind Jozef Pronek & Dead Souls," in his collection of stories *The Question of Bruno* (2000). As a teenager in Sarajevo, Hemon's alter ego, Jozef Pronek, studies English and starts a rock group that sings only Beatles songs. The city itself was famous for its tolerant mixture of nationalities and religions, at least before the Bosnian War set neighbor against neighbor. "Sarajevo in the eighties was a beautiful place to be young—I know because I was young then" (49). Pronek's father, like Hemon's, is Ukrainian, but Pronek's father uses the international culture of English and rock to carve out a space separate from his parents, to which they have no access. The rebellious young Pronek comes to hate his father "for being a fucking foreigner: displaced, cheap, and always angry" (89), and hates old men in general for their patriotic nostalgia for the world of their childhood, with its bitter nationalistic rivalries. In Ukraine he feels no interest in visiting his father's hometown.

Both Pronek, who migrates from Sarajevo to Chicago, and Shteyngart's Girshkin, whose family hails from Leningrad, are at the cutting edge of a new globalism; cut loose from their origins, they are at once contemptuous and yet envious of complacent native types who seem so secure in their simple loyalties and firm identities. At times they feel like ciphers, voyagers from nowhere to nowhere, hollow men, ungrounded. Girshkin imagines that 'real' Americans, out of confidence or insensitivity, feel at home everywhere, especially in their own bodies. Both writers are instinctive postmodernists for whom immigration epitomizes the instability of modern identity. For Shteyngart, a much more light-hearted writer, this involves the picaresque adventures of a shape-shifting con artist as antihero. Hemon, perhaps more rigorously, deploys Pronek as his equivalent of Philip Roth's Zuckerman, a surrogate whose "counterlife" enables him to examine his own experience as if from the outside. He does this in part by shuffling the time scheme and observing him through the eyes of narrators who change mysteriously from chapter to chapter. Pronek himself has the constant experience, typical of a writer as well as an immigrant, of standing outside himself, probing the limits of who he is. "Why couldn't he be more than one person? Why was he stuck in the middle of himself, hungry and tired?" (198). The novel begins: "Had I been dreaming, I would have dreamt of being someone else, with a little creature burrowed in my body, clawing at the walls inside my chest—a recurring nightmare. But I was awake . . ." (3). In the Chicago suburbs, campaigning for Greenpeace from door to door, Pronek fears being laughed at, patronized. "He imagined good Americans opening their doors, hating him for his foreign stupidity, for his silly accent, for his childish grammar errors" (167). In one bravura passage he confounds these ordinary Americans by altering his identity at each stop, making himself up as he goes along, yet behind it all feeling like "Nobody," like "Someone Else" (180).[11] Yet he could just as well be seen as Everyman, the immigrant as Woody Allen's Zelig (or the blank-slate protagonist of Jerzy Kosinski's *Being There*). In Ukraine in 1991 Pronek turns up just in time for a revolution and a visit by the first President Bush. Around him Hemon creates a fluid fictional space influenced by the writers he most admires, including Bruno Schulz and Danilo Kiš, central European masters who were also hybrid Jews.

For Shteyngart that fluid space, where almost anything can happen, is the expatriate world of Prague in the early 1990s, with its would-be writers starting little magazines, its Russian mobsters and callow American students. Back in New York he had been exasperated by "this being Vladimir Girshkin business, this being neither here nor there, neither Leningrad nor Soho" (92). In Prava Girshkin feels more American than in New York, more Russian than anywhere else. He experiences himself as a Jew only in his sense of marginality, or when he sees himself as schlemiel-like, inept, physically clumsy, or when he's cursed out as a Jew, or begins an affair with a wholesome American girl. Most Russian immigrants brought little positive Jewish culture with them from the Soviet Union. Their residual Jewishness was often represented by little more than a stray grandparent, a figure in the background for Shteyngart, Vapnyar, and Bezmozgis. In some of their stories, the grandparent is like a living relic, eccentric or ill, their almost shattered link to a Russian Jewish past.

As writers from Eastern Europe, they rarely feel the pressure that Jewish writers like Bellow and Malamud exerted on their American contemporaries. Instead they bring their own influences: Kafka, Nabokov (himself a master of émigré fiction), Schulz, Kiš, Russian classics like Gogol, Chekhov, and Babel, but also Philip Roth, who developed a special connection to "Writers from the Other Europe" (as he called his Penguin series). But a story like Bezmozgis's "Minyan" moves in Malamud's path as the young narrator pursues his "nostalgia for old Jews" (134), his quickened feeling for a tradition he never really knew. The story deals with the tenuous survival of a daily minyan, or prayer service, in a housing facility for the elderly, where the narrator's recently widowed grandfather has moved. (The illness and death of the grandmother had been part of the previous story, "Choynski.")

The plot focuses not on young Berman's grandfather, who has somehow adapted to his new life, but on two widowers who share another flat in the building, men whose tender relationship is rumored to be more than friendly. When one of them dies, after a life beset by all the upheavals of Jews in the twentieth century, the survivor is stricken with sorrow. At the funeral, "his worn tweed jacket and crooked back delivered a eulogy before he reached the coffin. His posture was unspeakable grief. What could he say that could compare with the eulogy of his wretched back?" (142). His measureless grief adds to suspicions of an unnatural attachment. The fate of the coveted apartment hangs in the balance, as does the minyan itself, which is by now as imperiled as an old man's life. Mostly not religious men, the prayer-goers, like the narrator, have been "drawn by the nostalgia for ancient cadences" (134). The wise beadle, with Malamudian generosity—but also with a determined self-interest—awards the apartment to the elderly survivor, despite the scurrilous rumors: "My concern is ten Jewish men. If you want ten Jewish saints, good luck. . . . They should know I don't put a Jew who comes to synagogue in the street. Homosexuals, murderers, liars, and thieves—I take them all. Without them we would never have a minyan" (147). This God-like judgment is hardly a compliment but its message is tolerance, inclusion. Here, a fable about dying old men, and perhaps a dying tradition, takes on a humane contemporary moral. In its wide embrace, the minyan will be like life itself. Diversity and tolerance spring from the notion that we may be sinners but are all God's children.

"Minyan" is about death and survival, as well as the young narrator's attraction to old Jews and the customs that helped them survive. Vapnyar's grandfather story, "Mistress," on the other hand, is a delightful if improbable account of rebirth. While the young protagonist's grandmother cooks up grand old-world meals and spends much of her time visiting doctors, where her nine-year-old grandson must translate for her, his grandfather, with no role to play and little to do with his time, lingers in a mute, listless state. The boy, too, is in immigrant shock, bright with potential yet unable to speak up in class, though he knows the right answers. He does his homework eagerly but cannot show it. "It wasn't true that he didn't talk at all. When asked a question, he gave an accurate answer, but he tried to make it as brief as possible." Instead he lives vigorously in his own head, imagining all he might say. The same thing happens when his divorced father calls. "Misha spent a whole week preparing for his call; he had thousands of things to tell him. . . . But when his father called, Misha went numb. He answered questions but never volunteered to speak and never asked anything himself."[12]

To fill up his time, the grandfather is urged to take English classes; the boy and the old man do their homework together. When the grandfather strikes up a relationship with a woman he knew back in Russia, his long walks with the boy enable him to see her. When challenged, he shows new backbone. "The grandfather was firm, almost as firm as he used to be back in Russia. He said the boy needed exercise and that was that" (110). Thanks to this new friendship, both the old man and the boy emerge from their shells for the first time, as if licensed to live again. They make this their secret and forge a quiet, conspiratorial bond, suggesting the affinity that Vapnyar herself, like David Bezmozgis, feels for an earlier generation. She writes as if old people—and older writers—have something to teach her. In one of her best stories, "Love Lessons—Mondays, 9 a.m.," an aged aunt, twice married, once perhaps a beauty, educates her inexperienced niece with tales from her colorful love life.

Because of her training in Russian literature and her love of its greatest writers, Vapnyar's bond with her elders reaches even further back. In her first novel, *Memoirs of a Muse* (2006), she enlarges the immigrant narrative by giving us a young woman who identifies with Dostoevsky's mistress and muse, Polina Suslova.[13] Even back in Russia, the bookish Tanya, awkward with boys, inexperienced in love life, had imagined that she too was destined to become the muse of a great writer. But when she acts out this fantasy by moving in with a young writer in New York, who treats her as little more than an appendage and a convenience, she lets herself in for a heavy dose of humiliation. This motif of self-degradation may well be Vapnyar's tribute to Dostoevsky, whose troubled affair with Polina she recounts in vivid detail. But the parallels between Tanya and Polina are strained, and nothing can disguise the improbability of Tanya's gross self-deception and her sudden awakening, as she comes too quickly to detest everything that appealed to her about her lover, including his writing. The theme of *Memoirs of a Muse* is closely linked to the role-playing, the insecurities, and the confusions of identity of other young immigrant characters coming of age, but is built on an idea that never quite comes off.

Vapnyar encompasses history more effectively, reaching back to a darker past, in the superb title story of *There Are Jews in My House*. All her stories center on characters who feel stigmatized, on the brink of rejection, people living on other people's sufferance. In "There Are Jews in My House," set during World War II, this is literally the case. A Jewish woman and her daughter take refuge with a gentile friend and her young daughter when the Nazis occupy their town. Despite the terrible danger, despite differences of taste and class, the two women gossip about everything like sisters, even their intimate lives with their husbands, who are both off in the military. But this suffocating proximity leads to jealousy, even hatred, which we see through the eddying emotions of the would-be Russian protector, who is not quite up to the role of the righteous gentile. As she grows more irritable and impatient with the Jews in her house, the Jewish woman feels increasingly vulnerable, then desperate. She rightly worries about being betrayed, an overwhelming temptation her gentile friend can barely resist. In the end she does resist, just barely, but the tension has grown unbearable. The fugitives decamp for what looks like certain death.

On the surface this is a powerful Holocaust story, but more symbolically it portrays the deep but hostile kinship, almost twin-ship, between Russians and Jews, and its disastrous consequences. As the title suggests, the Jew is the secret sharer of Russian culture, the perennial Other, fated to become the chosen victim. For the Russian woman, despite her good intentions, the Jew in her house, her alter ego, gradually becomes an alien presence, an encumbrance, not for anything she says or does but for who she is. Like Europe with all *its* Jews, she feels a mounting need to cast them out. This pressure is cultural rather than personal. The story has touches of allegory, for Russia itself is perhaps the house to which the title refers. Unlike most Americans, writers from Eastern Europe have invariably felt the weight of history in their lives and they've searched for unconventional techniques to express it. Whether they are Jewish or not, their lives have been knocked around by history and dislocated by culture and geography. The disintegration of Yugoslavia and the siege of Sarajevo run like a thread of blood through Hemon's novel, as the history of persecution runs through the work of Russian Jews. It may not be possible for anyone from Eastern Europe, Jew or gentile, to avoid the legacy of World War II, the genocide of the Jews, and the Communist occupation that followed, though older writers like Norman Manea in *The Hooligan's Return* (2003) are more likely to deal with these traumas directly, since they experienced them at first hand.

Once these writers arrived in North America, they all turned more Jewish, as if licensed by the strong Jewish presence in American literary culture, but also by a multicultural environment that equates ethnic identity with personal authenticity. They know that immigrant writers all run the risk of telling the same story about their coming of age, their sense of estrangement and cultural displacement, the ordeal of language, the conflicts between generations, and their need for acknowledgment within their new world. So they have worked hard to cultivate their own voice, sardonic and picaresque for Shteyngart, Chekhovian for Vapnyar, quietly ironic for Bezmozgis. All of them arrived young enough to learn to write in English, which has become the new international language, the lingua franca of the global imperium, and all have been published in *The New Yorker*, a magazine that styles itself a guardian of the language and the marker of a new fiction writer's arrival. In the terminology of the Cold War, they "chose the West," yet brought with them some valuable Eastern baggage, including literary traditions that show how endangered our separate lives may be, how susceptible to the crosswinds of history. Where immigrant writing was once naturalistic and focused on the material conditions of life, and later (beginning with Henry Roth) more modernist, probing the immigrant's psychological formation, these new writers have concentrated on questions of identity in a world in which both the geography of the planet and the geography of the mind have shifted and turned more fluid. Today, once again, immigration has become the catalyst for momentous changes in American life. By channeling the rhythms of another culture (and of their own insecurities) into English, these writers have become fully American yet have also added new wrinkles to the ongoing story of immigrants and American literature.

Notes

1. See the revealing memoir by his daughter, Janna Malamud Smith, *My Father Is a Book: A Memoir of Bernard Malamud* (New York: Houghton Mifflin, 2006), which I reviewed in the *Times Literary Supplement* (May 12, 2006): 8.

2. David Bezmozgis, "Roman Berman, Massage Therapist," in *Natasha and Other Stories* (New York: Farrar, Straus and Giroux, 2004), 21. (Further references by page number in the text.)

3. Aleksander Hemon, *Nowhere Man: The Pronek Fantasies* (New York: Doubleday, 2002), 47. (Further references by page number in the text.)

4. Gary Shteyngart, *The Russian Debutante's Handbook* (2002; New York: Riverhead Books, 2003), 36. (Further references by page number in the text.)

5. I quote here from eight pages of excerpts from enthusiastic reviews that appear at the beginning of the Riverhead paperback edition.

6. See David Fishman, ed., *Wild East: Stories from the Last Frontier* (2003; New York: Random House, 2004). This anthology includes not only stories from Eastern Europe but also stories by young American writers like Arthur Phillips who set their work there. Other American writers who have been drawn to Eastern Europe, past and present, for material include Jonathan Safran Foer, Nathan Englander, Dara Horn, and Nicole Krauss.

7. Gary Shteyngart, "The Mother Tongue between Two Slices of Rye," *The Threepenny Review* (Spring 2004). Available at http://www .threepennyreview.com/samples/shteyngart_sp04.html (accessed February 8, 2008).

8. Mary Antin, *The Promised Land* (Boston and New York: Houghton Mifflin, 1912), xi, xiv–xv.

9. Lara Vapnyar, "Borscht," *Harper's* (February 2006): 79, 80, 82.

10. Donald Weber, "Permutations of New-World Experiences Rejuvenate Jewish-American Literature," Chronicle Review, *Chronicle of Higher Education* (September 17, 2004). Available at http://chronicle .com/free/v51/i04/04b00801.htm (accessed February 8, 2008).

11. This theme reminds me of a favorite passage in *The Great Gatsby* in which Tom Buchanan, racist and xenophobe, dismisses Gatsby as an outsider, a man of no consequence: "I suppose the latest thing is to sit back and let Mr. Nobody from Nowhere make love to your wife. Well, if that's the idea you can count me out. . . ." A few lines later he

adds, "next they'll throw everything overboard and have intermarriage between black and white." This nicely links the poor young man from the provinces with the ethnic or racial outsider. F. Scott Fitzgerald, *The Great Gatsby* (1925; New York: Scribner's, n.d.), 130.

12. Lara Vapnyar, "Mistress," in *There Are Jews in My House* (2003; New York: Anchor, 2004), 107. (Further references by page number in the text.)

13. Lara Vapnyar, *Memoirs of a Muse* (New York: Pantheon, 2006).

A Displaced Scholar's Tale

The Jewish Factor

— *Geoffrey Hartman*

This is a story without suspense, drama, or crises of conscience. That will make you suspicious. But you cannot be more suspicious of myself than I am. Having the privilege of choosing where to begin, I do so with my arrival in the States; and this puts behind me as unremarkable, no, fortunate, given the deadly and uprooting era in which I grew up, the fact of having been evacuated to England in March 1939 with a *Kindertransport*.

I was nine years old. My father divorced when I was still an infant and went to Argentina after the Nazis came to power. My mother, having emigrated to America the month following Kristallnacht, hoped I could join her soon, a hope frustrated by the outbreak of the war and the submarine menace. I was reunited with her more than six years later, in August 1945. My grandmother on my mother's side, ill with diabetes, could not leave and died in Teresienstadt.

Memoirs all contain an amount of ego fiction. The "I," Pascal sternly remarked, is to be hated (*haïssable*), and to forestall that reaction, which could easily add itself to the suspiciousness already mentioned, the "I" in this story freely admits it is in flight from overstatement. The idea of publicizing my story came as an irritable response to an academic question I kept being asked about my shift from Wordsworth, Romanticism, and issues of critical style to Holocaust Studies, and also to Midrash as a neglected resource for contemporary nonreligious modes of interpretation. Does this shift matter, and does it indicate a sharp turn in my self-image or sense of vocation? Or was there, as a dear friend put it, a hidden continuity in my work responding to the discontinuity in my life?[1]

Although I cannot answer these questions decisively, two uncanny albeit not extraordinary facts emerge from the past, and point to an underlying, obstinate-bass tonality from early on.

For many years I hoarded an essay called "Cultural Memory and the Passion Narrative." The Passion narrative has received a new injection of relevance through the wide appeal (at least in this country) of Mel Gibson's film, *The Passion of the Christ*. Only when I began thinking back did it occur to me that, in the 1950s, aiming to be a poet, I actually wrote fragments of a Passion Play removed from a Christian context and adapting the words of a Holocaust survivor. My play aspired to the form of a Greek tragedy, featuring a Chorus, a protagonist bent on self-sacrifice, and a survivor's flashback conversation with a Nazi officer in a death camp.

That this play, as well as a further drama about Saul, failed to be completed, was not due to the pains of what Eva Hoffman's *Lost in Translation* has called "Life in a New Language."[2] The very attempt, however, to write so ambitiously *was* affected by my first displacement. Exposed at an early age to the great literary exemplars of my adopted country, I developed a love for these while entering more into their formal architecture, musicality, and diction than into a mature content I barely understood. I did not lose anything "in translation."

Of course, I was still unripe; I had not become a writer when having to leave Germany for England and eventually coming to

America. In England I gained a new language without repressing the mother tongue I rarely used but preserved in silence together with the image of an absent mother. I also gained, if it was a gain, a hankering after sublimities I could not live up to, even in maturity. Without abandoning what Blake called "the rough basement" of colloquial English, I was attracted to the high Romantic mode, as well as by what I read in the Bible about protagonists who shouldered the burden of a divine election.

The second detail pointing to an uncanny continuity needs more of a prologue. Lacking the benefit of an early religious education, nothing came to me predigested. This proved to be an advantage in one respect. I read not only the King James version of the Bible but also other books for their own sake, absorbing them without external pressure or conscious aim. The Bible, especially, attracted and intrigued, and kept the imagination going.

Later, as a teacher, I found myself more interested in examples of daring interpretation than in the problem of chastening these by criteria of correctness. Not a libertarian attitude inspired me but the pleasure of allowing texts to lead my thoughts, then to work them through with students, collectively, in class. In deciding among interpretive choices, I only reluctantly abandoned the rejected or marginal ones. Interpretation, I felt, should be a feast not a fast.

This interest in the process of interpretation, rather than proving or fighting for a particular view, led to an "object all sublime" for my studies. I formulated it after two hard and tedious, if also at times hilarious years as a draftee in Uncle Sam's army, from 1953 to 1955. My intent was to write a History of Interpretation: not just of its contemporary, mainly secular phase, but also to uncover the eight-ninths of a hidden iceberg consisting primarily of a mass of biblical exegeses overlooked by modern literary thinkers.

I had become fascinated by Christian as well as Rabbinic interpreters, by their very extravagance, quite often, their perverse elaboration (or so it seemed) of sacred texts. I quickly realized my lack of resources for such a history; and, to make headway on the Rabbinic side, spent the mosquito-filled summer of 1957 at the Jewish Theological Seminary. It only confirmed that I would never catch up, given my advanced age at the time—all of twenty-seven.

In order to access the Talmud and its accompanying corpus of midrashic texts, one must begin training as early as a ballerina: latest at age seven, not twenty-seven. Yet Akiba, who became the patron sage of *Akiba's Children*, my only book of verse,[3] was probably even older, when, as it is told, this illustrious rabbi, once an illiterate peasant, eavesdropped on a school to begin his education.

Given my own belatedness, and that I needed to be more proficient at ancient and modern languages, I relinquished the projected History of Interpretation. Still, for many years—at least until *Midrash and Literature* was published in 1986—I continued a scholarly flirtation with the freer form of Midrash, midrash aggada.[4] Its imaginative development, often within the framework of legal issues, prepared me for a broader engagement with Judaic Studies, which I helped to organize at Yale in the 1980s.

The uncanny fact for which all this is prologue involves ancestry. While a visiting professor at the University of Zurich, I recalled that my maternal grandfather, a rabbi and teacher of religion at Frankfurt's Philantropin (the oldest secular Jewish school in Germany, founded in 1804)—my grandfather had studied for a time at Zurich before receiving his doctorate. He died when I was a year old. I consulted the university library, and, behold, it had his dissertation, a product of the *Wissenschaft des Judentums*. Its title: *The Book of Ruth in Midrash Literature*.[5] On returning to Yale, I hastened to look in *its* Library and found the same booklet right there.

What has been said so far recalls a cliché that contains a difficult truth. Am I portraying an exile, living in the company of great books, making them his homeland? But I did not feel like an exile. I was the Unexile. While it is hard to remember precisely one's thoughts at an early age, I do not recall worrying about my identity. Being Jewish seemed a fact of nature. Eventually, though, possibly through my twofold displacement, I fell into the category of what has been called a "Jew of culture" (Philip Rieff) or "a Jew, but not of the Synagogue" (Amos Oz). Nonobservant in the main, I grew up as a person for whom, when it came to literature or the arts, no bright line separated Jewish and non-Jewish, or sacred and secular.

Nor did I turn against the classics of my native language. Studying German Romanticism I felt at home with Hölderlin and Goethe as with Wordsworth and Keats. I realized, of course, that cultural icons could be misappropriated and politicized, as in Nazism. Yet such misprision simply raised the ante: freedom of interpretation had to triumph over an ideologically induced distortion, so that hermeneutics as a disciplinary field revealed its essential place in the humanities.

Perhaps all who have a literary vocation build up a reserve that acts as a personal Scripture. The Bible continued to be, within that context, a resource. I sought to understand its portrayal of God and to envisage what existential functions might have been the reason for ritual law and such central, conspicuous speech-acts as naming, vowing, blessing, curse. The contextual frame of nonbiblical literature, however, always accompanied the comparatist-to-be. Franz Rosenzweig has a Bloomian insight in which he views the Bible through Kafka: "The people who wrote the Bible seem to have thought of God much the way Kafka did. I have never read a book that reminds me so much of the Bible as his novel *The Castle*."[6] This perspective, Rosenzweig added, was not a comforting one.

Like Rosenzweig, moreover, I experienced an "insatiable hunger for forms . . . a hunger without goal or meaning." I did not share, however, his revulsion at that libidinous knowledge drive and the endless cultural differences exposed by historicism. Rosenzweig, though offered an academic position—a rare thing for a Jew in the Germany of 1937—felt he had to reject it.[7] "Cognition," he told the historian Friederich Meinecke in turning the offer down, and, indeed, renouncing academic life entirely, "Cognition no longer appears to me as an end in itself."[8]

In my case, the choice of academic life occurred without conflicting thoughts; and the gift of studying provided by four years of graduate education, then by the enforced isolation of army life, and finally by university appointments, allowed me to be shielded, for a time, from pressures of the public sphere.

Rosenzweig, of course, worried heroically about what kind of Jewish community was viable. His rejection of Meinecke's offer meant he would devote himself totally to the revival of Jewish learning among Germany's rapidly assimilating Jews. A new translation of the Bible, not as an accommodation, but as an attempt to influence, like Luther, the German language itself, and his return to observances with a *kavanah* that should characterize ritual acts, these became crucially important for the Frankfurt *Lehrschule* he helped to found. He also disputed those among the Zionists who believed a revival of Jewishness would occur only by adopting in Palestine a new Hebrew totally free from burdens of the past. So the language question, the unavoidable spiritual influence of what we speak and read, comes to the fore once again.[9]

During my time in Heidelberg, courtesy of the U.S. Army, a friend and I recruited a Shoah survivor to help us through the Book of Job. (It was Herr Sprecher's camp experiences that I later adapted for my Passion Play.) The Hebrew of Job was not my only difficulty. Reading the Bible I often felt disconcerted. Could one understand so strange a phenomenon as a God infinitely far away and yet so near that he heard Sara laugh and reproached her? Or why calamities and tortures should be inflicted on Job, on the Single One (to cite Martin Buber's Kierkegaardian concept), even if all this was staged as a limited ordeal and redeemed by the sublime pathos of Job's pleas and attestations, or that improbable Happy End, the *Wiedergutmachung* of thousands of sheep, camels, oxen, she-asses, and children?

It was not that I lusted after a spiritual intimacy characteristic of Christian notions of grace and mediation. My need was, well, ethnographic or anthropological. I wanted to understand the strangeness of Yahwe, not to evade it: to see what sociopolitical or psychic factors were involved. I also needed to be assured that human intermediaries had not intervened to skew the Bible's portrayal.

Yehuda Halevy's *Kuzari* eventually eased my sense of being too removed from an original revelation. Halevy claimed that an uninterrupted tradition (the kind suggested by the opening saying in the *Pirke Avot*) was equivalent to direct experience. This bolstered my own, Job-like wish to stand in the presence, to hope that vision, at least its echoes or "daughters" (the *bat kol*) had not ceased. I retained an instinctive belief in the possibility of an unmediated relation to truth—unmediated except by literary texts and arts associated with them.

Looking across the writing I have done over some fifty years, I see how important the call of literature was: how it sustained both a verbal discipline and an imaginative hope. It did not foster, though it might have, the solipsism of a youngster who grew up without a family and depended on the kindness of strangers. Instead, the idea of literature and that of community came together in viewing teaching as mutual learning. That was the ideal motivating my study of canonical texts: they enabled a sharing not basically different from what I later recognized as the spirit of Midrash. Literature became secular Scripture and literary commentary secular Midrash.

An allusive, Bible-oriented poetry, moreover, like Halevy's, taught me the power of pastiche; and this influenced fledgling poetic ventures. The Song of Songs was the model justifying the sacred dictions in Halevy's exilic love songs for Zion. But given my verses' distinctly nonsacred subject matter, I had to find a contrafactura style to emphasize the disparity between diction and content: a style strangely similar to what John Barth, referring to metafiction, called "cool riffs on the classical tune."

———

My trust in literary texts, their potential to express as much as could be expressed, led me to think about the ubiquity of figurative language with a religious cast. The great literary survivals of the ancient world are full of a ritual vocabulary and divine actors (or, it may be, Pretenders); this holds for a vast number of literary ventures throughout history. The idea that a displacement called secularization explains the later persistence of such "oriental" themes or figures of speech does not satisfy: more is surely involved than a theft of aura. I was intrigued, in any case, by Wordsworth, who used biblical colors of speech very sparingly, while seeming to stand on biblical ground.

In Wordsworth's autobiographical *Prelude* I found not only an account of the growth of a poet's mind but a recap of the developmental link between structures of feeling and ancient religious conceptions. Wordsworth conveys through powerful vignettes how as a youngster he was deeply affected by certain rural places, charged spots comparable to Jacob's Beit-El. A rotted gallows and its admonitory inscription, a tree, a tower, or other cosmic navel might open into vision. That "one" place could lead to the "One." Such "spots of time" were deeply, memorably frightening, even as purely virtual theophanies. The poet's vivid descriptions show that local revelation, its place-bound character, is part of the "incumbent mystery of sense and soul."

In the Bible, places marked by a theophany are given a name or a new name and held to be sacred. Without a relation of *nomen* and *numen*, could literature have come into being? The name localizes the event and recalls or even generates an explanatory story. Wordsworth tells of nature experiences inscribed on his memory, experiences that became a source of unalienated affection after they originally terrified him. By calling them "spots of time," he metaphorically merges "spot" as place and "spot" as an indelible mental mark with an underconscious influence.[10] Gradually, though, Nature frees the imagination from sensory (especially ocular) fixations that are the sign of psychic arrest and could lead to idolatrous fantasies.

Returning from Wordsworth's biography to my own: was the scholarly focus on spirit of place sensitized by my displacements? Did it contain a tacit hope that another country might inspire the homeless boy? Could he sing in a foreign land? I had been brought up in a big city, in Frankfurt; so the first and lasting impact on me of open nature was the English countryside during the very time I encountered Wordsworth's poetry.

Making this point, I feel like an imitation Kierkegaard. His "Prelude" to *Fear and Trembling* scans repeatedly the story of Isaac's sacrifice and shuttles between it and a narrative of traumatic individuation, of how the child is weaned from its parents. The role of fear, even terror, experienced early, is remarkable from a developmental point of view. That fear factor often translates into religious awe, into "fear and trembling," although not in my case. I was in awe only of Creation itself, of what I felt Wordsworth expressed: that a great force was masking itself, or gently deployed its majesty, spreading life in "widest commonality."

I cannot explain why that mask did not morph into a death's head, despite an increasing awareness of the Holocaust and of the barely controlled predominance of malignancy and outright aggression in the world. How much illusion was there in me at that time, and how much is there still? Reading Norman Manea's memoir, only my having escaped his incomparably severer situation, the mental as well as physical oppression he lived with, first in a Transnistrian camp, then under the all-pervasive political masquerade of Romanian communism, keeps me today from being afflicted by the disillusioned hope he mentions so often. "I had thought," Manea writes, "I could . . . imagine myself the inhabitant of a language rather than a country."[11] Though I too was bewitched by "the Promised Land, language," and could write about the intricate relation of words and wounds, I did not have to suffer, with little possibility of escape, the political traps of informers or the hysterical rhetoric of betrayer and betrayed.

I browsed Freud and Jung, as well as the exotic tomes of the Eranos Association with their admixture of classical and oriental studies. Also eagerly read were Van Gennep on rites of passage, the later (and politically quiescent) Mircea Eliade on the ritual abolition of contingency or of history's intolerable weight on consciousness, and Rudolf Otto on the *tremendum*. Most intriguing, though, was myth criticism. It became popular in the wake of speculations by the Cambridge (post-Frazer) school of anthropology that posited a primal archaic event, a ritual mime evolving into drama by adding actors and the *legomenon* of a narrative verbal reinforcement. Yet exactly what "mystery" or initiation was represented proved beyond reach.

Aristotle acknowledged the religious origins of drama, and left it at that. But Jane Harrison, Gilbert Murray, and others writing in the wake of Frazer went behind the purely structural, nonreligious categories of his *Poetics* to uncover shadowy outlines of an original sacred drama. There was methodological daring as well as literary discovery in these efforts. *Form-Geschichte*, a promising branch of the *Wissenschaft des Judentums*, without finding its Jewish Aristotle, suggested an analogous evolution of the Psalms from a central dramatic ceremony.[12]

Judaism differs, in any case, by refusing to be a mystery religion. Even if what happened in the Temple's inner shrine was covert, the ceremonies surrounding the Temple Mount, which were the primary occasion for the biblical Psalms, did not breed a mysterious initiation drama centering on what Aristotle, in his fragmentary *Poetics*, called *the [scene of] pathos*. The psalms are an open celebration, though with something invisible at its core, a vacancy eventually filled by the elaboration of a shared Scripture. Once the Temple cult with its sacrifices passes into history, the psalms as part of that celebration are integrated into decentralized, home-based rituals and the interpretive vigor of the B'nei Yisrael as a whole.

As my own bio-bibliographer, I glimpse a common axis to my early books. The axis is not primarily a theory correlating human psychological development with basic religious conceptions. I would define it rather as bookishness itself; more elegantly stated, as the problem of literary mediation.[13] That I find it impossible to empty "mediation" of a religious overtone is frustrating. But except for a Marxism that re-envisions mediation in terms of the circumstances and means of production, and frames the story of human liberty as entailing an emancipation from religion, not only of religion, there is no way to circumvent what Kenneth Burke in *The Rhetoric of Religion* calls logology: that all words are also about words as generative, as akin to the Logos. The anarchist philosopher Proudhon pointed to a parallel quandary when he lamented that language was full of Jove,[14] and Derrida's major effort was spent outwitting the logocentric character of the human sciences without giving up their rich, verbal constitution.

—

My Ph.D. thesis, published in 1954 as *The Unmediated Vision*, was minimally influenced by graduate teachers. Yet René Wellek, Henri Peyre, and Erich Auerbach, all refugees or displaced scholars, helped me by their high standards and broad perspective. Auerbach provided the example of *Mimesis*, which always used the close reading of a passage as the starting point for insights into a large historical development.[15] Even more important was his magnanimous rather than pale cosmopolitanism, his ability to take pleasure in the diversity of the national vernaculars as they developed their own literature. What I learned about the Nazis' so-called cleansing of German culture in order to create a purely "Nordic" or "Aryan" canon, placed the refugee scholars who taught me in an even more appealing light.[16]

A certain idea of Judaism may already have informed this first book. Simply stated, I tried to show that an unmediated relation to matters human or divine—unmediated except for a consecrated text—was similar to the mindset of the modern poets I wrote about. Wordsworth, Hopkins, Rilke, and Valéry, I argued, lived this lack of mediation; and it became a model of mediation. Existentially, they are Moses figures. The book's epigraph was from Deuteronomy: "The Lord talked with you face to face in the mount out of the midst of the fire. I stood between the Lord and you at that time, to show you the word of the Lord: for ye were afraid by reason of the fire, and went not up into the mount" (5:4–5).

Even a devout Christian like Hopkins relies on the plot of

the senses (though this was partly authorized by the practice of Ignatian meditation) and endeavors to report realities as directly as possible. One of my concluding chapters goes so far as to claim that poetry's symbolic process reflects an imaginative quest pitting the senses against each other in order to undo their confines and gain an "imageless vision." Mysticism (I was sporadically reading Meister Eckhart as well as Maimonides) and a desire for purity join here with a more than adolescent fervor; and I took the side of those who wished to limit the anthropomorphic imagination, or, rather, expand imagination toward "unknown modes of being."[17]

The book remained a questioning, however, rather than a taking of sides. Had I known Wallace Stevens's poetry at that time, I might have considered what I was doing as "Notes toward a Supreme Fiction." Should that supreme fiction be identified with the transcendentalism of a world seen in its idea, or with the realism of a world substantiating William Carlos Williams's "No Ideas but in Things"? Stevens, in his poetry, opted for things, but things "Washed in the remotest cleanliness of a heaven / That has expelled us and our images."[18]

A decade later a second book (apart from a short monograph on André Malraux) was entirely on Wordsworth. By that time my understanding of mediation, especially the role of language and textuality, had grown so complex, not to say confused, that it was tantamount to a fall from innocence.[19] In tracing Wordsworth's *itinerarium mentis*, the concept of originality complicated itself. It still entailed, as in *Unmediated Vision*, a heroic dismantling of defenses so that a new, more direct intuition of reality might be achieved. But to the danger of confronting the world in its immediacy was added a second peril. Under the influence of Hegel's *Phenomenology*, I understood that reality in its immediacy was abstract rather than real, so that progress toward a reality principle beyond this phantom immediacy had to be viewed in terms of an odyssey called history and a form of cognition the highest form of which was thinking in language. The "unmediated" turned out to be a construct, the historical outcome of an extraordinary collective synthesis.[20]

In 1955, the year I began to teach at Yale, even a purely cultural interest in Judaism was merely tolerated by the university's distinctive, if quietly assumed, Christian ethos. Ironically, while there was doubt that someone not brought up Christian could teach in a sympathetic way literary traditions based on Christianity, I found myself having to inform students about the basic symbols of their faith, so that they might understand the major English poets.

There was no visible sign of Judaic origins anywhere, except on Yale's escutcheon. Jewishness was a private matter; the student organization Hillel a hole in the wall in a basement on the Old Campus. The number of (putative) Jewish professors in the College of Arts and Sciences did not outnumber the fingers of one hand. My interest in Judaism was confined to sneaking into classes textual nuggets from classical Jewish sources and meeting irregularly with a faculty group.

But I met Harold Bloom, like myself on first appointment; and our conversation (which has lasted) made me attend more closely to the example of Blake and his deceptive use of traditional apocalyptic imagery. A ghostly dialogue started in my mind between Blake and Wordsworth. Allegorists might even say between Bloom and myself.

I cannot overlook how much Bloom and I shared. Both had made significant use of Martin Buber's *I and Thou* in the dissertations that became our first books. In the opening chapter of *Unmediated Vision*, in order to define the basic intuition backing Wordsworth's sense of being-in-the-world I recalled Buber's premise that relationship was not a matter of reasoning or logical systematization. A person, quite simply, found himself/herself "in relation." I characterized that fundamental certainty not as a variant of the Cartesian "I think, *therefore* I am" but as "This river: I am," where *river* stood for all natural objects of nonhuman creation and their influence.

Adapting Buber, Bloom argued in his Shelley dissertation (which preceded his work on Blake) that poets enter an "I-Thou" rather than "I-It" (reifying or neutral) relation. The "Thou" is myth-inspiring: an object—if an object at all—at the limit of desire. Shelley's "Thou" addresses nature, or a beloved person, or the perceptible if "unseen Presence" of an inconstant "Spirit of Beauty."

To this day I remain astonished at the closeness of our early thinking. I say "early," for the later Bloom is, as the expression goes, "something else." He has become, like his Yahwe, a formidable man of war. Bloom will not cease from mental fight against what he considers to be illnesses or corruptions of both the academic and the religious imagination. When, fifty years after our first conversations, I gave a series of lectures at Notre Dame on Religion and Literature, I found that part of my talk on Shelley had unconsciously recreated the early affinity between Bloom and myself. Even the title of the series, "Theopoesis," was in relation to our relation.

I left Yale in 1962 for the University of Iowa and then Cornell. (Already trying to escape, I had previously spent a visiting year at the University of Chicago.) Called back to Yale five years later, I learned through a colleague who had been at Yale since the 1940s about the fuss made when Lionel Trilling's nomination was proposed early in that decade. He also revealed that a superior committee had in an unusual move overturned the recommendation of the Yale English Department that placed two junior colleagues with a lesser record of publication above Harold Bloom and me in the annual contest for a faculty fellowship.

I had not observed any *overt* sign of prejudicial behavior during my first appointment at Yale. Disinterest, yes, but not open discrimination. It did strike me as peculiar, however, when, after receiving the tenure offer from Iowa, a distinguished elder of the department, who had rarely spoken to me, journeyed across a large room in the university library to shake my hand and congratulate me on the offer.

Gradually, the atmosphere changed. Judah Goldin, an eminent scholar of Midrash, settled in at Yale before 1960; the admission criterion of "character," code for non-Jewish, especially non-New York Jewish, became less important than intellectual promise, and this propelled the number of Jewish students well above the previous 10 percent as Yale's entering classes were diversified in the mid-1960s. A general expansion of the university also brought more Jews into the humanities faculty. But there was minimal change in the Department of Religious Studies when it came to enriching a sparse Judaic Studies curriculum.

One eventually sees what is before one's eyes: a lack, a bias, a distortion. So, at Yale, my interest in changing the situation and creating more than a token Judaic Studies program did not come primarily from a frustrated sense of community. Rather, my growing impatience to have the university curriculum enriched was moved by a strong sense of what was missing. Where was the harvest of German Jewish scholarship before it was brutally cut off; where the fatally wounded Yiddish culture of Poland and Eastern Europe? There was instruction in conversational Hebrew, yet the teaching of a two-millennia-plus tradition of Jewish history, and even biblical commentary, was left to one senior faculty member added to non-Judaic scholars of the Scriptures and the intertestamental period. I pointed out that, in contrast, there were five tenured appointments in Pagan Studies, a.k.a. the Classics.[21]

Chance intervened in the person of Bart Giammati, Yale's new President, who came to a similar conclusion about that imbalance. He asked me to head a fund-raising drive to expand teaching resources in Judaic Studies. Together with William Hallo (curator of the Babylonian collection as well as a biblical scholar and translator of Franz Rosenzweig's *Star of Redemption*), I began to coordinate policy for the new major. Between 1981 and 1987, most of my time was spent on these tasks. I did not consider Judaic Studies as an identity-affirming program but as the recovery of a historical source whose neglect was impoverishing secular education as well as leaving dangerous stereotypes intact. Eventually, too, through the persistence of James Ponet, Director of Hillel at Yale, the Slifka Center replaced makeshift lodgings and created a campus-wide gathering place for Jewish and interfaith activities.

It was also around 1980, as I passed my fiftieth year, that the opportunity came to do something active about the memory of the Holocaust. A disturbing and extra-academic route of inquiry opened up. Even though my wife, Renée, a child survivor of Bergen Belsen, warned me against getting involved (she feared it would become an obsession), I joined her in supporting a grassroots New Haven group that had begun videotaping Holocaust witnesses; and the question was how to expand this effort to reach beyond New Haven.

I was struck by the project's relevance for education in an audiovisual age. Yale might archive and curate its collection properly, catalogue it for intellectual access, and allow it to expand nationally and internationally. The program was accepted by the university in 1981, and I became its adviser and project director. The Fortunoff Video Archive for Holocaust Testimonies has set a standard for careful taping, brought the video recording of witnesses to Europe and Israel, and helped to overcome the prejudice against oral history that met us at the outset.

I thought of myself only in terms of organizer and fund raiser. Yet the complex presuppositions of such an archive, one that combined oral documentation and the medium of television, gradually overtook the mundane necessity of having to "sell" the undertaking to foundations and individual donors. Developing the archive also meant visiting many countries to establish affiliates that recorded varied cultural perceptions, and especially the survivors' postwar struggles for social reintegration. These stories of resettlement and return to life are as moving as the passion narratives brought from the camps and hiding places.

As Renée had foreseen, most of my recent work has been touched by what I learned from collecting Holocaust testimonies. It is influenced no less, however, by the issue of how we face catastrophe in an era of *souffrance à distance*, as the French sociologist Luc Boltanski has named it. Through the media we have become involuntary spectators and impotent bystanders of widespread political terror and the misery it leaves behind.

Memory, whether it is the reflection of scenes directly experienced or those transmitted by the media, is more than a mimetic and retentive faculty. It is a field of strife, given that the perpetrators continue cultivating falsifications responsible for the outbreak. The war against memory often flares up. Holocaust denial is only one, if extreme, example. Memory action, through historical research, testimony projects, Truth Commissions, and organizations such as *Nunca Mas*, has a chance of overcoming a helpless grief.

I am often asked about my turn to catastrophic trauma, the Holocaust, and the collective memory. My response is that the study of literature, like literature itself, does not shy from the painful task of considering mankind's inhumanity. Because of the excess characterizing genocide—an excess that also exceeds explanation, so that the very attempt to explain, to figure out the *why* rather than the instrumental *how*, has been called obscene— we tend to fall into an apologetic stutter about the ineffectiveness of the humanities. But the "obscene" is that which may not be shown, or may be shown only indirectly, off-the-scene; and this is a judgment artists continually make and critics have to confirm. It is at the heart of all attempts to face what happened in the Holocaust and the difficulty of pursuing normal life in its aftermath. It is also at the heart of other massive traumatic events.

The contemporary literary interest, then, in issues of representation derives from more than the challenging presence of new, supervisual media. A moral rather than technical matter, it is linked to the necessity of having to make decisions about what should be transmitted and with what degree of graphic virtuosity.

In my case literary studies were not displaced: there was no discontinuity when it came to representational issues involving extreme or traumatizing events. If the turn to Jewish and Holocaust Studies did not strike me as a radical change, it was in good part because literature and the finding or restoring of voice—the "Philomela project," it might be called—went together. Building an archive to create conditions in which unheard voices would be heard differs from what we do in literary studies only by adding a careful application of information technology and encouraging a communiversity.

—

Today the surge in trauma narratives suggests that the legacy of humiliation, anger, and powerlessness left by massive collective crimes must still find a creative rather than destructive outlet. I do not believe, however, that we are paying too much attention to the victims. In this one respect I totally disagree with Nietzsche's attack on compassion ("Mitleids-Moral") in his *Genealogy of Morals*. Effective or not, the meditation on suffering has its place. Passion narratives multiply and are not confined to religion. They often surface as personal memoirs, or as testimony about violence in a genocidal age.

Theories of progress can no longer be based on Hegel's thesis that "the wounds of the spirit leave no scars." A memory scar remains. Can it lead to the pursuit of justice instead of politicized resentment or revenge? The history each of us carries within, and the trajectory it makes us envision, should not stifle lament by turning away from harrowing testimonial narratives and the beleaguered personal memory.

—

In conclusion, I want to look more broadly at my relation to Judaism. Is that relation idiosyncratic, in the sense of being typical only of a displaced child, now an Ancient of Days, or is it more general in our time?

I lack childhood associations with prayer services or communal ceremonies. To this day I can't sit in a synagogue for very long, and envy Renée's careful and happy participation. While she *davens* with patience and warmth, I fidget. I want to understand better what is being read or prayed, and wander over the pages of the Siddur with a critical eye, trying to become interested, finding food for thought in certain ritual formulas, regretting the lack of poetry in many of the translations — in short, relying on my intellect to engage the emotions. Profane thoughts are not the trouble, and they rarely distract me; it is the words of the prayers themselves, or aspects of the ritual, like swaddling and unswaddling the Torah scrolls, that make me at once reflective and frustrated. There is considerable anguish in knowing how excluded I am from an emotional identification with religious or similar kinds of ritual.

Those words, those rituals, ask respect for their strangeness. They want to be restored to some "ur" meaning—bare, essential, existential. In that quest, I try to become the child I never was, or rather a poet who responds to some original, faint residue, like a remembered scent in revisiting a city one has known, but with a feeling that here, half-hidden, are heartfelt cries that need the unison of a community to be heard. Yet I hear only the void shouting back.

Sometimes I am guided by what William Blake called a "Memorable Fancy." He could imagine himself dining with Isaiah and Ezekiel, or talking with Milton and Shakespeare. I am not free of regret for a lost *chevra*, for the scattered company of German Jewish scholars in exile. Some, like Gershom Scholem, Ernst Simon, Hannah Arendt, and Abraham Heschel, I still met fleetingly; others, like Martin Buber, Hugo Bergmann, and Nahum Glatzer (I continue to treasure his *Lesebuch* of Jewish sources, edited with Ludwig Strauss, picked up secondhand in Tel Aviv on my first visit there in July 1952), I know only through their publications. There is no craving to identify with them, to imitate or directly emulate: simply to preserve a measure of their greatness. In the absence of father, grandfather, and all family except a mother I had grown away from during more than six years of separation, I adopted myself out to words blowing in the wind and insights that detached themselves from what I read promiscuously in the little tomes of the Schocken Verlag I carried about like a talisman.

I had no deliberate return, then, to Judaism. Brought up without any formal or family-based knowledge of the tradition, I remained a raider and explorer. I did not have to break away to find myself. Midrash and other aspects of Judaism opened their peculiar riches through a belated intellectual acquisition.

Which leads me to think again of my one direct scholarly effort in the area of Judaic Studies. I initiated a semester's teaching stint at the Hebrew University's English Department in the fall of 1958. Harold Bloom and I split a year's part-time teaching. Those few months in Israel gave me the opportunity to attend a Midrash class of Nehama Leibowitz. My knowledge of Hebrew at that time was (and, alas, remains) minimal, although I sense magic in that strange alphabet whenever I turn to the Hebrew Bible. Its script, like stony relics of a distant civilization, has the aura of an elemental simplicity. In contrast, the rich, elliptical outgrowth of midrashic divinations comforts like desert flowers after the rains.

These inauspicious beginnings led to an avid if sporadic study of Midrash, mainly in English and German; and when Sanford Budick of the Hebrew University founded the Institute for Literary Studies circa 1980 and invited me to help inaugurate it I suggested that its first year be devoted to the midrashic mode of interpretation. From that came our jointly edited volume, *Midrash and Literature*, in 1986.[22]

Can Midrash prove fruitful for literary interpretation? This mode of exegesis, which has remained invisible in literary circles, is worth exploring and may even bring back a part of the laity we have lost. I cannot ignore, in any case, the worry that returns to me at almost every academic conference. The very power of intellect exhibited there, as colleagues go about the task of close reading, also makes them desperate to extract, like preachers, relevant political and social messages. This tells me two things. It will not do to keep the religious imagination, deposited in texts, rituals, and modes of exegesis, out of the liberal arts classroom, and confine it to divinity schools, seminaries, and religious studies departments. That's too much, in effect, like putting it in quarantine as one would a computer virus. It also tells me that the communitarian instinct does not die off as we pursue the teaching profession in the secular university.

—

If I opened a chink into the *pardes* or sacred jungle of Midrash, it was also in the hope of dispelling the deadly slander that Judaism was crippled by a narrow legalistic and materialistic literalism. There was another reason too: Midrash showed that commentary could be a form of literature. It continues to be an extraordinary blend of intellectual and imaginative, legal and inventive thought.

My greatest pleasure, though, was tempting the Muse. I wanted to write beyond the middle style. Like the Romantics, I was unwilling to give up a visionary kind of verse, even if it meant raiding a sacred treasure and risking profanation or pastiche. I started and never sustained a long poem in which Spenser, Shelley, the masters of Midrash, and God knows who else kept me aloft. The poem's allegory was to represent all those that "in the wide deep wandering are" and whose path crossed mine. That wandering continues, with poetic moments surprising me like markers in a mist.

Why, finally, despite the prosaic nature of the critical act, and pressures coming from political and social issues that seem to increase daily, have I not given up thinking and writing about poetry, and especially Romantic poetry? On the verge of retirement, some time ago, I looked forward to devoting myself to the study of Hebrew Scripture, its commentators, and German Jewish writing in the time between World War I and the Shoah. It did not happen. I could not simply close my Keats, Wordsworth, Blake, or Shakespeare. Or, for that matter, Thoreau and Whitman, or the

Wallace Stevens who said that the great poems of heaven and hell had been written but the great poem of earth was still to come.

My adherence to the poets and a poetic kind of thinking has a realistic basis. There is a contest between poetry and divinity, between those subsuming passions. The history of religion and religious politics has provided many Great Awakenings, many self-anointed prophets and redeemers with enormous influence and often catastrophic consequences. This eternal return of religion, or what Matthew Arnold named epochs of concentration, cannot be ignored. Northrop Frye's last chapter in his *The Secular Scripture* is "The Recovery of Myth." Religion is sustained by ritual and romance, intensely imaginative conceptions that too often are skeletalized by a dogmatic theology or exploited by extreme nationalist or fundamentalist politics. From that historical perspective the mental fight of the Romantic poets, in particular, is exemplary. Reading Keats's unfinished *Hyperions*, I glimpse the remarkable drama of a poet "shamed by the knowledge that the gods are born once more of him, that great poetry must survive, if at all, in a cockney's breast." Who was more secular than Keats? Yet he had to approach the great poem of earth through this divine overhead, what he once called a "load of immortality."

At the end of this academic tale I append verses from *Akiba's Children*. Belated, and indebted to visionary imagery, they remain a post-Romantic fragment.

MARINER'S SONG

After He had maimed the dragon deep
And throned us in new limbs of everlasting
Opening to fable the mortal stars
We wept praises and harped the flood of His word.
Our tears might have filled an ocean our blood a sea.
We followed or wantoned before Him,
He was our serpent, flexible and brazen,

On His broad back we crossed the seas
Or stood precipitously between worlds.
Come now, with a staunch heart, a steady love,
Redeem His river-bones from Egypt,
Fetch home His visions, and out of His grave
Make a vineyard to plant the voice of the dove.

Notes

The present essay is an independently developed section of a larger memoir to be published by Fordham University Press as *A Scholar's Tale*.

1. Mark Krupnick, *Jewish Writing and the Deep Places of the Imagination*, ed. Jean Carney and Mark Sheckner (Madison: University of Wisconsin Press, 2005), 71.

2. In "The New Nomads," however, her contribution to *Letters of Transit: Reflections on Exile, Identity, Language, and Loss*, ed. André Aciman (New York: New Press, 1999), 35–65, Hoffman describes the change in the severity of the condition, or rather concept, of exile between the era of Nazism and Stalinism and the present time. "The basic revision," she writes, to the concept of exile and the "contrapuntal concept of home," a revision that corresponds to a changed reality, though that is unevenly realized, is "to attach a positive sign to exile. . . . today, at least within the framework of postmodern theory, we have come to value exactly the qualities of experience that exile demands— uncertainty, displacement, the fragmented identity" (44).

3. Between *The Unmediated Vision* and *Wordsworth's Poetry* I did not give up writing verse and also went against the contemporary tide by reviews that questioned the turn to confessionalism and an aggressively intimate diction. The new, supervernacular orthodoxy was leading to a forgetfulness of the high Romantic style as well as to bouts of exhibitionistic self-exposure.

4. I take this opportunity to name Nehama Leibowitz, whose seminar I audited while teaching at the Hebrew University in 1958; Judah Goldin, after he came to Yale; and then private sessions in Israel with

Michael Fishbane, Moshe Greenberg, and Uri Simon, and also with Daniel Boyarin when he spent a semester at Yale. David Stern's understanding of the contribution Midrash might make to secular criticism, and the matchless erudition yet open quality of thought in David Weiss Halivni's books, were important to me at a still later stage. Moshe Idel's work on the Kabbalah as inward rather than simply a reaction against rabbinical interpretive modes has also been a guide.

5. Dr. Phil. D. Hartmann, *Das Buch Ruth in der Midrash-Literatur: Ein Beitrag zur Geschichte der Bibelexegese* (Leipzig: Bär & Hermann, 1901).

6. Nahum N. Glatzer, *Franz Rosenzweig: His Life and Thought* (New York: Schocken Books, 1961), 160.

7. Here is what Max Weber wrote in 1917 in "Scholarship as a Vocation" when stressing how academic appointments in Germany were a gamble: "The responsibility [of giving advice on the chances of qualifying for a teaching position] . . . is scarcely to be borne. Of course, if the student is a Jew, you can only say: *lasciate ogni speranza . . .*"

8. See his letter to Friedrich Meinecke, in Glatzer, *Franz Rosenzweig*, 95, 97.

9. Gershom Sholem too, in his famous letter honoring Rosenzweig, did not think that the "apocalyptic thorn" implanted by Scripture could be removed from everyday Hebrew.

10. Not in *The Prelude*, but in "Hart-Leap Well" and playfully in the "Poems on the Naming of Places," names become a factor as the poet thinks back to oral tradition.

11. *The Hooligan's Return: A Memoir* (New York: Farrar, Straus, and Giroux, 2003), 175. The next quotation is from the same source, 291.

12. Theodor Gaster, however, comes close in *Thespis*, which ends with a consideration of the Psalms as well as Near Eastern poetry. See his *Thespis: Ritual, Myth, and Drama in the Ancient Near East* (Garden City, N.Y.: Doubleday, 1961), 442ff. He discerns a "punctual Seasonal Pattern" being projected into a "durative myth" in the biblical prophesies of the Book of Joel.

13. A. B. Yehoshua, in a controversial speech to the American Jewish Committee celebrating an anniversary, comes close to blaming an

absorption in the "texts" and cultural achievements of Diaspora Jewry for blindness to the mortal danger that culminated in the Holocaust, a blindness that might have been avoided had they striven to attain a "sovereign homeland." See "People without a Land," *Haaretz Magazine* of May 12, 2006: 6–7.

14. I should quote, however, a canny observation of Ortega y Gasset. He writes in *Toward a Philosophy of History* (New York: Norton, 1941), 35–36: "Everything ancient that is no longer understood seems to acquire an electric charge of mysticism that transforms it into a religious phenomenon."

15. Its vast literary circumspection went much further than I could; yet Auerbach omitted most Romantic and post-Romantic poetry. Like E. R. Curtius he lessened the gulf between medieval and modern, making his contribution to modernism by a mimesis concept based on the post-Christian realism of the nineteenth and twentieth century novel.

16. While I do not want to engage in odious comparisons, and still recognize now as I did then the vigor of English seventeenth-century poetry to at least Milton, I was reluctant to play the game of canon and refused the dogma of the New Critics that the tradition of the modern was preeminent in that or any doctrinal Christian matrix. The downgrading of Wordsworth and most Romantic poets indicated a narrowing rather than expansion of the canon. It was an attempt to fend off or even supersede the larger anthropological view of religion to which Eliot himself pointed in the notes accompanying *The Waste Land*.

17. Yet in the Hebrew Bible there is a figure who dwells with God from the Beginning. She is called Wisdom in Proverbs; and this Sophie or Sapientia is important for the Jewish Kabbala and religious poetry. Did this figure also entice my imagination? Sheer visuality is a good thing, but hardly an end in itself; indeed, I associated that organic pleasure with the delight of intellectual discovery. A compromise between sensuous and intellectual is made possible (though I was not clear about it at the time) by poetic and ecstatic imaginings of the human body as a glorious body, enabling a fit partnership with the immortal Sophie.

18. Wallace Stevens, "Notes toward a Supreme Fiction." My wild

thesis would never have made it through the mill of publication reports and committees. But Henri Peyre, head of romance languages, took the manuscript personally to the director of Yale Press, and with affidavits from my teachers in comparative literature it was accepted—going out of print after selling a grand total of nine hundred copies over many years.

19. So my Malraux book contained a final chapter on his theory of the pictorial arts as an antimimesis, that is, as involving the competition between artists, or mediation of one artist by another leading to an intertextuality of images.

20. Unlike Hegel, Wordsworth kept to the ontogenetic growth of the individual mind, not raising—in *The Prelude*—the issue of historical or phylogenetic progress. Yet everything that he had tried to purge returned in his own later poetry. The clichés of poetic diction and classical allusion recovered their expressive density. Also in the later poetry, a vision of religious progress confessed the poet's allegiance to the *via media* principles of the English Church.

21. This was an exaggeration, but only in the sense that the ancient cultures of the Middle East, among which Judaism arose, were represented by professorships such as that of William Hallo, and that the Hebrew Bible was also, of course, the object of study in the divinity school and by teachers recruited from there to form the religious studies department in the 1960s.

22. I do not say enough about numerous visits to Israel beginning as early as the summer of 1952, of how deeply the landscape and the friendships affected me. Where is the poet-patriot and journalist Haim Gouri, whose three-part documentary film centering on the Holocaust was so important for me? Where my conversations with Saul Friedlander, Aharon Appelfeld, Yaron Ezrahi, Sidra Ezrahi, Ruth Nevo, Elizabeth Freund, Emily and Sandy Budick, Shira Wollosky, Shuli Barzilai, Leona Toker, Lilach and Zvika Lachman, as well as other long-standing friends? See also the title essay of *The Longest Shadow: In the Aftermath of the Holocaust* (1996 and 2002).

Exile
Inside and Out

— *Bronislava Volková*

Going into exile happens almost unnoticeably. You may think about it for a long time before you actually "commit the crime"; however, nothing prepares you for the brutal impact of actually doing it or for the extent of its implications. Suddenly you are in exile—outcast, alone, without people who know you or want to know you, without parents or ancestors, without language, without friends, without a past, and seemingly without a future. You weep over what has been lost, over what was and what will be, and mostly over what won't ever be.

Suddenly every memory becomes as sharp as a knife and every step a fatal step that cannot be reversed. *Alea iacta est*—for better and for worse, this is your life now, life in the middle of nowhere. You are no longer a member of a society or a member of a family, but a long-distance runner of the universe. In the country of your origin, you have been declared undesirable, and even your scholarly, completely nonpolitical writings are forbidden and declared nonexistent. Articles in print are torn out of journals, and your books cannot be owned by anyone, much less reviewed. You find new friends—not among the people you now encounter—their life is too complete, too different, too quiet, too satisfied to feel like a place for your raw heart. You find new friends among those you were previously not allowed to know much about, like the great poet Osip Mandelstam and his remarkable wife and writer Nadezhda, who inspire you and open a road to your own poetic adventures. You read their books and your heart opens to new vast expanses. But you never stop missing your old friends, who are now divided between those who dare to reply to your letters and those who consider their careers too important to be endangered in this way or who consider a relationship with you as futile in your new circumstances. You suffer pangs of guilt about not being able to be there for your aging parents, who miss you painfully. You don't know if you ever will be able to hug your mother; you know you will almost inevitably miss their dying; you know you will never spend a regular afternoon with them again in your lifetime. You wonder if, in fact, you will ever be allowed to see them again.

The next station feels even more remote, a place where you find absolutely nothing that connects with who you are: America. You lead the strange existence of a nonperson. You have a certain image you put on every day when you go out—to work, shopping, to parties, and so on. It is an image of a person who comes from a strange land that nobody knows much about, and this person is now trying to use her skills or knowledge or feeling in a different setting. That is all. Inside, you go on crying for the friends you can no longer call up, for your aging parents whose sharp pain of loss you sense more and more each day, for your old apartment, for every little piece of furniture you were forced to abandon, for your old doll, which is now part of the irretrievable, for the view out of the window of your study, for the street you used to take to school, for the greengrocer's shop next door.

At night, you have nightmares about the distance you put between yourself and your loved ones and everything that is familiar. Your partner is trying to fit in, so he does not want to hear your moaning and grieving and your sense of feeling lost. Your relationship with him dissolves gradually, as it is not solid enough to bear this new weight. Thus you are even more alone. You try to carve out an existence for yourself in the new environment. You find minor ways to fit in. You write in a language nobody can read, and you start publishing in the exile press and become a poet. First, you write about your acute sense of loss—a typical émigré topic, but your heart gradually moves into places where your old audiences cannot follow you so easily. Your next books take you to more universal spaces and explore new horizons, seeking sublime and intimate connections to transcendental truth and to an internal and metaphysical home, which is unfamiliar and foreign to Czech literature, preoccupied as it often is with satirizing disgust with the totalitarian regime and the general decomposition of values. Your closet gets filled up more and more with letters, diaries, and poems. For many years you write diligently, often to your parents and old friends. And yet you do create a new life and invent new identities. Since every old context is gone, you can now experiment with some exciting new ones. Having lost all, you gain freedom to expand into areas you otherwise would never have touched, be they spiritual, artistic, intellectual, or physical. This makes your life very dynamic and expansive. But you are always somehow different, and you always feel alone. The people who come into your life in your new country are different from your friends at home. They are often emotionally wounded in some way as you are, or they are socially marginal in the society in which you live. This adds to the sense of isolation you experience.

If we feel compelled to leave our native environment, something clearly breaks in us. It is almost as if our innocence is lost, as if we no longer can rely on very basic securities in the world that surrounds us. For me, this happened even before I was born.

To save their lives, both of my parents had to flee Czechoslovakia during the time of Hitler's occupation of the country. True, they returned after the war, hoping to create a new life. But what awaited them? Their property had been irrevocably stolen by the Germans and by their friends or coworkers, who no longer expected them to return, and later by the Communist government. For many years, they were not allowed to work at the level of their qualifications, nor could they even return to the apartment where they had lived before the war or easily rent another one. Instead, they were housed for a time in a communal apartment in the Sudetenland (border area), where I was born, and later in a small, one-room apartment in Prague. It took them three years to achieve the luxury of two rooms. Out of all their previous possessions only a few pieces of furniture and a few pictures were saved and returned to them by a friend. My father's innovative automobile, which he had single-handedly built in his workshop, my mother's Amati violin, their family house in Mladá Boleslav, and many acres of fields, as well as their life savings, were all stolen, never to be returned. All this loss was minor, though, after having twenty-six members of their family murdered by the Nazis.

So when I grew up, I had no good reason to trust my environment, an environment in which there were people who spat into the baby carriage simply because they found out I was a Jewish baby. Little wonder, then, that I never felt very attached to my surroundings. Given that my parents were virtually hiding their identity (as being Jewish and speaking German were not well regarded), I grew up somewhat incognito. My parents revealed my Jewish identity to me only when I was thirteen years old, after I had been ridiculed in school for the "crime" of being a Jew. As my parents were both atheists, no Jewish observance was passed on to me. I secretly experimented with the available religions and continued to do so. All religions were, of course, proscribed in the Communist state, but some people pursued them in spite of it. I assume I would have investigated the Jewish religion as well, were there someone nearby cultivating it to whom I could turn. But everybody was dead or dispersed around the world. We had virtually no Jewish friends. Later, when it became apparent that communism with a human face would not succeed and that the Russians had got the best of us again, it seemed almost natural to decide to flee. Fleeing Czechoslovakia in the nick of time had saved my parents' life during the German occupation. They were forced to leave separately—my father on a legal permit to France, while my mother, who was refused one, went later illegally, passing through many countries where she was not permitted to leave, sometimes for prolonged periods of time, until she eventually ended up in England, where my dad happened to be later stationed with the Czechoslovak army-in-exile.[1]

I thought perhaps leaving would save my life, too, even if not in the literal sense of the word. So I left. I did not succeed in fleeing right after the Soviet occupation in 1969, as Charles University had lost the doctoral diploma that I had just acquired. Since the border closed in 1969, I was effectively stuck in the country indefinitely. In 1974, however, my husband and I were allowed (it seems by mistake) to go on vacation to the West. We had purchased a round trip ticket through Austria, Italy, Spain, France, and Germany, and even though we were childless and thus did not leave a hostage behind, we were given permission to leave. This meant, of course, leaving everything and everyone behind, taking a suitcase with summer clothes, and leaving for the unknown. A relative of my husband placed our diplomas in sealed meat cans in order not to attract attention. This appeared perfectly natural, as Czechs typically traveled with tins of meat, not being able to afford to purchase food in the West. The cans just had to be weighed down with stones to match the exact weight of real cans that would have been purchased in the stores.

My first shock was to realize that Western intellectuals empathized with the Communists. Our first encounter with them was in Bordeaux, where my husband and I were invited to present papers at the World Congress of Hispanists. When the president of the Association of Hispanists heard of our intentions to defect, he chastised us, saying that we threatened to disrupt the dialogue between the East and West, apparently fearing that we would give a "bad name" to his organization in the eyes of his socialist colleagues. Later on, we were forced to settle in Germany, as France was inhospitable to refugees and America had a waiting period of up to two years, and I taught briefly at universities in Cologne and Marburg. There, I ran into students who were creating intense propaganda for communism, explaining to their fellow students what a humane system it was. If perhaps there were concentration camps in Communist countries, it was only for the good of mankind, they explained, as people simply did not understand the goodness of the system adequately and thus needed to be treated this way. (I have heard a similar philosophy occasionally on American campuses from leftist professors, some of whom have even justified torture.) All this made me wonder why on earth I left! At least in Communist Czechoslovakia everybody understood what a sham communism was! In France, Germany, or America, people did not have to put up with the everyday realities of this perverse system, realities that made the lie immediately obvious to everyone who was not mentally challenged, so they had the luxury of dreaming it up to be a social ideal. Most of the people I encountered in America did not go so far as to idealize communism, but even there, people often thought that government propaganda against communism was exaggerated and that their regime was possibly just as oppressive as ours was.

I found, nevertheless, an important difference between the Americans and the West Europeans among whom I lived. While the Europeans were often dependent on theories and were blind to realities, most Americans seemed much more practically oriented and usually minded their business and were therefore not so susceptible to such political dreams. I found Americans to be much more interested in looking within and dealing with their own problems than in theorizing and politicizing. On the other hand, the lack of emphasis on culture and art in daily American life seemed to impoverish the human soul, whose only spiritual outlet then is often religion. While religion can and does play an essentially positive role in many people's lives, I came to see that if it is the only spiritualizing influence, it can make people's worlds somewhat narrow and sometimes susceptible to certain delusions. Thus it might lead to unreasonable and even dangerous cults, characterized by violence similar to that which one observed for centuries in Europe. The only saving grace is that in America such cults include relatively small numbers of people and do not force the whole community to submit to them. In Europe, unfortunately, the violent cults came from the leaders of the nation or community, often intellectuals, who have taken with them whole countries into the disasters of world wars and the postwar Communist societies. Millions of people paid with their lives, and the lives of many others were destroyed. And the damage has not stopped with one generation, but continues to affect the victims' children emotionally, mentally, and economically. Even today, the former communists are in possession of most of what has been nationalized (i.e., stolen) half a century ago. Most of those who were robbed have not been able to recover possessions stolen by the Communists or Nazis, due to huge red tape designed to make it impossible. Only those with strong contacts in the former Communist structure have had no problem.

Exile is essentially a tragic experience. Feeling expelled directly or indirectly from one's country of origin, being repeatedly robbed of one's possessions, and not being welcomed back leaves scars. At the same time, feeling only reluctantly welcomed or unable to fit in the target country (or so-called country of choice) again leaves a permanent mark on one's identity. Of course, one can create another identity, one can find a degree of acceptance elsewhere, but the process is much more difficult and one is never the same. One feels empowered by being accepted "in the world at large," but it is also sad to be ignored or mistreated by what one would like to call a home country. There is a part of the soul that forever longs to go back to where it originated. The double nature we acquire as exiles never leaves us. We almost have two sets of values and feel somewhat schizophrenic, with two personalities, the original and the acquired. We also have two sets of friends, and some of us have two careers. A substantial part of our lives has been lived abroad, and the new country we settled in has become our second home, which is after a certain time just as difficult to give up as the first one was. Should we forever commute between our two homes? Perhaps we do not have another choice: this eternal split has become by now our nature.

Exile is something that has repeated itself numerous times in the history of Czech culture, starting with the expulsion of the educated monks who introduced original Slavic liturgy, language, and literature in the ninth century, continuing with members of Unitas Fratrum, who were the well-educated heirs of the first European church reformation after the 1620 defeat of Czechs at the White Mountain (in America, they are referred to as the Moravian Brothers). The most famous among them was Jan Amos Komenský (Comenius), the so-called teacher of the nations. Finally, the eighteenth century saw a vast emigration of Czech musicians, who became the teachers of the prominent German, French, and Italian masters and created their own schools abroad. Nineteenth-century emigration was primarily due to economic factors, resulting in large farming settlements in areas such as Texas or Nebraska.

The twentieth century has experienced three major waves of exiles from Czechoslovakia—all of a political character. The first one was primarily the wave of escapees from Hitler's occupation of the country in 1939 and consisted almost entirely of Jews who were trying to save their lives. The second came shortly after World War II, following the Communist takeover of 1948, when a variety of people left, sometimes to save their lives, sometimes their possessions—or at least a part of them—from Communist confiscation, and sometimes simply to protest against the new totalitarian government, which made any meaningful participation in the political, cultural, and economic life of their country impossible. Finally, the exile wave I belong to left after 1968, after the failed attempt to institute the so-called "Socialism with a human face," also known as Prague Spring. After the total crushing of this democratizing process by the armies of the Warsaw pact, additional hundreds of thousands of people left, including large numbers of artists and intellectuals, who formed a powerful force for political, intellectual, and cultural dissent abroad. They organized publishing houses, journals, and scholarly conferences around the world, whose participants formed immediate friendships that never would have cemented back home. Had those people remained in their native country, they would have been somewhat separated from each other by both professional field and social status, as academic and intellectual spheres of established societies tend toward certain class formations and behaviors, especially in Europe. The condition of exile, however, brings about more interaction between those in different fields of specialization, as the exile society is much smaller and there is even a certain solidarity among its intellectuals, scholars, writers, and politicians. Many barriers have fallen in the face of common misfortune, and an exciting cross-pollination has taken place.

The most important publishing houses for Czech literature were created in various countries around the world, such as Ger-

many, Canada, Switzerland, England, and Italy. The best known
were Publishers 68 (Toronto), Poetry Abroad or PmD (Munich),
and Index (Cologne). It is interesting that hardly any have appeared in the United States, where many émigrés live, perhaps
because the geographical distance between writers makes it difficult for them to meet each other in person. The heavy focus in
the United States on other values and opportunities than literary
expression may have played a role, as well as the lack of audiences
and financial support for foreign literatures. Czech literature was
fervently smuggled back and forth during all this time between
Czechoslovakia and the free world. Works deemed unpublishable back home were smuggled to the West, and then some of
these were smuggled back to Czechoslovakia in published form,
together with the publications of exiled writers themselves. And
a very vibrant literature it was, indeed. Important samizdat libraries were created, especially in Germany and Canada. In this way,
Czech literary culture, which was thwarted and suppressed at
home, was kept alive.

This situation lasted exactly until the Velvet revolution of
1989, which, as if by a magic wand, dissolved the strong bonds
of the émigré society; and most of the wonderful cultural activities ceased, with the exception of the Czechoslovak Society
of Arts and Sciences, which continues to be active, organizing
scholarly conferences every year and building relationships with
scholarly organizations (universities and academy of sciences) in
the Czech Republic. Among literary people, though, the slogan
"every man for himself" seemed to replace the former solidarity.
Every writer tried to suddenly assert himself in the newly democratic Czechoslovakia, having been starved for recognition of his
or her existence at home for many decades. The ones who were
most welcome were, paradoxically, predominantly the former
Communists (and some non-Communists), who were still known
from the time of the cultural window of the late 1960s (Kun-

dera, Škvorecký, Lustig, Kohout, Tigrid, and Mlynář, to name just a few). From the younger generation only the clearly political writers were embraced (protest song writers and guitar singers such as Kryl and Hutka, political scholar Jacques Rupnik, etc.). Many others who entered professional lives in the 1970s and later and therefore remained in greater or lesser obscurity never really reintegrated into the culture they helped to keep alive and develop during its forbidden time under the totalitarian Communist regime. This is true also of those who stayed home and were forced into silence and inner exile there. In a way, they have been skipped over in favor of the next, louder generation of writers including Topol, Třešňák, Pekárková, and Pelc, whose books shock the public by their nihilistic and often sexualized portrayal of the life and values of the impoverished working classes, émigrés, and criminal youth.

Many efforts were and still are being made in the Czech Republic to create new histories of literature, integrating the formerly official culture with the one that went into underground or exile. Thus many of the exile writers, including myself, have recently been included in histories of literature without ever having been published or read much in our native country. And after the brief boom of émigré literature immediately following the revolution, the attention of the public turned toward practical and commercial literature, and some writers might never get their day. Publishers, who previously could not issue works by those who refused to comply with the Communists because of political reasons, now refuse to do so for economic ones, for they feel the need to produce books that will be commercially successful. Poetry has been treated especially badly. While poetry of the few permitted poets during communism used to appear often in tens of thousands of copies, today a book that is printed in a few hundred copies is considered successful. Most poets nowadays resort to self-publishing in editions of twenty to sixty copies. Booksellers typically refuse to buy poetry. If they have it in stock, they do not display such books to the public but rather store them in less accessible places in the bookstore, creating the self-fulfilling prophecy that poetry doesn't sell. The distribution system has become haphazard and broken down. An absence of educated criticism also creates a situation in which publishers often produce poetry books that, indeed, do not sell. In general, the book market is rather conservative, paying a lot of attention to classics and to what publishers consider certain cult figures or writers from older generations (often already dead) who still have not been published. Thus, new underground or samizdat editions are being developed even in this new democratic regime and abroad under very different circumstances. The yearly generational collection *Listopad* ("November," according to the November revolution of 1989) or my own Explorer Editions are just a few examples.

My poetry has gone through a long development since I first started writing. I am currently celebrating thirty years in exile (by releasing a CD under the title *The Slightest Reminder of Your Being ... Three Decades of Exile: 1974–2004*). Last year, I published my ninth book of poetry in a twin edition of Czech and English corresponding books. Some time ago, I started to produce my books bilingually, printing them in limited editions with my own color collages. I have written of love, loss, alienation, of emptiness and the spiritual nature of life, of inner transformation into a place of compassion and power, peace and bliss, and even of the inner connection to the absolute. I often sense that some of the feelings I express and make an effort to transform are not just my own but reflect the consciousness of a whole culture. We all carry such feelings in ourselves and are conditioned by them, often subconsciously. Bringing those feelings to the surface, living through them to the point at which we are capable of releasing them, owning the pain of generations of thwarted lives without reacting in destructive ways, and going even further, raising our vibration to the places where we can find the awareness that we are all one, are among the main ambitions of my poetry. Some of my poems aim to grasp a moment in time in order to reflect it in a new light; others have a deeper transformational design; and still others have the futuristic character of bringing a vision of heaven to earth. In my last book, in which I have visited my dead as well as civilizational diseases and entrapments, I was compelled to go back once again to the persistent issues of the Holocaust, which appear intermittently in various of my works as motives. Although not always conscious of it, it appears that the Holocaust, just like my exile from the Communist reality, is something that has formed who I am most profoundly. It is that which I periodically am forced to revisit, that which has left the deepest traces in my emotional psyche and made me who I am more than anything—a wandering Jew who only feels at home with God. Is my God the Jewish God? Perhaps not in a conventional sense. But as the Jews have known possibly before everyone else, there is only one God.

Many investigators of the condition of exile question whether it is possible to return after the political situation that originally triggered flight has changed. There are many stories of attempted returns both after the Nazi occupation of Czechoslovakia ended and after the Communist regime fell in 1989. Many have a tragic end. Going back after many years of absence is like undertaking another emigration, no matter what the external circumstances might be. I have already described the sad situation awaiting my parents after their return from England at the end of World War II. Today, many exiles who returned home, or attempted to, feel poorly accepted, as many of those who stayed in the country during the totalitarian period feel in some ways disadvantaged and thus jealous of some of the possibilities the exiles had—the broad intellectual horizons they were able to acquire due to their life in the West, as well as financial assets they were able to accumulate.

Most opt to continue living in the West and, thus, to remain in exile, and if they go back home to live, they do so almost as a return to inner exile again. Exile, it seems, has marked us for life. Many feel that they cannot understand their old friends any longer or their friends them (this situation is depicted in Kundera's latest novels); the insecurity and mistrust have now been reversed; and the economic differences also play a role. Those of us who have lived in the West and are usually not particularly wealthy feel upon our return home like millionaires, as the countries we left have been so impoverished by the Communist regime that it will take them decades to catch up.

At the same time, exile can be a great gift. It makes it possible to have more than one life, more than one country, more than one culture, and more than one perspective on political and cultural reality. Exile is a gift of broad horizons and can lead to the dropping of racial and cultural prejudices. Thus, along with the alienation and displacement of exile, so characteristic of life in the twentieth century in general, there come great freedom and greater authenticity. Not only has every exile had to struggle hard to make it in a new and foreign culture, but those who are exiled also cannot rely on cultural stereotypes or family and close friends to make them feel successful. More likely than not, they have had to rely on who they really are in both professional and personal situations.

As a social factor, exile has had an enormous international impact. More than anything else, it is helping people to cross boundaries, to globalize, to wipe away the borders between separate worlds. It is an enormously important catalyst for cross-pollination, making the world one big melting pot. This is the suprapolitical meaning of exile—its cosmic role, so to speak. Exile is largely responsible for making even the most peripheral local population aware that there is something besides their little world; and not only because they hear it on the news, but because they meet real persons carrying different values, habits, having different appearances, believing in different things, behaving in different ways.

Finally, there is another aspect that one does not usually associate with exile. When we live in a native community, we take
very many things for granted, from the sounds we hear once we
open our eyes in the morning to the tone of voice of a taxi driver
when he tells us how much we owe him. All of us have been exposed to the same children's literature, to the songs that linger in
our subconscious and that remind us of our first youthful awakenings. As exiles we suddenly have lost all that and have very little
in common on the surface with the people who now surround
us. This is when we realize that there are much more important
things than those we feel so naturally attached to. These are character, honesty, innate intelligence, decency, kindness, openness,
a willingness to help another in need, love. . . . Exile makes us
bigger people, with bigger hearts. Thus, if it does not break us,
exile, paradoxically, makes us more humane. And sometimes it
appears that those who have not been forced to undergo such a
humanizing process are the ones living in exile—in exile from
their own selves.

The notion of exile is thus multifaceted and can be considered
from many different perspectives. All depends on whether we see
ourselves from the inside or from the outside. What appears as
exile from the outside is actually coming home to oneself on the
inside, and what appears as being home on the outside ends up
intrinsically being expelled on the inside. This was true even in
the political sense of the word. If you weren't willing to risk a life
in prison or at least experience expulsion from your profession,
you needed to live as an exile inside your home country in the
form of pretending to express certain opinions or values on the
outside while believing others on the inside. If you dared to be
honest, you lived in exile again, this time ostracized by the rest

of the population and by the powers that ruled, which often deprived you of your job and sometimes even of freedom. So exile, as we usually think of it, is only the most extreme variation on something that happens in our everyday lives in any type of oppressive society, and even in so-called free ones. While Western societies cannot be compared with Communist or Nazi society with regard to their level of oppression, they are not entirely free from driving a portion of their population into inner exile either, due to their growing bureaucratization and cartelization. Thus, I can only say that at this stage of my life I experience my exile existence on many levels and as an unending state of mind. In the social sense of the word, I want to claim my exile status with pride. It has helped me to come home to myself. And that, I believe, is the only true home.

Note

1. I have told her dramatic story in a piece called "Escape," which appeared in the journal *Witness*, issue on Autobiography (March 1992): 68–96. It also was mentioned on the occasion of the Annual Memorial Day of the Shoah Memorial Foundation Yad Vashem, Jerusalem, Israel. A surrealist version of my mother's story is part of "Moje maminka, hrůza a já" ("My Mother, Terror and I," a story), in *Listopad* (Liberec, 2002).

From Country to Country
My Search for Home

— *Zsuzsanna Ozsváth*

I left Budapest on a cold, windy morning in March 1957. I had lain in bed wide awake throughout the night before, and even when I dozed off for a minute or two, I was stabbed by a sharp pain that compelled me to cry constantly. The separation from my parents, a threat with which I had lived ever since my early childhood, would now become real. But this reality had a grotesque twist: it was not the Germans who would separate us from one another. It was I of all people who would depart, leaving behind forever my father, my mother, my past, my friends, and whatever had remained of the rest of my family after the Holocaust.

Early in the morning, I heard my mother preparing breakfast in the kitchen. We ate very little, and none of us could talk. Afterwards, I picked up the two books I had set aside the night before: Thomas Mann's *Doctor Faustus* and Radnóti's volume of poems, *Foamy Sky*. I stuck both into the pocket of my winter coat: "I'll keep you for a hundred years," I whispered. It was time to leave. I hugged my mother with unbearable pain, kissed the forehead of Renny, our huge, funny, and beautiful, black-brown German

Shepherd, and left the apartment with my father. We took the streetcar to the East Station. Arriving in fifteen minutes, we went to the platform. I sobbed in his arms for a while, then boarded the train. One last touch of his hand, one last smile of his anguished face. I waved farewell. Tears rolled from his eyes. The wheels of the train started to move.

Opposite me sat Gustaf, the orchestra conductor, who was helping me escape. I wanted to tell him about our life during the Holocaust, about my father, the greatest and best of all men I knew, about his repeated resolutions to leave Hungary but also about his frequent last-minute changes-of-mind in doing so, and, then, about my sudden desperate decision to break the pattern and run away. But I couldn't. Gustaf was smiling and seemed quite happy. Obviously, he wouldn't know what I was talking about. An acquaintance of my parents, he had visited us just a few weeks ago, explaining that he had heard from common friends about my wish to leave the country. Then, he assured my father that for four hundred dollars, he could bribe someone he knew at the Ministry of the Interior, who would be able to get a passport for me. In this way, he and I could leave the country together, claiming that I was to play piano solo with his orchestra in Austria. There was nothing "strange" about this offer. At this point in Hungarian history, many people were involved in smuggling others out of the country. The problem lay in the sum he had asked for. To raise four hundred dollars at this particular time seemed impossible. With the chaos the revolution created, with hundreds of thousands of people fleeing, things left behind lost all value. Still, my parents tried to scrape together whatever they could, selling my Steinway, our remaining silver, in addition to the Persian rugs, all of which miraculously had survived the Holocaust in our old apartment. Borrowing more money from their friends and acquaintances, they paid Gustaf the sum he wanted. In this way, the heretofore unthinkable became reality:

I got a passport. The next day, my father bought my train tickets. I was free to follow István, my husband, who was waiting for me in Hamburg. Registering as a Ph.D. student in astronomy at Hamburg University, he also had a small job at the observatory in Bergedorf. Suddenly, I was free to be free for the first time in my life, free to leave behind Hungary, the Holocaust, the Russians, the mass arrests, the hellish world my family and I had lived in ever since I was born.

The wheels of the train were moving faster: it was heading for the border town, Hegyeshalom. But upon arriving there, it stopped for twelve hours. Troops of police and an army division virtually took apart all the railway cars. They looked for "insurgents," "spies," weapons, "evil-doers," for the so-called enemies of the Soviet-supported Hungarian Communist regime. Dismantling the toilets and the seats of the train, they searched the passengers as well, questioning us one by one, going through our suitcases, investigating all our belongings. The search went on until midnight; then, it petered out. The guards withdrew. We were on our way. I knew I could never return to Hungary; and I also knew I might never see my parents again.

That my fate took such a sudden, unexpected turn, and that I could tear myself away from my parents and everything that had been my life up till now, was directly intertwined with the tumultuous political events that had shaked Hungary over the previous several decades. From my early childhood, I was aware of the terrible danger threatening us. This knowledge had eaten itself into my consciousness, becoming part of my very being. I believe it started to take hold of my mind after the *Anschluss* and the escape of some of my mother's Austrian friends and relatives from their country to Hungary. Their horror stories, which I overheard, told of atrocities committed by the Germans against the Jews. I held my father's hand tightly at night when I asked him questions about our friends and relatives who had remained in Austria. Listening to his answers, I had yet another question for him that kept on terrifying me: what would happen to us and other Jews if the Germans occupied Hungary? He assured me again and again that the Germans would never invade our country, and even if they would, even if it came to a war, in the end, we probably would survive. He assured me over and over that he and my mother would always take care of us. And to make me feel better, he proposed that I come to him and press his hand whenever I was frightened. I did just that during the weeks, months, and years that followed, during the German occupation, during the firebombing of Budapest, and even after the war, when a new wave of deportations was initiated by the Communist government to eradicate "the enemy within."

Yet despite my father's reassurances, I ran away when meeting people who talked about the humiliation and torture to which the Germans subjected the Jews. There were times, however, when I had to pay attention. In August 1941, we heard about the arrival of my father's childhood friend, Robert, and his family, in Budapest: the four of them fled from the German-occupied Netherlands. Soon, they came to visit us. And they spoke of nothing else but the horror they had experienced: the threats, cruelty, and humiliation the Germans had meted out to the Jews. "They will kill us in the end," Robert said, and I could tell he was terribly frightened. He was right; they did just that in the spring of 1944. But for the moment, his family felt lucky, as they had managed to obtain false papers and leave the Netherlands. Since Hungary was still relatively independent, Robert, his wife, and children hoped to be able to hide and survive the war in Budapest. Still, I couldn't avoid noticing that they were different from other people I knew. I observed that when invited over, they were anxious to leave before darkness fell on the streets. They always looked out the window, wondering whether or not they were being followed by the police, and they constantly discussed possible ways of hiding, in case the Germans invaded Hungary.

We also knew others who had fled from German-occupied Europe. And they, too, spoke with horror about the Germans' brutality they had observed or heard about. To me, however, the most frightening of all was the story a little Polish girl my own age told me. She recounted what happened when the Germans arrived in the town where she lived with her family. One day, she said, all the Jews were herded into the marketplace. Then, separated from their families, a group of men, including her father and grandfather, were driven on to a bridge, to undertake some repair work. Laboring all day, they were taken to the synagogue at night, where the SS shot them. In the meantime, the Germans marched Hanna and her mother to the ghetto, with the rest of the town's women and children. Some months later, the two of them were smuggled out of the ghetto by her cousins, who helped the pair escape from Poland to Hungary. Now she went to my school. "But I don't want to live without Daddy," she said, her face distorted by crying. "To die by suicide would be better: I would suffer less." I have never forgotten this discussion. Afterwards, I had recurring nightmares that would not leave me, seeing my father, mother, and brother shot, while I was running down the streets, homeless, alone.

By now, I was obsessed with the fear of separation from my parents. And I was terrified of the Germans. But soon, I started to be fearful of the Hungarians as well. With the country joining in the war, tens of thousands of young Jewish men were drafted into the labor service. Transported to the Russian front, they were subjected to the torture of the officers and guards of the Hungarian Army. Most people my parents knew had family members who were deployed as slave-labor servicemen on the front. A small fraction of them came home after awhile and gave account of what happened with their comrades in Ukraine. Hence, it was through these eyewitnesses that we started to hear about the atrocities and torture the unfortunate servicemen had to endure. Their accounts shook my father to the core: his brother, our beloved uncle Pali, was among them. A highly gifted young lawyer, Pali loved to read poems and play chamber music. And he could invent the world's most interesting fantasy games. We adored him. He left behind his pregnant wife and a two-year-old baby girl. Forced-marched in rain and snow, across fields and towns, tortured, ill-clothed, hungry, deprived of food, sleep, and water, he was shot into a mass grave in January 1943. We heard the details of his murder from one of his comrades who stayed alive and returned a few months later. But my father didn't want to accept these rumors. He wouldn't give up hope, he said, repeating again and again his belief that despite everything, Pali had survived. He just was trying now to hide in some Russian village. And he would return when the war ended, my father said, and we would continue to have him around and play with him for many years to come. After awhile, however, as the story of Pali's murder and its circumstances kept reemerging from several sources, and he did not return after the war, my father lost hope and turned despondent for the rest of his life.

Living with bad news and the constant threat of atrocities, I was terrified when the Germans occupied Hungary in March 1944. I feared their brutality that, I knew quite clearly, would soon be unleashed against us. But I was most afraid of separation from my parents. In comparison, hunger, humiliation, pain, and even death seemed significantly less frightening to me. I lived through the next ten months, then, with this fear on my mind and the foreboding vision of our murder. But I was wrong; we were spared. While in the countryside more than 437,000 Jews were dumped into the ghettos and sent to Auschwitz during the spring of 1944, with most of them gassed and cremated during that summer, the

Jews of Budapest were ghettoized but not deported. The reason for this lay in the state of the war; that is, in the combination of the American invasion of Normandy and the rapidly moving Russian offensive from the East, auguring the impending victory of the Allies. Fearing Russian occupation and the Allies' retribution, the regent, Horthy, cancelled the entrainment of the Budapest Jews. While the threat of deportation didn't disappear, it didn't come to fruition either. Still, our fate hung on a fragile thread. We wore the yellow star and avoided the streets except during the hours allotted to Jews. Also, four people were forced to move into our apartment, because the house in which we had lived for years had now been turned into a "ghetto house." But we were enormously lucky: we didn't have to give up our home and move elsewhere. Staying in our apartment where we had always lived, our family was neither separated nor deported throughout the summer. In fact, after awhile, the children of our ghetto house started to meet regularly, developing deep friendships and forming a "children's group" that played games, rehearsed, and performed theater pieces from morning till midnight. Although we had less and less to eat and ghetto-living was not only deeply humiliating but also unbearably difficult and threatening for most adults, we played throughout the whole summer and, by the early fall, we even started to believe that surviving the war with all of us staying together in Budapest was perhaps possible.

But then, on October 15, 1944, with German help and support, the Hungarian Arrow Cross Party assumed power. Things changed. Our lives were now threatened. We didn't die, however, because Erzsi (Elizabeth), our former playmate and babysitter, who lived nearby, took care of us from the beginning of the German occupation until our liberation by the Russians, risking her own life for our sake a thousand times over. Rather than going back to the countryside where she came from, and where her parents lived, she stayed in Budapest, helping us survive. First, she tried to line up places for each of us to hide, in case we needed to move out of the ghetto; but she also shopped for food and other necessities for us and helped my parents in every way she could. After the Arrow Cross coup in the fall of 1944, she saved us from immediate death, again and again risking her own life in a variety of rescue operations. She took each of us to different places, finding people who were willing to take in Jews for money, at least temporarily; and she came to pick us up when we had to leave. As she had stood in line for food for us throughout the summer, she now stood in line at times for genuine, at other times, for falsified protective passes. She even found some exemption certificates for my father so that he didn't have to report for slave labor. To find such papers and certificates, she had to cross the streets during the shelling and bombing of Budapest. Finding places in protected houses, she visited us wherever we hid, even when the city was under a deadly siege, and often she had to stop her movement on the streets and run for protection from house to house, from shelter to shelter.

Indeed, by November 1944, the Arrow Cross caught up with the remaining Jews of Budapest. At this point, Erzsi got "Vatican passes" for us; and we spent two weeks in a protected "Vatican house." But at the beginning of December, the Arrow Cross started to eliminate the "protected houses," among them those that stood under the protection of the Vatican, marching Ivan and me to the ghetto. Erzsi was not to be defeated, however. She came a few days later, found us, and smuggled us out from there before the Arrow Cross sealed off the area. In the course of the next six weeks, she took my parents, Ivan, and me to a variety of places to hide, roving the streets even during the city's carpet bombing. She took me first to a Red Cross home to hide from the Arrow Cross, and then, after a few days, to a "Swedish house," and then to a convent I had to leave after I told a playmate that I was Jewish. From there, we stayed with a woman Erzsi had known for some time. Staying with her for only one night, I was on the street the next morning. Undeterred by all the difficulties, Erzsi still found a new place for me. But by then, the siege of Budapest had grown into a full-fledged, bloody battle, the likes of which only Warsaw and Berlin suffered during World War II.[1] Erzsi gave my new host my mother's last gold bracelet, promising her that she would return and pick me up in a few days. Accepting both the bracelet and me, the lady disappeared by next morning, however. When I woke up, I was alone in the apartment; and all I could find to eat there was a small box of cookies. I lived off them for the next two days. In the meantime, from the suburbs, the Russians started to shell the house where I was staying. This was on the Pest side, facing the Danube; so that the tenants, here and in every other house on the street, moved down to the shelters. But I knew that I must not do so, because, as Erzsi had told me before she left, the concierge as well as the standing committees responsible for the people living in the house and moving to the shelter would immediately call the police, when seeing me, a new, unaccounted person, and ask them to check me out. Fearful of being discovered, I stayed in the apartment, which during the morning came under increasingly heavy artillery and mortar attack. Within a few minutes, all was broken: windows, lamps, and most of the furniture. I ran to the kitchen and saw from there that fire had broken out in the neighboring apartment. I didn't know what to do. Hearing voices, however, I ran back inside the place where I was staying. But not only were parts of the house burning in which I hid: wherever I peaked out the window, I saw heavy black smoke billowing toward the sky. I prayed and played and cried all day and all night, crawling into a closet filled with blankets and pillows, covering myself with them as I heard bombs whistling through the air, falling and exploding. By next morning, the series of explosions stopped; instead, I heard a series of popping sounds. Thinking the Russians had arrived, I slunk to the window. But what I saw was worse than anything I had ever seen before, worse than the most frightening accounts I had ever witnessed. Two Arrow Cross men were standing on the embankment of the river, aiming at and shooting a group of men, women, and children into the Danube—one after the other, on their coats the Yellow Star. I looked at the Danube. It was neither blue nor gray but red. With a throbbing heart, I ran back to the room in the middle of the apartment and sat on the floor, gasping for air. Then, I returned to the closet, burying my head in the pillows and continued praying, singing songs, or loudly reciting my favorite poems so that I wouldn't hear the sound of the shootings.

After three days in the closet, I started to be very hungry. I also became increasingly weak. It was the morning of the fourth day when Erzsi got me out of there. How she walked from one end of Pest to the other, I don't know. Nor do I know how she had the courage to take me amidst the bombing, shelling, and the Arrow Cross checkpoints from the house next to the Danube to Kisfaludy street, where my parents were hiding in the basement of a louse-infested makeshift hospital. It took a whole day, but we made it. A week later, she brought Ivan. The four of us were together now, hiding with 150 other Jews for three weeks in that basement. And we survived despite the bloody siege, despite the Arrow Cross's reign of terror, despite their murder of tens of thousands of Jews.

The Russians liberated us on January 17th, and we walked home the same day. In the following weeks, the population of Budapest was further decimated by typhus, influenza, other epidemics, and death by starvation. I got typhus, but within one week, I recovered. Erzsi included, all of us survived.

Life moved slowly after the war. We went back to our old apartment, which had not been looted after we left and Erzsi moved in; nor had it been destroyed by the bombardment. But lacking coal, we were freezing; lacking food, we were starving. To escape from Budapest, we set out in a group, walking to Békéscsaba (about 150 miles), a town near the Romanian border. We knew the place; we had lived there for some years before moving to the capital. I don't remember much of this journey, though, for I was very weak and unable to walk. My father carried me in his arms most of the time. Arriving at the house of Erzsi's parents, we ate for several weeks, day and night. To eat real food again was truly wonderful; but otherwise, life was frightening. My parents found none of their friends at home alive. Neither did I: nobody among my friends and schoolmates in Csaba had survived Auschwitz.

Slowly, a few men returned from labor service; after awhile, a few survivors arrived as well. But, of course, no children came back from the camps. Talking with everybody they could reach, my parents sat stunned. It was the spring of 1945. They began to suspect that all their siblings and most of their relatives had been murdered. Time proved them right. My father lost his beloved sister and his brother, and my mother lost three sisters and one brother in the Holocaust. This loss hit my parents hard; they suffered tremendously. Their only solace was our survival. In addition, besides the terrible personal tragedies, the general devastation of the Shoah was almost unbearable to face. The entire Hungarian Jewish community, except that of Budapest, was destroyed. And even the families of Budapest's Jews were significantly torn apart. Most had lost several of their members.

After awhile, however, slowly and clearly, people began to move beyond death and destruction. Living for the time in Békéscsaba, we found not only food, but my father regained his strength as well. He started a new pharmaceutical laboratory, realizing a dream he had had for years but could never carry out because the country's anti-Semitic policies had restricted Jewish business activities as far back as the early 1930s. He worked hard, and soon his lab, producing serum for animals, employed three workers. Within the next three years, it developed into a serum institute employing more than one hundred people, filling the instant needs of the impoverished countryside.

At the end of the summer of 1945, my mother, brother, and I returned to Budapest. My father, on the other hand, traveled back and forth between the capital and Békéscsaba, to oversee the operation of his business. In the meantime, my brother registered at his former school and started to prepare for his high school diploma, making possible his enrollment in medical school three years later. I, on the other hand, did not reenroll in a public school. Taking my yearly exams, I continued at the music academy as a child pianist. By then, the boards replacing the windows in our apartment house were replaced by glass. Soon we were eating bread instead of beans, and, I remember, by 1947–1948, my mother was baking cakes as often as we wanted her to do so, at least for awhile.

Some of our friends and acquaintances, young men and women who had survived the Holocaust, married and had children after the war; some left for Israel or for countries willing to accept them. My parents, too, were considering such a move. In early 1948, they even found two young Zionists who volunteered to walk with us across the border to Romania, and from there, they promised, we would be picked up by others, who would take us on a boat to Israel. But my parents felt uneasy starting a new existence in another country. They decided to stay and do the best with what we had.

Two days after their decision, they heard from neighbors that one of my father's closest friends, whose wife and son had been killed in the Holocaust, encouraged his second, remaining son to go to Israel, where the young man died in the War of Independence. Hearing this news, our friend committed suicide.

—

As life went on, the question "how did you survive," which Jews asked of one another as soon as they met in the months following the Shoah, gave way to more immediate concerns about the present. What took place *then* became a topic of discussion only among close friends. The reason for this silence might have lain partly in the incapability of most Jews to face the tremendous devastation the Shoah created, partly in the reaction of the rest of the country to what had happened. Most Hungarians were unwilling to discuss either Jewish losses or their own participation and involvement in the Shoah—political, economic, intellectual, or emotional. Aware of this uneven ground, by the end of the 1940s, at a time when the Communist Rákosi government decided to suppress all discussion of the Holocaust and concentrate on the "crimes" of the capitalists and independent business alone, much of the humiliated Jewish community was terrorized into obeying the official line. Nevertheless, the events of the Shoah remained deeply engraved in the memory of Hungarian Jews. Beginning to make a decisive impact on the literature of the time, elaborations on this calamity grew significantly in volume over the years. Especially when examined against the background of the ban on Jewish remembrance, an amazingly large number of memoirs, eyewitness accounts, and novels appeared in Hungary immediately after the war, calling attention to the power the Shoah held over the remaining Jewish population.[2] Even in the 1950s, 1960s, and 1970s, when official policies intensified the pressure on erasing Jewish memory, almost all Jews eagerly read whatever was published on this subject.

—

But by 1948, everyday life had become hard and political pressure grew ever-more threatening. Because of unjust demands on the peasants, food was scarce in the villages. And in the towns, it simply was not available. Again, we had barely enough to eat, and the general economic gain achieved immediately after the war declined. Within a few months, a new exodus started. Once again, we, too, seriously considered leaving the country. But it wasn't easy to do so by then. The number of places that would accept refugees was even more limited; and, as before, the sense of uncertainty of a future in foreign lands was more frightening to my parents than the intensifying tension of politics in Hungary. By the early 1950s, I recognized, however, that remaining in my "homeland" was a huge mistake. A Communist terror emerged in Hungary. What I had read earlier in my father's library on the violence of the Communists in Russia now became a way of life in Hungary. I had to realize that the deeply human and moral Hungary of the future, which my father had so often de-scribed to me during and after the German occupation, includ-ing the world's interest in helping us, would never materialize. Overnight, Hungary became a center of Stalinist terror. Show trials were arranged. People were arrested, tortured, sentenced to physical labor, and deported from Budapest to distant villages or towns. Suddenly my parents wanted to flee, but it was no longer possible. Hungary had been barricaded; on its borders, guards, fences, and mines made any escape impossible.

Living under the terror of the state, intellectuals as well as or-dinary people, dreamers as well as realists searched for theoretical justifications for the new developments. They became interested in the texts of Marx, Lenin, and Stalin. Some of these people we knew; some of them were my parents' friends. In fact, some intel-lectuals even believed, or at least tried to believe, in these texts' basic assumptions. But I didn't. In fact, at first I couldn't even ex-plain why anybody would take these ideologues seriously. To me, they were just like "Stalin's best Hungarian disciple," Rákosi, the leader of the Hungarian Communist government, who would

lie, cheat, and murder to curry the favor of the Russian dictator. Their aim involved nothing more than extending their power
and gathering people into groups of a creed, secular in nature,
but religious in structure. Depicting the world as based on two
conflicting ideological camps, they maintained that the first one
followed the "working class" and was therefore redemptive, while
the second wasn't. These leaders as well as their followers were
in my eyes either lying, deliberately falsifying both reality and the
future, or truly naive. But I couldn't speak about this with strangers. Whoever questioned the doctrine of the Party was arrested,
even schoolchildren. And the rest? Most acted as if suddenly they
had found "the true and rational" explanation for everything, including the present and future development of the world.

As for the Holocaust, several of our best friends, some of whom
were Jewish and who had lost their family in the Shoah, claimed
that mass murder could only happen in a capitalist world, where
the rich exploit the poor and everybody is the enemy of the other. I knew that this was nonsense. Anti-Semitism had nothing
to do with capitalism. I knew from my parents that the "believers'" charge of deicide, the Crusaders' denunciations of the Jews,
and the ritual myth of "blood libel" were accusations that had
played themselves out over nearly two millennia in the Western
world. Historically, these accusations resulted in the incitement
of people to murder Jews and, when that took place, the masses
regarded the killing as the "Christ-killers'" divine punishment. I
knew that these accusations were still alive, accepted by many,
even in nineteenth-century "enlightened" Hungary—as the trial
at Tiszaeszlár had demonstrated. I also read about the Russian
pogroms and the Dreyfus Affair in France; and after the end of
World War II, I knew what had happened in Auschwitz. In addition, I was well-acquainted with the details of the mass murder
of six thousand Jews in 1919 by the Hungarian counterrevolu-
tionary army, and aware of the atrocities against Jewish students

at Hungarian universities in 1920.[3] Growing up on these "lessons of Jewish history," by the 1950s I knew that the problem was larger than the suddenly surfacing, ideologically shaped Holocaust analyses imported from the Soviet Union. In fact, I knew that those statements were lies. But there was almost nobody with whom I could discuss these matters. Several of our friends and acquaintances were caught up in the process of becoming good Communists and were overjoyed by this "new vision of the world" toward which the "legendary leadership" of the Soviet government would lead them. With such mindless adaptation of the new political system and, of course, direct military and political pressure from the Soviet Union, it is no coincidence that within a few years after the war, Communist Hungary became a partner to everything Stalin proposed, including an anti-Zionist, anti-Semitic campaign to discredit the State of Israel, denigrate the Holocaust, and launch a war against the Jews. At this point, the system had highly discouraged, and after awhile forbidden, any kind of discussion of the Shoah.

Thus, what had become important at the beginning of the 1950s, in the Hungarian media as well as in educational institutions, among intellectuals, students, and professionals alike, involved a description of the world as being torn between the forces of the "future" and those of the "past": the forces of communism and those of capitalism. Suddenly, some people started to believe in the centrality of the "dictatorship of the proletariat," and became preoccupied with questions and statements of ideology that took the place of everything else. These questions surfaced in virtually every discussion in every school or university, including the Music Academy. We started to have classes in Marxism-Leninism, where most students were expected to demonstrate their beliefs in the importance of analyzing these "new" ideas, because without doing so, the world could again be overtaken by the "enemies of humanity." At this point, I separated myself psychologically from most of my colleagues and from most people I knew in any kind of position of power. I remember myself starting to refer to the lines of a verse I had first read at the age of fourteen, in a new volume of poetry by Miklós Radnóti, who was killed in the Holocaust: ". . . / such things one must forget, but I / have never yet been able to forget." "I have never yet been able to forget," I repeated again and again, "And neither would I want to do so."[4]

Reading through these pages, one might think that I felt isolated as a young girl in Budapest, after the world started to be twisted more and more toward the Left. But I wasn't. The gap between me and others emerged only in my relationship to the larger, more impersonal Hungarian community. In my personal life, I was surrounded by friends and continued to live after the Holocaust as I had before. I still saw life as divided into two groups of people: those who save and those who don't. While I know today that this recognition is not a realistic tool for judging the larger world, for judging mine, at that time of history, it worked well. That is, I understood and believed that in saving us from the Germans, Erzsi had demonstrated a level of heroic love without which life was unworthy to be lived. This criterion then became the measure of all my relationships. Seeing the world from the perspective of my experience of the German occupation, I was deliberately searching for friends who would, if need be, save my life, knowing that I would always do the same for them. I will never forget that in 1951, when I heard about the impending deportation of the parents of my friend, Vera, I went to their apartment to help. To my greatest astonishment, there I met István, my future husband. He had rushed there to help the elderly couple pack and move their belongings. Marked for deportation from Budapest, they were to report to the police station the next morning. One couldn't know whether or not the house was observed. But had the police found István there, he would have had to face accusations or worse. Yet he didn't stay away; he came and offered his help.

Besides the importance of saving people's lives, I felt there was yet another, albeit very different, quality I hoped to find in a person who would become my friend: "would he or she like to play?" I used to ask myself. For many years, I didn't know why I had such a need for "the game." But now I know that it was my desire for reliving the past. What that past meant involved my experience in 1944, in the ghetto house, where our so-called "children's group" was left to its own devices by the adults, who were sick of fear and humiliation, preoccupied with questions such as: "when will we be picked up?" "what will happen to my children?" and "how will we survive"? Hence, living virtually without parental supervision, I and my friends in the "children's group" passionately wrote and rehearsed theater pieces, played games and make-believe for days, weeks, and months on end, inventing a magical private world, separate from the realm of the adults, a world that was understood only by us, the self-chosen participants, who had created our own "stage."

As soon as we returned from Csaba to Budapest, I felt compelled to find new friends and continue to play our old games. This was not hard. During those years, the youth of Budapest, perhaps more than that of other cities in Europe, had a history of magical games invented in the settings of private worlds projected by children's fantasy.[5] Among students at the Music Academy and others who were very close to me, I had no difficulty in finding partners with whom I continued to listen to, relive, and recall these fairy-tale games, with everybody playing along, playing make-believe. Today, I know that what we did then as adolescents was nothing other than the repetition of our childhood experiences, which helped us escape the real world of atrocity and the threat of death. Caught first by the Holocaust and then by the post–World War II Communist world in Hungary, we continued to live in a hostile environment, from which only theater and games, inspired by make-believe, fairy tale, and a magical imagination, could shield us. We constantly spoke through poems to one another, sometimes using the same author, sometimes picking up lines from a variety of poets to express a thought or challenge one another or invent new combinations. We perhaps would have played all these games till we died had the revolution not broken out in 1956 and split up our group forever.

———

Although my life was highly active on the personal, intellectual, emotional, and professional level, I recognized under the pressure of change that the public world had deteriorated catastrophically. By the beginning of the 1950s, the conflict between East and West had intensified. Stalin was bent on spreading his stamp of power over all of Eastern and Central Europe's occupied territories. His Hungarian puppet government helped him to create the Communist terror. The unbearable "class war" continued; enemies were identified, and in 1951, mass deportations started from Budapest into the countryside.[6] By 1952–1953, the destruction of Zionist organizations became the aim of the Soviets and their followers. Everybody understood that this was an attack not only on the new Jewish state in Israel but also on Jews everywhere. Indeed, culminating in the infamous "Doctors' Plot," the new purges were openly directed against them. In Hungary too, many Jews were arrested, jailed, or sent to slave-labor camps. In fact, one of our friends and neighbors was imprisoned and tortured for years. I was kicked out of the Music Academy, probably not because I was Jewish but because my father appeared as a "capitalist" according to their records. It was the Secretary of the Communist Party at the Music Academy who told me that I could not remain there as a student: "You belong to the camp of the enemy," she said. "Why?" I asked desperately. "Well, we know that your father was an industrialist."

This was a frightening statement. For it was back in 1949 that my father's serum laboratory had been confiscated (he found, then, a job in a similar institute, owned by the state, in Budapest). This remark, made two years later, was a major threat. To be singled out was dangerous because it could have had political consequences; but even if it didn't, it made my career as a pianist in Hungary impossible. At this point, several of our friends were thrown out of their jobs, and more and more among them were imprisoned. "Why did we stay?" I asked my parents desperately, suddenly understanding the horrible consequences of our decision. "It's only a matter of time until they'll get us! Why didn't we move a long time ago to a country where people had never worn the yellow star? Where they had never been gassed? Where they had not been shot into mass graves or into the Danube? Where they were not bombed? Where they were not threatened with exile if their fathers became involved in business? Where people always had bread to eat?" I had come to understand the past: the catastrophic history of Hungary, Jewish fate in Hungary, Jewish fate in Europe, abandonment by the world, danger, vulnerability, and the hopelessness of escape.

Stalin died in March 1953. After that, life changed somewhat in Hungary. Antagonism against Jews ceased to be on the government's most pressing agenda, although silence about the Shoah still characterized national policies. What shifted to the foreground, however, involved the ideological differences of various factions of the Party. In October 1956, a planned demonstration developed into an all-encompassing revolution against the Soviet system. The revolution was won, and we believed ourselves to be liberated and free. But it was not the right time truly to believe this, not the right time to trust the world. The West was unwilling to face up to a political conflict with the Soviets. Hungary was left to its fate. Fearing American involvement for a short while, but soon understanding they had nothing to fear, the Soviets quickly reclaimed Hungary. In addition to their large army units surrounding Budapest, new Soviet military divisions entered the country to put down the uprising. Woken up during the small hours of November 4, 1956, I couldn't believe what was happening: the house we lived in shook from the shelling. Again. Within the next few weeks, 250,000 Hungarians fled. My father, too, started to search anew for possible, secure ways of running away, but he didn't seem to find one. Before I knew it, most of my friends had left. I suddenly understood that there was no secure way to leave; no secure future to run toward. Nonetheless, I understood that we must run away because if not, we would continue to live in Hungary, continue to live in misery, continue to be persecuted, continue to be oppressed, and, thus would allow the murderers to kill us. I finally understood that we had to leave Hungary. In addition, I understood that talking to my parents wouldn't help because they would agree, but then, they would step back, as they had always done. And in the end, we wouldn't leave. I started to beg my husband, István, to pack his bag and go, telling him that as long as we were waiting for each other, nothing would happen. But as soon as he departed, I could follow. And as soon as the two of us left, my parents would leave as well. I preached to the choir. He, too, was shaken by the bloodshed, disgusted by the Communists and the life they forced upon us, disgusted by the Russians, disgusted by the siege. And he, too, was outraged at the murder of the Jews, which nobody wanted to discuss and nobody was allowed to talk about. He, too, wanted to leave. And finally, he did. I was to follow him to Hamburg.

Pondering the past throughout my train trip and even after bidding farewell to Gustaf, I stayed for five days in Vienna, where

I received my new German "refugee passport," which István sent me from Hamburg. I then boarded another train that took me to Germany. I was delirious from a new sense of freedom, though at the same time I was also overwhelmed by pain for those I left behind. I arrived at my new destination with great expectations and a strange sense of heaviness and uncertainty. There was one thing, however, I was sure of: there wouldn't be any difficulties arising from the "cultural difference" between me and the Germans. For, I felt, there was none. Despite what had happened, I was, in many ways, like them; I felt part of German culture, part of Bach and Goethe, Schiller and Thomas Mann.

István waited for me at the train station and took me to the observatory, where we would live for the next six years. The same night, I met a number of his colleagues, astronomers, students, and scholars alike, all of whom seemed to be kind and pleased about admitting yet another "Hungarian" into their circle. In fact, all of them looked upon us with friendly admiration, as if we were representatives of the Hungarian Revolution; for they regarded the latter as the first major "galvanizing attempt" in Eastern Europe to try and resist, even defeat, the all-powerful Soviet army. Although the revolution of the Hungarians didn't prevail then, most Germans were tensely waiting for the next one. Confronted with the Russian occupation of East Germany, they were deeply concerned with the enormous tensions that a divided Europe posed as well as the dangers that the Cold War created. Despite the fact that neither of us belonged to the ranks of the Hungarian freedom fighters who forced the Soviets to surrender, we, too, were overjoyed about the defeat of the Russians, who perpetuated murder and atrocity in Europe, and about the collapse of the Hungarian government that terrorized, threatened, frightened, and forced us to lie for years: a government responsible for the murder of thousands of innocent people.

Of the Germans I met on the day of my arrival at the Bergedorf Observatory, many were still preoccupied with the horrors that World War II had bought upon them. But I immediately noticed a problem: we were speaking about different horrors. My experience with the Germans was similar to that of my discussions with Hungarians, with whom, in discussing the losses of the Jews, people compared them to the losses of Hungarians, identifying both groups as having suffered from the "evil of the war." To me, however, the Holocaust had not much to do with the evil of the war; rather it was about the deliberate, brutal murder of Jews, of all Jews, of men, women, children, the sick and the aged, their communities as well as their culture. To me, what happened to others, including the Germans (or the Hungarians) during World War II, however terrible, was of another nature. While these countries obviously lost large numbers of innocent people, not all Germans and not all Hungarians were sentenced to death. I had thought about this issue back in Hungary as well and saw much of my alienation from Hungarian society in general and from the Communist rule in particular rooted in these revised versions of Holocaust memory. During that night of our first meeting with people in the observatory, I spoke with several men and women about their experiences during the war. Some of them found rational explanations for the atrocities, and others condemned them; yet others spoke about the tremendous suffering the Germans went through during the years in which they lived under the pressure of merciless Allied bombing. These were the reactions to the past I encountered in Hamburg on the first night of my arrival; they were also emblematic of my discussions with most people throughout our sojourn in Germany.

At the end of March 1957, I applied for admittance to the Hamburg Academy of Music. I was accepted, and found some truly wonderful teachers there: first, Robert Henry, later, Mme. Zur. I also located an elementary school in Bergedorf that had an old and kind caretaker, Mr. Schreiber, who had been a Social

Democrat before the rise of Hitler. He and his wife allowed me to practice eight to ten hours a day there. Small wonder that István and I recognized that the path to achieve our goal was open. Working hard, we would be able to get our degrees in Germany: he his Ph.D. and I my Concert Diploma.

Yes, but what else? Weeks, months, and years passed by. We lived in Hamburg-Bergedorf, but my life remained overshadowed by the world of Budapest. In fact, time didn't close the gap between my present and past. Hurting from the separation from my parents, I wrote them a letter every day; and my father wrote back daily, too. The Hungarian mail was unreliable, however, so that our letters were often delayed or even discarded, confusing our communication, creating constant irritation, concern, and worries in all of us. This tension was intensified by the lack of communication via the telephone. We didn't have one and couldn't afford one. Thus, István and I went every Saturday afternoon to the "Inn of Frieda," a tavern near the observatory in Bergedorf, where we were allowed to sit down and place a call to Budapest. Sometimes we could speak with my parents within an hour or so; other times, it took two to five or more hours before we were connected; sometimes we understood one another clearly, sometimes, not at all. It was sheer torture.

And then, slowly, almost imperceptibly, I started to recognize that I was homeless and would remain homeless for the rest of my life. While there were people who were kind and good to us, I began to understand that I could never be free of my past and, in turn, that I could never live in a world where my past amounted to nothing, where it could never be translated or explained. These recognitions were new. However estranged I was from the larger world in Hungary, there had been many people around me who loved Radnóti, who expressed their thoughts and feelings through the "vortex of voices" of Hungarian, German, English, or French poems, who had been children, as I had, during the German occupation, who played, acted out, and recited poetry to forget or not to forget *"that* which had happened."[7] I started to see that no matter how well I knew *Faust* or the poems of Hofmannsthal and Rilke, I was a stranger in the German world of the late 1950s and early 1960s. I could never tell anyone who I was—although I tried to do so, never failing to mention that I was Jewish. This fact alone didn't create a relationship with people, however. How could it? Why should another person be responsible for that? And what could my Jewishness tell about me anyhow? And how could I say more? How could I speak about the pain and the fear that had been etched into me so many years earlier, the pain and the fear that are part of me forever? How could I speak about the place I came from? About our life? About the poetry that expresses it? About Radnóti, whose verse affirms my being? About Hungarian Jews? About my father? About Jewish religious questions; about the world of the Jews, and about what happened to them?

I felt estranged in Germany perhaps because I didn't know anybody else who had experienced life as I had. The major concerns of our closest friends, mostly young artists, young students, or young faculty, revolved around contemporary German-American policies. To them, wars were responsible for the deaths of millions of people; in fact, wars caused all the grief of the world. It was not as if these people ignored the past. But their outrage was essentially different from mine. They spoke about the extent to which the Nazis had disregarded people's constitutional rights during the Hitler era, the extent to which they had neglected people's individual needs, the ease with which they had turned racial discrimination into national policy, viewing *Gleichschaltung* as a process that interconnected with people's desire for fitting in, no matter *what* was expected of them. While I, too, regarded these concerns to be of great theoretical importance, other issues, more direct ones, more personal ones, hurt me more. I mourned the murdered Jews, the destruction of our family, and the injustice that separated me from my father and mother. Nor could István help me at this point. He, too, had been rather uncertain of himself during this period; he, too, had left his elderly parents behind; he, too, was looking for support. While I was more and more swept off my feet by the forces of the past, he, too, worried about the future, which he didn't see yet as settled. I missed my old friends in Budapest with whom I used to play all those games, and who would save me no matter what, and I missed my parents, terribly. I was devastated.

It was amidst these concerns that I obtained my concert diploma at the Hamburg Music Academy in 1961. Shortly afterwards, one of István's colleagues, our closest friend, decided to accept a job at the University of Texas at Austin and thought that it would be excellent if István would do the same. We came to Austin in November 1962. Deciding to give up my career in music, perhaps because I yearned for a new homeland in the realm of language, I enrolled in the German Department's Ph.D. program. I read day and night. A year later, we moved to Dallas, with István getting a job at the Southwest Center for Advanced Studies, which later became the University of Texas at Dallas. Gradually, I started to feel better. I found friends here. These people knew what had happened in Auschwitz; these people were interested in our past; these people knew about the Jews. I even met some who were interested in Hungarian poetry. I could speak with them and I could translate for them what had happened to us. I started to have great friendships. No, I didn't play games of metaphors with them, but I found myself closer to home.

⸻

While my lot improved tremendously in America, my parents' plight had not changed. The suffering my father had endured never ceased. He, the most loving human being of all the people

I have ever known, had lived in a never-ending state of anguish ever since his youth. The more I thought about it, the more I believed that the pattern could still be changed, that I and István and our daughter, little Kathleen, born in Dallas, and all of our friends here could, if not take back what had happened to him, at least make it good. I wanted to believe in the chance of my parents' visit, even in the possibility of their move to America. After all, we lived in America and my father loved America; this was the place, he told me, where he had always wanted to go. Also, by now, my parents were older. I thought they might appreciate that we were so well off. With our future secured, I hoped they would come, and we could lay to rest the events of the past.

But leaving Hungary at that time was still hard. Throughout our sojourn in Hamburg, my father tried to apply, and reapply, for a passport; his applications, however, were mercilessly turned down by the Hungarian government. Finally, in 1959, he received one for East Berlin. István and I flew to West Berlin, not yet walled-off from the East, and we spent five heartbreaking days together. Unwilling to stay and leave my mother and brother behind, my father returned to Hungary. But he continued to apply every six weeks for a passport. After three years, in the summer of 1962 he received one with permission to stay one week with us in Hamburg. A year or two later, the officials in the Hungarian Passport Office convinced him to retire from his job in the serum institute so that he and my mother could receive passports valid for one year in the United States. He did so. My parents arrived on September 1, 1964 in Dallas, Texas; my father died of a heart attack twenty-one days later. A year later, my mother went back to Budapest, where she died in 1971.

Our son, Peter, was born in 1967. By then, my love for life had returned with an enormous intensity. However hurtful the past, the world with our children turned out to be a wonderful and profound experience. Raising them with constant, enormous joy, we felt tremendously happy and satisfied. And while we wanted them to be at home in America, more so than we ever had been in Hungary, both of us felt that they would gain much from retaining part of our Hungarian heritage, which we would carry within ourselves for as long as we lived. And because the language I spoke at home with István was Hungarian and the poetry written in Hungarian had been so important to us, we decided to speak in this language with both children, teaching them all the games we had been playing throughout our life, all the folk songs I had learned from my parents, and later from Kodály and Sugár, all the most beautiful fairy tales, and poems, and stories, and novels, and Jewish jokes we had grown up on. And we did. Being with them in every free minute of our life, we spent together a beautiful, love-filled, miraculously free, enchanted time that continues into these days despite the fact that they grew up, despite the fact that they now live elsewhere. And we have been at home in Dallas, more at home than ever, anywhere, in my life.

There can be no doubt, however, that besides István and our children, my desire for studying the Holocaust and translating poetry have been the staple of my long search for finding home. First of all, my professional life began to progress well. Obtaining my Ph.D. in German literature in 1968, I began teaching in September of the same year. After a while, I began to publish as well. And I read—endlessly. Throughout my life, I have been preoccupied with the Holocaust. But now, I read about it systematically: studying its history, its literature, its social, political, and ideological background, with an emphasis on the history of the French, German, Russian–Polish, Hungarian, and Austrian Jews and their intellectual contribution in the course of the past two or three centuries. In 1976, I started to publish and teach courses on the Shoah. Some years later, with the help of interested individuals, the community, and the administration, the Holocaust

Studies program at the University of Texas at Dallas came to take shape.

—

There was yet another realm of great importance in my life, a realm that confirms my identity, recalls my childhood, and promises continuity. This is the realm of literary translation. Growing up speaking Hungarian, German, and French, I read much from these countries' literature in the original, especially their poetry. At the same time, I read the bulk of the nineteenth-century European novel in Hungarian. In this way, I have always been aware of the wide-ranging, creative significance of the act of translation. I have come to understand the role of changing languages, learning to understand oneself and the world in different ways, discovering the sound and color of other voices, and melting them into one's own being. Now that I was living in Dallas, I felt compelled to translate poems and stories from German and Hungarian into English. While starting with some works from German, I soon came to believe that rendering Hungarian poetry into English would be essential for the future, as there are just a few people in the world who know about the beauty, riches, and depth of the Magyars' literary tradition. With a chain of voices stretching back eight hundred years, a major cultural achievement has been realized in Hungarian poetry, which ranks among the greatest achievements in the Western literary tradition

While I dreamed about translating much of this huge and diverse material, in my thoughts I always returned to the work of the poet who had had the most significant influence on my life, whose poems I constantly recited with my friends in Budapest, whose tragic, never-waning presence had opened to me new and essential vistas on the Hungarian Holocaust: Miklós Radnóti (1909–1944). Radnóti was a brilliant poet with a heightened sense of beauty and an enchanting musical voice. But he lived amid a terrible conflict. Hoping to become a major force in the great Hungarian poetic tradition, he saw himself as being overlooked by Hungarian official, anti-Semitic, political and intellectual leadership. Humiliated first by the free-floating popular and intellectual anti-Semitism of the 1920s and 1930s, he was later directly attacked and, ultimately, dehumanized by the racist, anti-Jewish measures decreed between 1938 and 1941. Drafted three times during the early 1940s as a Jewish labor serviceman, Radnóti was taken finally to Yugoslavia. And when the German and Hungarian armies evacuated the Balkans in the late summer of 1944, Radnóti was force-marched back to Hungary. Ill-clothed, malnourished, mistreated, tortured, and driven for months through rain and mud and snow, he became exhausted and could no longer walk. Then he was selected and murdered by members of the Hungarian Army, who shot him with twenty-one of his comrades into a mass grave, where his body was found and exhumed almost twenty-months later. In the pocket of his raincoat, those who did an autopsy on him located a notebook containing ten poems that Radnóti had composed during his labor service in Yugoslavia and on the death march. These poems as well as much of his earlier lyrics have been, as Primo Levi says about the verses of Celan, "grafted into me" ever since I first heard them in Budapest.[8] I dreamed about translating them into English, thereby communicating Radnóti's belief in the redemptive power of poetry, his melancholic, deeply humane words, his heartbreakingly beautiful verbal metaphors that captured Jewish life and Jewish death in the twentieth century. I felt that he must be introduced and internationally recognized as one of the great poets of our time and as the chronicler of the *tremendum* that ruled Europe and killed millions in heretofore unimaginable ways. I started to yearn to render the dramatic force of his imagination and the beauty of his words, his musical-metrical patterns into English.

One day I met a new colleague, the poet Fred Turner, at The

University of Texas-Dallas, and we began to discuss the tasks, hopes, and potentials of translations. At this point, I already knew of Turner's lyrical output, and I found the music of his verse extraordinarily beautiful: graceful and lithe in its metrics, movements, and expressions, but also mystical, highly emotional, and visionary. He felt, as he said in our discussion, that besides finding equivalences between the source and the target language, a good translation must capture and recreate the rhymes, resonances, and metrical patterns that usually include the cultural memory of the original. He spoke of the hope for hearing and resounding the "Ur-language," a notion close to what Walter Benjamin calls a "pure language," a language that doesn't really exist, but always reverberates in the music of the original.

We had our first translation session three days later. Our work started with Radnóti's lyric, "Similes," one of the poet's tenderly smiling love poems that I adore. This piece also interplays with one of the games my friends and I played in Budapest a long time ago, describing a person in terms of color and sound, a game that at one point in his life Radnóti must have played as well. And then, I couldn't believe what happened: Fred saw the images of the poem, and he heard its music:

> And then you're indigo, and I'm scared, don't leave me,
> like twined smoke wandering,
> and sometimes I'm afraid of you
> hued like the lightening.
>
> And like the sunlit tempest
> —darkgold!—
> when you lose your temper
> you are the sounds of "ah" and "oh"—
>
> resonant, contralto, darkling.
> But now I'll scribble
> around you glittering
> smiles, ringlet within ring. (*FS*, 123–124)

There can be no doubt that what Fred calls "the Ur-language" resonates here somewhere in the depth of the words. And whatever echoes in the "Hungarian translation" of the poem echoes now in the English version as well. The reader hears the speaker's song and sees him scribbling "glittering ringlets" of smiles around his beloved.

Also the folk-song beat of "In Your Arms" resounds in English as if it were Hungarian:

> In your arms I am rocking, rocking
> hushaby.
> In my arms you are rocking, rocking
> lullaby. (*FS*, 105)

With the rhythm set, the words find their place and so does the voice. But even the poem's happiest moments take place on the edge of darkness. The ending of this "rocking poem" reveals the speaker's vision of death. Just as in Hungarian, exhaling again and again the h-sound, the speaker's last breath ("huge hushaby"), and reinforcing the hard beat of the d-sound, the voice moves between "death" and "dreaming," exhaling with the last word: "dreamingly."

> when you're holding me, not even
> death's huge hushaby
> can frighten me.
> In your arms through death as dreaming
> I will fall so
> dreamingly. (*FS*, 104–105)

Translating these lyrics, we went back to render a selection of Radnóti's work, one poem after the other. The metrically determined metaphorical language of the Magyars resounds now in

English, recreating the music, the colors, and the meaning of the Hungarian. Witness "Foamy Sky," which projects turbulent foamlike clouds, gushing toward the moon and contrasting the green streaks in the firmament. The images are as ominous in English as they are in Hungarian; at the same time, they inter-connect in both languages in the same uncanny ways with the persona's thoughtful, existential recognition of being:

> Foam gushes forth upon the moon.
> A dark green venom streaks the sky.
> I roll myself a cigarette,
> am slowly, carefully, a living I. (*FS*, 99–100)

And we started to work on the eclogues. On the one hand, a given here is the beat of the hexameter, pulsing in the ancient tradition of both Hungarian and European poetry; on the other, however, this is a structure with layers of echoes demanding to be heard and recalled. I was moved to the core: Fred recreated in English the metrics and the melodic line of the original composi-tion. He wanted to follow in the footsteps of Radnóti, his "brother-poet," who scanned the measure of his poems, taking their cry to the sky, paying great care and attention to the beat, even when in the camps, even when surrounded by his tortured comrades, even in the proximity of death, as in "The Seventh Eclogue":

Snoring they fly, the poor captives, ragged and bald,
From the blind crest of Serbia to the hidden heartland of home!
The hidden heartland. —O home, O can it still be?
with the bombing? And *is* it as then when they marched us away?
And shall those who moan on my left and my right return?
Say, is there a country where someone still knows the hexameter?
   (*FS*, 189–191)

Indeed, we wanted to follow Radnóti with utmost care, moving with him wherever he was forced to go, even on the death march. We imagined seeing what he saw, feeling what he felt, observing what he observed as he noted carefully and conscientiously, like medieval chroniclers, the suffering, destruction, and executions of the Jews. Witnessing his guards' shooting of hundreds of innocent people, he foresaw and captured in his last poem his own death, the Jewish death of the twentieth century:

> I fell beside him and his corpse turned over,
> tight already as a snapping string.
> Shot in the neck. "And that's how you end too,"
> I whispered to myself: "Lie still; no moving.
> Now patience flowers in death." Then I could hear
> "Der springt noch auf," above and very near.
> Blood mixed with mud was drying on my ear.
>   (FS, 212–213)

Having completed the translation of Radnóti's poems, Fred and I started to render into English the work of yet another great Hungarian twentieth-century poet: Attila József (1905–1937). József reveals an essential connection between the past and present in Hungarian poetry, resonating the ancient Magyar tonality as well as the voices of generations of Hungarian poets, but he also recalls the work of the national and international avant-garde.

I would not have imagined that József's sonorities and incantatory metrics could ever resound in English. But they do now. So it has become possible that in his early love poem, "Beads," for example, both the static and the glittery moving circles and spheres act within the poem and assume at once an audible and a visible presence:

> Beads around your neck aglow,
> Frogheads in the lake below.

Lambkin droppings,
Lambkin droppings in the snow.

Rose within the moon's halo,
gold belt round your waist to go.
Hampen knottings
knotted round my neck just so.

Skirted legs so subtly swinging,
Bell-tongue in its bell a-ringing,
River-mirror
With two swaying poplars' winging.

Skirted legs so subtly calling,
Bell-tongue in its bell a-tolling,
river-mirror
With the dumb leaves falling, falling.[9] (*IBV*, 75)

And to my greatest delight, we could translate (but may cite here only a few lines from) one of the most beautiful love poems of world literature, József's "Ode." This has been an important experience for me because there can be no doubt that along with its breathtaking sweep and glow, this poem has had an extraordinary influence on my life: it has shaped the ways in which many of my friends and I have learned to understand love in the world:

I love you as we who marked for death
Love the moment of their living breath.

Every smile, every word, every move you make,
as falling bodies to my earth, I press;
as into metal acids eat and ache
I etch you in my brains with instinct's stress,
beautiful shapeliness,
your substance fills the essence they partake.

The moments march by, clattering and relentless,
but in my ears your silence lies.

> Even the stars blaze up, fall, evanesce,
> but you're a stillness in my eyes.
> The taste of you, hushed like a cavern-pool,
> floats in my mouth, as cool;
> your hand, upon a water-glass,
> veined with its glowing lace,
> dawns beautiful.
> ... (*IBV*, 105–108)

But József composed poems not only about love and life and death; he also warned his people of the danger of nationalism and chauvinism and the threat these ideologies had created in Europe.

Fred and I hoped we would do justice to the art of József, not only to the harmonious sound of his words and to the mellifluous tunes of his voice, but also to the projection of his visual power and the clarity of his thinking, so that his English-speaking reader would appreciate József's poetic presence as well as his penetrating insight into twentieth-century European culture. For there were not too many writers and poets in the mid-1930s who could produce such insight, who understood *both* "wolfish" ideologies of the time, that created wars and killing centers, ultimately murdering more than fifty- or sixty million people. Unlike most of his internationally well-known colleagues, by 1937, József had recognized and warned against the murderous aggression inherent in Nazism and communism alike.

Our collection of Attila József's poetry came out in 1999, and soon after, Fred and I started on a new project involving the translation of a selection of eight hundred years of Hungarian poetry. Having completed this Hungarian anthology, Fred and I are now involved in translating a representative volume of Goethe's lyrics.

Changing countries several times in my life, I arrived with István in America in the fall of 1962. I was homeless, burdened by pain, guilt, my parents' tragic life, and the memory of the Holocaust. Despite this burden and despite this memory, however, I have found my home here. Of course, it has been my family—István, Peter, Kathleen, her husband, Gary, and baby Elizabeth—who are mostly responsible for my change of consciousness over the years; and so are my close friendships with people whom I love. But there have been other factors shaping my life, my perception of identity, authenticity, and memory as well. It was my book on Radnóti and my constant reading, writing, and thinking about the Holocaust, my ongoing discussions with students, friends, and others, including the interest many people express for the Shoah, which have played an important role in my understanding of the past. Furthermore, it took some time for me to comprehend that my past is not mine alone: I share it with the lives and deaths of many people, my family, my friends, and millions of Jews. That I am allowed, even encouraged to ponder their lives and deaths in freedom and with dignity and to think about the ways that led to the Shoah and the ways in which this event has affected my future and the future of the world are some of the major reasons for the deep gratitude I feel toward this country.

But then, besides my passionate desire for reading and teaching about the Holocaust, there is one more, deeply personal reason for my sense of being at home in America. Despite my life-threatening experience in Hungary, my love for Hungarian literature has not diminished over the years. In fact, it has been intensified by my experience of living in this country and listening to all those who speak English around me: my students, readers, friends, and the world that surrounds us. They urge me to keep on translating poetry. And despite my outlandish accent, a constant reminder that I wasn't born in this country, I feel that I express myself as comfortably in English as in Hungarian and enjoy moving between these two worlds. In addition, the poems Fred and I translated have sharpened my sense of hearing and understanding the huge variety of both languages' musical material and visual textures, with both becoming just as vital in shaping my intellectual–emotional world in English as in Hungarian. I hope to translate with Fred much more Hungarian and German poetry; and I hope to study further, and continue to write about, the major issues of the Holocaust.

Yet there are questions the reader may ask, questions that emerge despite my sense of "rootedness" in America: have my old nightmares left me? Have I learned to believe that my house will be here rather than destroyed when I return? That those whom I bid farewell to will return? That I will return? That the horrific memories of the past will become part of a bygone world? The answer to these questions is of course *no*. In my nightmares, I am still running down the streets, homeless, alone.

Notes

1. See the analysis, description, and exploration of this major attack on the Hungarian capital by Krisztián Ungváry, *The Siege of Budapest: 100 Days in World War II* (New Haven and London: Yale University Press, 2005).

2. Zsuzsanna Ozsváth, "Trauma and Distortion: The Ban on Jewish Memory in Hungary," *Congress Monthly* 1 (2006): 11–15; and in *The Holocaust in Hungary: Sixty Years Later*, ed. Randolph L. Braham and Brewster S. Chamberlin (New York: Columbia University Press, 2006), 337–347.

3. As my poor father could never forget about the brutal attack unleashed against him. This happened after he underwent surgery for

a life-threatening head wound he was afflicted with on the front, in World War I. His recuperation took almost a year. In 1919, he enrolled in the pharmacology department at the university, where he was captured and brutally beaten up by a group of "Awakening Hungarians," as they called themselves, lying in wait for Jewish students outside the classrooms of Hungarian universities. His sacrifice for the "fatherland" was quite meaningless, apparently.

4. Zsuzsanna Ozsváth and Frederick Turner, trans. *Foamy Sky: The Major Poems of Miklós Radnóti* (Princeton, N.J.: Princeton University Press, 1992), 100.

5. Even before World War II, though, Budapest's youth had been involved in playing and inventing magical games. See, e.g., Antal Szerb, *Journey in Moonlight*, trans. Len Rix (London: Pushkin Press, 2001).

6. According to Paul Lendvai, about one-third of these deportees were Jewish; see *Anti-Semitism without Jews: Communist Eastern Europe* (New York: Doubleday & Co., 1971), 309.

7. Paul Celan, "Ansprache Anlässlich der Entgegennahme des Literaturpreises der Freien Hansastadt Bremen," in *Paul Celan Gesammelte Werke* (Frankfurt am Main: Suhrkamp, 2000), 186.

8. John Felstiner, *Paul Celan: Poet. Survivor. Jew* (New Haven and London: Yale University Press, 1995), 331.

9. Zsuzsanna Ozsváth and Frederick Turner, trans. Attila József: *The Iron-Blue Vault: Selected Poems* (Newcastle upon Tyne: Bloodaxe, 1999).

Finding a Virtual Home for Yiddish Poetry in Southern Indiana

— *Dov-Ber Kerler*

How uprooted is a person who insists on writing in a language that is itself homeless? Other writers represented in this book on contemporary Jewish exile literature have moved between countries, cultures, and languages, ultimately reaching and settling on the shores of America. Some have adopted English as their new linguistic medium or even began their creative work entirely in English; others have continued to write in their first or native language. I, however, have chosen another course (or has it chosen me?) and write poetry in a language that is perceived to be inherently a language of exile. Yet, for a long time Yiddish was not a language *in* exile. Indeed, in prewar Eastern Europe, Yiddish had a homeland. It never had a state of its own, but it indeed had a homeland, a clearly discernible geographical space of its own, with its special ethnographic, cultural, and even sociopolitical properties. Otherwise, Yiddish literature and culture would not have come into their own, nor would they have almost simultaneously expanded to other lands and shores. Hence, while Hebrew was broadly adopted or recalibrated as the national Jewish language, Yiddish, with the nearly global expansion of Ashkenazi Jews during the last few centuries, became for a considerable time the international Jewish language and maintained its role as a leading medium of Jewish national, literary, and cultural creativity.

Given the fact that I myself was born in the postwar Soviet Union, the issue of uprootedness becomes even trickier. Moscow, in the early 1960s, was of course a far cry from the prewar East European Yiddish homeland from which my own parents hailed. There is also a subtle distinction between *uprootedness* and *deracination*. Immigrants who came to America, whether they were fully bent on becoming Americans or grappled with maintaining some version of their pre-emigrant identity, could indeed be characterized as subjects of various degrees of uprootedness, a state that invokes geographical rupture and separation. By contrast, the phenomenon of Russia's Jews turning, as it were, into Soviet citizens "of Jewish nationality" was heavy-handedly encouraged or in fact forced by the State. And many accepted this changeover willingly and had no reservations about becoming deracinated, uprooted from their own pre-Soviet, often traditionally Jewish upbringing and culture. As matters transpired, you did not have to travel very far, or even travel at all, to become deracinated in your own country. By the time I was born, the deracination process was more or less complete. The physical devastation of the Holocaust was successfully augmented on the mental or spiritual plane by postwar Soviet policies, which brought about the transformation just described.

So how did it happen that an ostensibly deracinated person born in Moscow in 1958 was to take up writing Yiddish poetry in the early 1990s in England? Before I attempt to answer this question, it's important to clarify a number of things, many of which are known only in the very narrow circle of today's devotees and readers of contemporary Yiddish literature.

One of the advantages of being a postwar Yiddish author is

the privilege of being considered even today a "young Yiddish author"—*young* meaning someone who is not well over the age of sixty even in the first decade of the new century. The sad and inevitable logic here is that if, for some ostensibly inexplicable reason, a person born in this increasingly "post-Yiddish" era began writing and publishing in Yiddish, he or she must be "young." Secondly, while it would be a folly to maintain that Yiddish literature is doing well, it nonetheless is quite remarkable that there are today about forty "younger" Yiddish authors, most of them poets (and some "poem writers"), a somewhat smaller but growing number of journalists and essayists, and finally a markedly small number of fiction writers and playwrights—all born after the war. Most began publishing in the 1980s and quite a few later still. (My estimate of about forty authors does not include those who penned and published less than a handful of "literary texts.")

This, of course, is a far cry from the situation that characterized the animated, though steadily waning, Yiddish literary life of the last prewar-reared generations in the 1960s, some of whose members wrote even into the early 1990s. With very few exceptions, the "younger" Yiddish writers make their living doing something else. Some have successful academic careers, and others work as professional teachers, translators from Yiddish, or journalists (in some cases in Yiddish). A few are producing new Yiddish translations of European children's literary classics, although this kind of work is hardly a reliable source of income. All things considered, there must be something other than a sheer drive for fame or literary conquest that drives these people to be creative in Yiddish.

This is not the place to analyze or offer even a brief overview of the Yiddish writers of this younger, postwar generation. It is, however, noteworthy that members of this very small and often disconnected group reside in Austria, Belarus, England, France,

Lithuania, Russia, Ukraine, Wales, and, of course, the United States, Canada, and Israel (outside of Israel and the United States, we are, in fact, looking at a very solitary literary existence, with not more than one or two, at best three, persons per country, or even one person divided between two countries). Many hail from the former Soviet Union; in particular, from Moldova, where Yiddish as a living language was, it seems, particularly well entrenched—as evident in the cases of Moyshe Lemster, Mikhoel Felzenbaum, Boris Sandler, Lev Berinsky (born in 1939, Berinsky is nonetheless included in the postwar generation). But quite a few were born and raised elsewhere—Yitskhok Niborski and Daniel Galai in Argentina; Heershadovid Menkes (pen name of Dovid Katz), the song writer Joshua Waletzky, and the prolific *haredi* pioneer of Yiddish "blogging," known only by his literary name "Katle Kanye" in the United States; Armin Eidherr and Thomas Soxberger in Austria.

Most of these "younger Yiddish writers," although certainly not all, are, in my view, accomplished poets and prose writers; some write in Yiddish as well as in other languages (multilingualism was always a particular strength of Yiddish literati); others, including some non-Jews, have adopted Yiddish as their primary language of creativity. I should add in passing that the few, actually five, non-Jewish authors with whose works I am familiar exhibit a remarkable grasp of Yiddish poetic diction and its deep Jewish cultural resonance. Thus, the vexed question of what constitutes Jewish literature is not an issue in Yiddish. When Aleksander Belousov (1948–2004) began publishing poetry in the early 1970s, Eleanor (Leah) Robinson debuted with her stories in the early 1980s, and Haike Beruriah Wiegand's first poems appeared just a few years ago, there was no doubt that their work belonged to Yiddish creativity and, therefore, was an integral part of the Jewish literary process.

Yet, writing Yiddish poetry in the new millennium is a very lonely enterprise, which no e-mail, Google Talk, or Skype can help to fully remedy. In May 2005, coinciding with the sixtieth anniversary of the end of World War II, three "younger" Yiddish poets met at a Yiddish studies event in Vilnius, two of them in their late forties, the third in his thirties; all three had been born in Russia. This miniscule group included the poet and scholar Velvl Chernin and myself, both Moscow-native Israelis living elsewhere, as well as our younger colleague with the resounding name of Yisroel Nekrasov, who lives in St. Petersburg (his native Leningrad). Each one read not more than two or three of his recent poems, and Chernin also recited a number of poems by some of our absent contemporaries. The amount of poetry read and shared was not of the essence; rather, it was this particular coming together of three Yiddish poets in the former Jerusalem of Lithuania that mattered. Such meetings are so few and far between—and like this one, incidental to some academic or other event—that a more sentimental participant easily could have mistaken it for something more than what it really was, namely a small, happy gathering of friends and, above all, pen colleagues.

When I was very young and incorrigibly individualistic, I tended to frown upon the social and public aspects of literary creativity. Reception (especially commercial success), audience, readership, and even a creative collegial environment—they all seemed to me to be of secondary importance. At the center of my own preoccupation with literature was the work itself, be it a novel, poem, or play, as well as the author's discernible craftsmanship, genius, and creative individuality. Interestingly enough, this stubbornly naive attitude developed in my late teens, more or less coinciding with my own brave decision to stop writing poems (which I earlier had attempted to compose in Russian, then in Hebrew, and somewhat later in Yiddish). Suppressing my own "creative" urges was indeed a source of lasting personal pride, for there were too many peers especially in Russia and particularly among other writers' children who devoted themselves to rhyme-stery and various types of verse production. Little did I know then that a time would come when I would cave in to those urges and devote myself to writing poetry in a language that forces oneself to yearn for the things I had earlier disregarded—a measure of reception, a wider readership, and, above all, a vibrant creative environment. For Yiddish poets writing today, none of this can be taken for granted; indeed, these factors hardly exist.

Growing up in a literary home—my father Yoysef Kerler was a leading Soviet Yiddish, and, later, Israeli Yiddish poet, I had more than ample opportunity to directly witness literary creativity in action by observing his work. I was also that proverbial fly on the wall at some lively debates and exchanges among his colleagues—Yiddish poets, writers, critics, actors, singers, and artists, in Moscow, Vilnius, and Odessa in the 1960s and then in Jerusalem and Tel Aviv in the 1970s. Sometime in 1969, I asked my father to teach me the Hebrew alphabet and soon thereafter began copying his then new and audaciously courageous poems of protest, many of which I could remember by heart. A significant number of these poems were written by him during his imprisonment in Stalin's Gulag in the 1950s, and many others were written, so to speak, in front of my eyes, when he and my mother were among the first Jewish dissidents in the USSR of the 1960s. However, most memorable, apart from my father's work and his own very artistic poetry recitations, were the numerous private readings by a number of excellent, though often unknown, Yiddish poets. These took place first in my parents' home (in Russia, and from 1971 in Israel) and later at various private and public evenings and literary gatherings in Israel. Whenever I read and reread the poems of such masters of Yiddish verse and song as Yosl Kotliar, Borukh Bergholtz, Shike Driz, Rokhl Boimvol, Ziame Telesin, Meir Kharatz, Khayim Maltinsky, Kadye Molodowsky, Malka

Heifetz Tussman, Yankev Tzvi Shargel, and Avrom Sutzkever, I often hear in my mind's ear their voices' timbre, intonation, and diction. Of these, perhaps only the names of Molodowsky and Sutzkever, who are considered by many to be among the top masters of Yiddish poetry, are known outside of the by now miniscule circle of Yiddish poetry cognoscenti.

It may well be that had I not been privy to such a wealth of live Yiddish poetry (and in some cases prose, humorous sketches, and critical essays) read by the authors themselves, my much later surrender to the hitherto suppressed "creative" charges never would have occurred. It is this counterpoint or perhaps polyphony of very different and individualistic poetic voices that continues to echo and, to some degree, reverberate in my own attempts at marrying rhymes and meters with more elusive sense and reason. However, the more "prosaic," though not less creatively challenging, cause for the invention of the Yiddish poet "Boris Karloff" was the constantly evolving personality of my teacher and later colleague Dovid Katz, who began to publish original and highly sophisticated Yiddish fiction in the early 1990s, only after the death of his father, the distinguished and much beloved Yiddish poet Menke Katz. At that time, under Dovid Katz's inspirational leadership, Oxford University developed into a spirited new center of Yiddish studies that boasted a growing number of graduate students, a series of academic conferences, symposia, hefty academic publications, and an internationally acclaimed intensive summer program (which he and I "relocated" to Vilnius in 1998).

After publishing fiction in a number of important Yiddish periodicals as well as his first book of stories, Dovid challenged me in 1992 to try my hand at writing prose that would be more "creative" than our usual academic Yiddish texts. And a few weeks later I gave in. I believed then that I might have a perfect plot for a satirical novel, which would meet the "style-and-sarcasm-over-action" requirements of some kind of an early-late-pre-postmodern sustained narrative. My protagonist would be a certain type of American Yiddish, or better still, an American Yiddishist *nudnik,* named Hentl-Pentl, who despite his classic schlemiel constitution becomes astonishingly successful. In other words, my character was an American Yiddish schlimazel studying Yiddish philology in Europe, who nevertheless is far from becoming a "loser" upon his return to America.

One night after getting bored and frustrated with drafting the first outline of my great Yiddish novel, I took another piece of paper (at the time it seemed still sacrilegious to use the PC for creative writing) and quite unexpectedly wrote a poem, which projected the schlimazel idea onto myself; it's a poem about a tiny blade of grass looking up to mighty tall trees and begging them to be accepted into their "grown-up" company. To this the trees reply, "Don't worry, you grand little grass, it's not so bad to be who you are, after all!" A few days later when Dovid asked again about the progress of my novel, I instead showed him my first two poems. Since then, it seems, I have been lost to prose forever. At that time one of my graduate students, Gennady Estraikh, himself a published author and former editorial secretary of the Soviet Yiddish monthly *Sovetish heimland,* suggested that we should start publishing our own literary periodical. The idea appealed to our whole group, it seemed, because the establishment periodicals in Israel and the United States were, we felt, beginning to show signs of fatigue and apathy to new and "younger" literary works (one of the few exceptions was my father's *Yerusholaimer Almanakh* that was always on the look out for new creative talents). Indeed, in 1994 we launched a new literary monthly, *Di pen,* which closed down two years later when the halcyon days of Yiddish at Oxford, a period that had lasted for eighteen years from 1978 to 1996, came to a close.

Dovid was, however, eager to launch my "literary career" well before our new publishing venture began to materialize, and the same evening I showed him my first two poems, in early 1993, he promptly keyed them in on his Mac 512 (or was it MacPlus?) and drafted an accompanying letter to a highly esteemed editor of an eminent Yiddish literary magazine in New York. Dovid Katz — as I said, the son of Menke Katz — publishes fiction under the transparent pseudonym Heershadovid Menkes. In my case there was a similar need to employ a pen-name in order to avoid confusion between different Kerlers. Also, in the case of both Dovid Katz and myself, there was a need to differentiate between our ongoing academic work and our then more recent attempts at belles lettres, with no intent of effective identity disguise. My choice fell on a combination of my Russian first name and a Russified form of my surname: Boris Karloff (the spelling style in English courtesy of the late William Henry Pratt).

A month or so later, I was helping to edit parts of the twenty-third volume of the "thick" literary journal, *Yerusholaimer Almanakh*, which was founded and edited by my father in Jerusalem from 1973. Before sending the materials off to Jerusalem, I dared to include a selection of my own poems. At the time, the editor insisted on publishing a brief bio-bibliography of every new author, so together with Dovid I devised a parallel but totally fictitious biography for "Boris Karloff" (according to which he was exposed from a young age to all three languages: Russian, Yiddish, and Hebrew). Then came one of the longest weeks of my life. Upon receiving the materials, my father called me to compliment me on my editorial work and, among other things, inquired about Boris Karloff. I stubbornly stuck to Karloff's "biography," and that was it. Two days later, not being able to wait any longer, I called my father and told him that this Boris Karloff, while not a bad person, is a bit of a nudnik who keeps calling me day and night asking about the fate of his poems. My father's reply was:

"Boris Karloff? Ah, yes, of course, he is a poet! Tell him that we will publish him."

I can't be entirely sure whether my father's judgment wasn't a tad rash, but I am quite certain that at the time he was not aware of my close association with that particular Boris. Then three years later, in 1996, we jointly published a collection of poems by father and son, *Shpigl-ksav* ("Words in a Mirror," in which each poem by Yoysef Kerler was matched by one of Boris Karloff's).

It was my good fortune to experience first-hand the still vibrant Yiddish literary scene of Jerusalem and Tel Aviv in the 1970s and early 1980s, and it also has been my sad lot to witness its near complete disappearance at the turn of the twenty-first century. Yiddish literature, while marginalized and estranged in mainstream Israeli society and culture, was in the 1970s and 1980s still a powerhouse of literary life. In 1978 my father received a letter from the distinguished Hebrew poet Shin Shalom, accompanying Shalom's own unsolicited translation of one of my father's new poems. In that letter Shalom expressed his admiration of Yiddish writers who continue to be vigorously creative despite the fact that they have no audience. He compared them to his wife, who was a gifted musician but, due to her poor health, had had to stop performing. Nevertheless, a few days a week she would play at home all alone with the utmost concentration and care as if she were performing before a real audience. I remember how my father and I reacted with surprise: "No audience!? What is he talking about?" For although Shalom's admiration was sincere, his sympathy seemed to us a bit premature; there was certainly still a sizeable and active Yiddish readership and audience in Israel in those years. However, twenty-five years later, upon my return from a visit to Israel following my mother's death in early 2004, I was forced to recall that letter of the master of Hebrew poetry and wrote the following poem which is, I believe, more "Hebrew" than "Yiddish" in its cadence and diction:

Nokh alemen נאָך אַלעמען

I came to my land
when all were gone
and I saw that
my land doesn't miss
them at all

כ׳בין געקומען אין לאַנד
נאָך אַלעמען
און געזען
אַז עס בענקט ניט דאָס לאַנד
נאָך אַלעמען

Only your heart bitterly cries
with a lump in your throat
missing them all
after all

נאָר עס וויינט ביטער דאָס האַרץ
און עס וואַרגט דיך אין האַלדז
נאָך אַלעמען
נאָך אַלעמען

Lost
in your land as in a foreign land
you ask of God*
How can one bear all this
after all are gone
after all is said and done

אין לאַנד ווי אין אויסלאַנד
אַ פאַרפאַלענער
פרעגסטו ביים מקום
ווי קאָן מען פאַרטראָגן דאָס אַלץ
נאָך אַלעמען
נאָך אַלעמען

---

* lit., "Omniscient"; *Mokem* — lit., "place" is also a traditional designation for God.

In December 2000 my father succumbed to a protracted illness. He passed away a month before I left Oxford after spending more than sixteen years there. The last year of the twentieth century was, as it seems now in retrospect, the final moment in the life of secular Yiddish literature as we know it. The long awaited demise of the prewar-nourished Yiddish literary creativity became for me a painful reality. By then there was already no crisis of Yiddish publishing left to talk about. Secular Yiddish publishing in America collapsed even earlier, and since the year 2000 Yiddish book production in Israel has been further reduced to a minimum. Even the partial statistics are quite sobering: out of some thirty-two new books of Yiddish poetry published to date since 2000, only twelve are, to the best of my knowledge, by authors of the "younger" generation. They include three new poetry volumes by Velvl Chernin (2004, 2005, and 2007), two by Lev Berinsky (2001 and 2005), as well as collections of poems by Alexander Beiderman (2002), Gitl Schaechter-Viswanath (2003), Boris Karloff (2006), Aleksander Belousov (2006), Moyshe Lemster (2007), Yisroel Nekrasov (2007), and a collection of original songs by Dmitry Yakirevich (2002). Still, many new young voices and works were published in the few Yiddish literary periodicals remaining; for example, in the journal *Naye vegn* ("New Paths," which has been appearing periodically in the years 1992–2006), the new literary quarterly *Toplpunkt* ("Colon," launched in Israel in 2000), in the new rather slim journal *Der nayer fraynd* ("The New Companion," launched in St. Petersburg in 2004), and, on this side of the ocean, in the not-too-regularly published issues of the famed New York *Di tzukunft,* the recently rejuvenated by "younger" staff Yiddish weekly *Forverts* (which is the only surviving regular secular periodical, formerly the *Daily Yiddish Forward*; http://yiddish.forward.com/), and the traditional, Chabad-oriented, but culturally broadminded weekly *Algemeiner zhurnal* (http://www.algemeiner.com/generic.asp?cat=4) that was established in 1972 by Gershon Jacobson (1933–2005) and revitalized by his talented children Rabbis Simon Jacobson (as publisher) and Yosef Yitzchok Jacobson (as editor in chief). In addition to including secular authors from various generations, the paper (in a *haredi* first, it appears) has begun to republish, in cooperation with the Vilnius Yiddish Institute, works of classic and modern "secular" Yiddish literature (http://www.judaicvilnius.com/en/main/yiddishtextsonline/classic; http://www.algemeiner.com/archives.asp?expand=462).

Today there are virtually no publishing houses for secular Yiddish books, the sole exception being the Israeli Yiddish Writers'

Association's Leyvik Farlag and the terminally paralyzed Y.L. Peretz Farlag. Publishing a new book costs money, but even if one indulges in what colleagues working in other languages may deride as "vanity publishing," there is still the most acute problem of distribution. When a new book appears, it is virtually impossible to purchase it unless one happens to be in contact with the author or the person responsible for the book's publication. It is a sad fact that in our "global" age with several popular intensive Yiddish summer programs and many Yiddish culture clubs and centers in a dozen countries, both the local and the international channels of Yiddish books and periodicals distribution are completely in tatters.

In 1998 Sholem Berger, a young Yiddish journalist and author (in addition to his professional medical career), launched the first Yiddish online literary journal, *Der bavebter yid* ("The Webbed Jew"; http://www.cs.uky.edu/~raphael/bavebter/). Its issues are quite short, but most contain original works by new young authors. Back in 1998 the journal was still inaccessible to many Yiddish readers. However today, when the so-called information age has engulfed both young and old, these texts are out there on the World Wide Web, readily retrievable and accessible to all.

Of course the glorious Internet revolution cannot solve all the existential problems of contemporary Yiddish literary production, but it does provide a novel and in many respects effective type of virtual publishing. By the time I moved to Bloomington, Indiana, in January 2001, it had become clear that this was a viable new avenue. By 2004 the phenomenon of blogs had become visibly popular and blogging had turned into a fast-growing activity. Yiddish blogging by Hasidic bloggers also began to take hold around that time, inspired, since 2002, by the prolific Yiddish blogging pioneer Katle Kanye (a Yiddishized Aramaic pseudonym, meaning "woodchopper"), who later also began to publish stories and articles in the *Algemeiner zhurnal*. Once I stumbled upon the blogger program that was acquired and launched as a free service by Google, I registered and created my own Yiddish poetry blog in August 2004. The few technical queries I had were answered in Yiddish by an anonymous *haredi* Internet *maven* on a special Yiddish technical advice weblog, called *bloger eytses* ("advice for bloggers") that closed down a few years later. I believe that among the faithful, regularly returning readers of my blog there must be quite a few *haredi* Yiddish native speakers who wouldn't have otherwise bought or kept a Yiddish poetry book or a secular magazine at home (for fear of being discovered or providing a bad example for their children).

The one-time, much esteemed nineteenth-century Hebrew poet Yehuda Leib Gordon (the YaLaG) once bemoaned in a poem, "Lemi ani omeyl" (or "L'mi ani oml"; "For whom do I toil"), that in effect he is writing poetry for "one person in a city and for two in a whole district." He was of course lamenting the then-growing ignorance of Hebrew or indifference to the language among many "modern" Russian Jews who instead chose to read Russian, German, and Yiddish. As a matter of fact, he was forced to publish a volume of his Yiddish verse (even though he wasn't a great patriot of the *Zhargon*, "Jargon") in order to earn money for the publication of his Hebrew poems. A poem with an almost identical content and title easily could have been written by a contemporary Yiddish poet. However, yearning for a receptive readership is not the only stimulus of creativity. There is a famous Russian dictum that says "If you can abstain from writing poems, then abstain!" (literally: "If you can [manage] not to write poetry, don't!" which is in fact a witty travesty of the saying "If you can't write poetry, don't!"). In other words, poetry should be written only out of an irrepressible inner need.

As I have discovered over the last few years, maintaining a po-etry blog is an unobtrusive and yet open and accessible way to satisfy one's creative impulse. With luck a good poem can still find a reader, which is certainly not the case with an unpublished, or an unwritten one. My friend and colleague Velvl Chernin writes in a poem published in 2004:

I live in Tel Aviv,	וואוינען וואוין איך אין תל אביב
But I exist in the internet,	און לעבן לעב איך אין אינטערנעץ,
And through the cables my heart	און דורך די דראָטן לויפט מיין האַרץ
zigzags to and fro.	אַהין און צוריק, אַהין און צוריק.
I rinse myself [clean] in the virtual luck	איך שוועִנק זיך אויס אין מיין ווירטואַלן גליק
And everything is divided between black and white.	און אַלץ איז צעטיילט אויף ווייס און שוואַרץ.
Days and nights, countries and cities,	טעג ווי נעכט, לענדער און שטעט,
An elevated top without a bottom, without a ditch.	אַ דערהויבענער שפיץ אָן אַ דנאָ אָן אַ ריוו.
I live there where my body is.	וואוינען וואוין איך דאָרט, וואו ס'איז מיין גוף.
But I exist there where I am.	און לעבן לעב איך דאָרט, וואו איך בין.

About the same time, and before Velvl's poem reached me, I myself was experimenting with the new Yiddish word *virtuel* in the following manner:

A Virtual Poem	אוירטועל ליד

I live quite well	איך לעב זיך אויס
Quite to the fullest	גאַנץ וואויל
In the virtual mode	ווירטועל
And who knows how long	און ווער וויסט
I will stay	ווי לאַנג דאָרט
There	פאַרבלייבן כ׳וועל

Somewhere at the lap	ערגעצוואו אין שויס
Of the electronic infinity	פון עלעקטראָנישן אין־סוף
I let my word roam	בלאָנקעט מיינס אַ וואָרט
As an advance	ווי אַן אַדעראויף

And I gamble away	און אין קאָן איך שטעל
Quite virtually	גאַנץ ווירטועל
My rhyming venture	דעם גראַמען געשטעל
That brims with tunes	וואָס ניגונט און קוועלט

If you wish to —	ווילט איר — גיט אַ קוק
Come in,	ווילט איר — שעֶנקט אַ בליק
Grace it with a glance	ווילט איר ניט, —
And if not — no sweat	אויך גוט
For virtual is	ס׳איז ווירטועל
My luck	מיין גליק

So I live quite to the fullest	לעב איך זיך גאַנץ וואויל
And I know for sure	און כ׳ווייס אויך געווייס
I am dear	מיך לייענען דאָרט

To those who read me	הױך
From high above	די, װעמען איך בין זיס
As long as I don't go mute	כּל־זמן איך בלײַב ניט שטום
My fresh greeting line	ניט װערן װעט אַ תל
Will not go down	מײַן פרישער שורה־גרוס
The one I send to them	װאָס כ'שיק זײ
Virtually	װירטועל

I wish it were possible to conclude by saying that despite all, contemporary Yiddish poetry is alive and well, but that would certainly be more fiction than truth. Then again, what would our life be without fiction, and what kind of a reality would we have denying ourselves the brave new dimension of virtuality, or as Velvl would have put it: virtual existence?

So, how does a deracinated (and at least twice uprooted) person born in Moscow in 1958, and raised in Jerusalem, who embraced the writing of Yiddish poetry in the early 1990s in England, continue to be a Yiddish poet in the new millennium in his new home in southern Indiana?

Perhaps deracination, bad as it was in Soviet Russia, was not so complete in my case after all. My parents' and their friends' natural, unaffected Yiddish, which still reverberates with traditional Jewish culture, live Yiddish poetry, song, artistic performance, and heated debates—all of these must have played a decisive role in imparting to me more than just a superficial familiarity with some rudimentary Yiddish expressions and half-forgotten idioms.

As for uprootedness, I recall bringing my mother to England in 1984 for the first time to see my gothic cloister college in Oxford. She was perplexed: "mayn zun, vi kumen mir, fun kreminetser yatke-gas—bizn kloyster do in oksford!?" (in a very rough translation: "My son, how do we fit in here in this Oxford *kloyster* [literally, "church"], coming as we do from the butcher shop street in Kremenetz?!"). Of course I felt proud that she included me in her personal life saga, thereby allowing me, too, in some sense to be rooted in her native Kremenetz (in her childhood Krzemieniec, Poland and now Кременець, Ukraine). But if truth be told, I did not feel at all uprooted in the splendidly cloistered Oxford setting; nor do I feel so in the genuinely hospitable environment of Bloomington. For I still remember how my father pointed more than forty years ago to the bulky, protruding bare roots of fully grown trees that were brought to be replanted in our new Khruschevite neighborhood in Moscow, telling me: "You see, my son, people are like trees; when trees are moved they should be moved with their roots intact . . ."

Afterword

— *Eva Hoffman*

The history of exile—understood in its broadest sense as long-term displacement from one's native region—is by now very long and informatively varied. In its strongest form, exile refers to forcible expulsion, to leaving your country or place of habitation under duress. But as we scan the vast panorama of collective and individual migrations, we can see that there are shades of exile, occurring within widely differing political and social conditions and for an almost ingenious array of reasons, ranging from sheer state oppression to economic deprivation. The circumstances surrounding individual migration, and the wider context in which it takes place, can have enormous practical and psychic repercussions, reflected in the various designations we use for those who leave one country for another. There are *refugees, émigrés, emigrants,* and *expatriates*—terms that point to distinct kinds of social, but also sociopsychological experience, including, crucially, different degrees of personal choice.

Historically, too, the symbolic meaning and, therefore, the inward experience of exile has gone through many permutations. In medieval Europe, where an individual's identity was defined by one's place and role in a specific society, exile from a village or a city-state was the worst punishment that could be inflicted, amounting to a sort of psychic death. For religious Jews living in the Diaspora, on the other hand, it was the countries in which they actually lived that were seen as sites of symbolic exile; the spiritual center and home toward which they were imaginatively oriented was located in a territory, at once allegorical and geographic, called Jerusalem, or Israel.

The essays in this richly revealing and valuable collection are reports from a late stage and distinct kind of exile, one marked by stark dramas, and quiet ambiguities. Of course, as these personal and subtle statements show, each emigrant story, and trajectory, is unique and filled with its particular details of difficulty and success, private sorrow and unexpected satisfactions. And yet, for all the divergences of their experiences, the emigrants whose biographies are considered here share some central dimensions of identity and of history: They are writers and they are Jews; and, with the exception of Geoffrey Hartman, they all emigrated from the Soviet sphere during the period of the Cold War. How do these salient facts affect their lived experience of cultural and political transplantation?

It is part of the essays' interest that their authors give us insight into the personal vicissitudes that have fed their writing; and that they give full and truthful voice to the multiple and sometimes contradictory elements of their experience. None of them diminishes the difficulties or the anguish of displacement; but all of them attest to the gains that accrue in the process.

To begin on the other side of the geographical divide: none of the writers included here was precisely forced to leave—but none of them left, precisely, voluntarily. They left because of political pressures; because the countries of the Soviet bloc in the postwar decades were materially uncomfortable and politically stifling places to live; because, as Jews, they were targets of ordinary anti-Semitism and official prejudice; because, as writers (for those whose literary careers began before emigration), they were subject to covert and overt censorship. It is perhaps moot, in such circumstances, to speak of entirely free choice. Moreover, although history reversed their assumption, for the emigrants of that era, Jewish or non-Jewish, there seemed to be no possibility of return. By deciding to emigrate, they in effect chose exile, with its aura of finality, its sense that departure was irrevocable. This awareness undoubtedly intensified the sense of rupture and loss attendant on all migration. Zsuzsanna Ozsváth and Bronislava Volková speak eloquently about the primary, human losses they suffered on leaving their countries: the acute pain of separation from parents, friends, and playmates; from people who understood their history and sometimes shared it ("Suddenly; every memory becomes as sharp as a knife," writes Volková); the loss of cherished possessions, documents, professional credentials.

It can be seen in retrospect that the period of the Cold War produced quite extreme forms of displacement. The Iron Curtain created a bipolar world, of radical divisions and chiaroscuro contrasts, of enormous and artificial distances, out of all proportion to actual geography. On the economic, political, and social levels, East and West became each other's antipodes, differing in culture, economic development, and tenor of life, to a degree unimaginable in today's increasingly globalized world.

It is a feature of exile which takes place in such a world that it encourages a construction of a bipolar internal world. Spatially, the world becomes riven into two parts, divided by a barrier that cannot be crossed; temporally, the past is all of a sudden on one side, the present on the other. Unlike Dante, say, who felt his exile from his beloved Florence bitterly, but who nevertheless continued to live within less than a hundred miles of it, and still within the sphere of similar cultural norms, the exiles coming to America, or indeed, the West, from Eastern Europe, were initially plunged into a truly unknown, and in many ways alien world.

In such a situation, it is easy to feel that one is split in two; that one's original identity, norms of feeling, pitch toward the world, is irrelevant in the new surroundings, and quite separate from the new persona the emigrant has to assume—or form. It is not surprising that tropes of haunting, self-division, and double selves run through these testimonies with a metaphoric consistency.

That self, especially for a writer, is intimately and inextricably bound up with language; and it is the problematic of linguistic uprooting that looms largest in many exiled writers' biographies. Other immigrants too suffer the shock of linguistic dislocation, the injury to the ego that comes with the loss of verbal mastery and competence. But for a writer, even more than for others, language is not only an instrument of communication, but a method of knowledge and self-knowledge, the means of production and the medium of the self. The internal language from which creativity proceeds constitutes nothing less than a psychic home. In "Nomadic Language," Norman Manea writes eloquently of his relationship to Romanian, the only language which—for all that it is also the tongue of those who have persecuted him—is a fully comfortable habitation. As many Jewish refugees from Germany can testify, one cannot disown one's native tongue because it has been used for wrongful or even perverted ends. Each language, after all, contains the sum total of human possibilities. But the first language holds a privileged place in the psyche, partly because we learn it unconsciously, so that it seems to correspond to the world it describes; but also, as Manea points out, because it is the language of our first relationships, our initiation into the human world. "The doctor and all those who assisted my difficult birth spoke Romanian," he writes. "Romanian was spoken in my home, where I spent most of my time with Maria, the lovely peasant girl who took care of me and spoiled me, in Romanian." In a similar vein, Zsuzsanna Ozsváth speaks of the deprivation she felt on not being able to play linguistic games with her peers once she left Hungary—games that depended on a shared repository of verbal allusions and, also, of experiences.

Shared experiences matter, because languages exist not only as syllables or sentences but also within a wider cultural syntax and social matrix. It is that embeddedness in an infinite web of meanings and implications that makes literary translation (and for that matter, self-translation) so difficult.

In order really to translate a text from one language to another, it would be necessary to transpose that delicate surround of implicit significance, references, and resonances. Ideally, a translation would also convey something of the original music, the stylistic valences, and the modality of an author's voice in the new text. Manea speaks wryly about the near-impossibility of such an endeavor; for it is in the course of textual translation—especially if you know both languages in question very well—that the gaps and disjunctions between them become most evident. (Nabokov, who wrote both in English and Russian masterfully, apparently came near breakdown when he tried to translate his own work; one can perhaps speculate that translating yourself reveals not only the ruptures between languages but, also, between the writer's disparate cultural selves). Henryk Grynberg writes about the vexations of being, in a sense, displaced from each of his literal and cultural languages: "And so I try to translate my Jewish culture for the Poles, and my Polish culture for the Jews, and both of my cultures for Americans—an unenviable task."

Of course, there are advantages, especially for a writer, in being, so to speak, disembedded. Dislocation from the familiar gives you new ways of observing and seeing, and brings you up against certain questions that otherwise remain unasked and quiescent. It places you at an oblique angle to your world and gives you a certain detachment and a vantage point. The perspective of distance can be a great stimulus to thought and creativity, which is surely why so many artists have actively chosen expatriation and exile: Joyce, with his motto "Silence, exile, and cunning," Samuel Beckett, with his decision to write in French—precisely for the advantages of defamiliarization.

———

What of the third point of commonality in these essays, the writers' Jewishness? The story of Jewish migrations and diasporas is vast enough to form a separate, thick chapter, in the wider saga of exile. But if the problematic of language is the diachronic constant of exile, expressing itself in recurring patterns in all epochs and conditions, questions of Jewish identity are strongly inflected by social and cultural factors. And, in Eastern Europe and the Soviet Union after World War II, "being Jewish" was a proposition fraught with ambiguities. After the near-total decimation of the region's Jewish world in the Holocaust, those who stayed on rather than emigrating immediately after the war tended to be well acculturated, if not assimilated; and most of the writers indicate that they come from such acculturated, nonreligious backgrounds. Aside from Dov-Ber Kerler, who in his youth moved within much-diminished, but still lively Yiddish-speaking literary circles in the Soviet Union, none of the essayists has adult memories of the richly textured prewar Jewish communities that inhabited Eastern Europe (although a few of them remember childhood glimpses).

And yet, as these essays attest, most East European Jews did not harbor uncertainty as to their identity, or feel the need, in the manner of their Western counterparts, to search for "roots." For those, including Grynberg, Ozsváth, and Manea, who endured terrible persecutions and incurred tragic losses during the Shoah as children, "what it means to be Jewish" was not a question that needed to be asked. Sent out from Germany on a *Kindertransport* at the age of nine, Geoffrey Hartman was also a child of that most somber of events. For those born after in its close proximity, the shadow of the Holocaust was long, even if the event was initially surrounded by silence; and writers such as Lara Vapnyar continue to be deeply affected by that formative catastrophe and trauma.

Moreover, while Eastern Europe after the war was a sphere of putative secularism, in which ethnic and religious affiliations were supposedly deleted from individual identity and collective awareness, the realities were, of course, quite different; and all of the autobiographers mention a general atmosphere and specific incidents of anti-Semitism, which were sufficient to convince them that they did not "belong" in the countries where they were growing up by natural right, or easy assumption. Lara Vapnyar writes with biting humor about her childhood discovery that she was Jewish, and the sense of estrangement that followed, both from the larger body politic and, more self-divisively, from her own, supposedly "Jewish" traits.

Perhaps it can be said that Jewishness for these writers was above all the first bifurcation of identity, the first marker of difference. They all had some training in being "Other"—but, also, in being hybrid. Not that this made emigration necessarily easier. On the contrary, such a radical rupture may be even harder for those who do not feel firmly rooted in the first place. It may be felt as an exacerbation of an original sense of impermanence or instability; or even, for those who had undergone horrific events, as a reawakening of an earlier trauma—of that deep dread which Ozsváth says was conferred on her by the Holocaust; or of what Manea calls "the psychosis of the provisory."

But it should also be noted that even if it was impossible for these Jewish writers to give full allegiance to their countries of origin, none of them slights the force of their early attachments or the degree to which their original homelands formed them. Various writers mention friendships, relationships with colleagues, and affection for aspects of their original cultures. Grynberg, for all his professed "anti-nostalgia," and moral anger at his compatriots, has fond memories of student theater in Poland, and his own comic gifts, which expressed themselves in a specifically Polish vein. Vapnyar writes about her childish admiration for qualities of Russian "character," and her love for Russian literature, even as she discovered that it is pervasively tainted by anti-Semitism.

Beyond that, "home" is constituted not only by the tangible present, but also by the past; and exile, as some of the writers note, takes place in time as well as space. Being ejected from the places that hold one's accumulated memories, or from sites holding family history, can be felt as painful, even if those memories come in mixed affective colors. It is as hard to discard one's first world completely as to extract the first language from the psyche; to do so would be to some extent to reject or discard oneself.

If leaving one's first home is surely never easy, the process of adjustment to a new world holds complex challenges. It requires, on the part of the immigrant, a stretching of the self beyond its original boundaries, a capacious curiosity, and a willingness to be deeply changed. Embarking on such a transcultural journey can be not only arduous but also fascinating; and it can lead not only to new practical opportunities but to an expansion of vision, an opening of new human possibilities and vistas. Bronislava Volková describes the transformation of her work wrought through her very struggles with her new environment, the enlargement of her poetic understanding beyond immediate and culturally specific perceptions, to an apprehension of universal human problems and values. For Ozsváth, the gains accrue literally from and through textual translation, as she transposes, with a gifted collaborator, the Hungarian poetry she loves into English versions that seem to her to have a magical correspondence to the originals. This is an enrichment for her new language and culture, no less than for herself. Vapnyar indicates that she may have turned to writing in the first place as a result of emigration and the isolation she felt in its first stages. For what, after all, do we write out of if not gaps and ruptures?

Vapnyar was young enough when she emigrated to begin her writing life in English, and she is the writer in this collection who most explicitly alludes to the uses of the exilic, or bicultural perspective in her work. Her fiction often draws on Russian themes and characters, many of them immigrants caught between past and present. While Vapnyar has been accused (as she explains in her essay) of acting as a kind of fictional tour guide for her American readers, she also suggests that shuttling between her imaginative coordinates helps her understand and orient herself in her new world.

It is one of the surprising motifs recurring in several of the essays that exile can have a paradoxically integrative as well as a fracturing effect, and that its great disruption can close up some of the earlier fault lines—particularly the ambiguities caused by Jewishness. In the American setting, writers no longer need to feel that Jewishness is a dangerous or an endangered fact, a curtailed part of consciousness, or a semi-secret aspect of identity. If they wish, they can now explore it as a theme, part of their history, or even a language. For Dov-Ber Kerler, that means actually writing in Yiddish. While that choice is so rare in his generation as to be eccentric, the possibility of making it is there; and clearly, he swims in the rich heritage of Yiddish poetry as in nourishing waters, even if the practice of it is a pretty pure case of art for art's sake.

For a writer, the inability to address a subject that lies most pressingly on the heart is a deprivation indeed; and the ability to do so can be a form of catharsis or solace. For Henryk Grynberg, the possibility of writing about the Holocaust past without external constraints has been a poignant liberation. He has used the freedom of his adopted country to undertake a labor of powerful and difficult witnessing. Norman Manea, who has experienced the constraints of censorship, also stresses the importance of being able to write freely about your chosen themes. In that sense, political freedom really matters, not only at the external level of social relations but for our inward lives as well.

⸺

Among the statements gathered here, the essay by Geoffrey Hartman stands as an illuminating exception. Hartman declares right up front that his "is a story without suspense, drama, or crises of conscience." The narrative he proceeds to unfold is indeed one of accumulation and enrichment rather than conflict or loss—of sheer addition. For this distinguished scholar, there seems to be no contradiction between being German and Jewish, between studying the English Romantics and the Midrash, between the exegesis of texts and the interpretation of oral testimonies. He does not consider it incongruous to write a Passion play—based on that most Christian of all genres—about a Holocaust survivor. Perhaps this capacity for inclusiveness is a matter of a generous and open temperament; but perhaps it is not too presumptuous to speculate that this kind of imaginative polymorphism is easier to attain if the transplantation from one culture to another takes place in childhood. Childhood, after all, is a kind of pre-ideological age, in which various elements of one's selfhood have not yet separated themselves out into ideologically defined strands, and in which impressions of the world, languages, and cultural influences can coexist in a happy, if not yet entirely conscious, hybridity. Such mental heterogeneity becomes more difficult to sustain, or to carry across to new circumstances, in one's adult years, especially if one becomes a target of persecution of prejudice; but the paradigm of accumulation points to a very real possibility within ourselves, and one that has a special relevance for exile and immigration. We *can* have hyphenated identities, in which the hyphen stands for a link, rather than division. (I am reminded of an interwar poet, Aleksander Wat, who, when asked whether he was Polish or Jewish, answered, "I am Polish-Polish, and Jewish-Jewish.") We are constituted not only by our pasts and received identities, but also by our minds and imaginations. We can open out to new experiences, languages, and cultures. We can, in some cases, absorb them deeply enough into ourselves so that we become truly bilingual and bicultural. There is, in other words, the possibility of addition as well as subtraction—and nowhere is this more possible, of course, than in the always polyvalent universe of literature.

If one has to emigrate, it is no small advantage to have the cosmopolitan treasury of texts at one's disposal. Zsuzsanna Ozsváth, as a last act before fleeing Hungary, put two books in her winter coat, and whispered "I'll keep you for a hundred years." It's a gesture echoing Nadezhda Mandelstam who, in "Hope against Hope," recounts that before going into exile in Siberia, she snatched a book to put into her basket, as the secret policemen were hurrying her to leave. The book was Dante's *Divine Comedy*, and in taking it with her, Mandelstam felt that she was transporting a fragment of her spiritual home. In Hartman's view, our experience of reality is always mediated; but through literature, we can have access to all its articulated forms.

—

Since the earlier emigrations described in these essays took place, the geopolitical conditions of cross-cultural movement have changed greatly. In the last decades the world has become vastly more mobile, intermingled, nomadic. Cross-national movement is as much the norm as the exception. And even if we continue to inhabit one country or spot, the processes of globalization are greatly decreasing imaginative distances between countries and parts of the world. As Morris Dickstein points out, the generation growing up in the Soviet Union in the 1980s and 1990s was much better informed about American culture and life than their predecessors. When we do leave our countries of origin, the means of communication and travel available to us today make the sense of rift, of separation between the past and the present, much less radical than it was for the Cold War exiles. Indeed, the identity of today's youth in the Western parts of the world may be generational as much as national. It is possible that the shaping force of the distinctive, historical cultures that were so defining for earlier generations is lessening. That means that the writing emerging from the younger generation of émigrés can be—as Dickstein also notes—tinged with comedy as much as tragedy; and with multiple ironies, rather than the intensities of loss and irrevocable choice.

In Europe, the era of enforced exile is over. The patterns of such exile persist in other parts of the world, of course; but there is currently no country on the European continent that prevents its citizens from leaving or expels them for political reasons. To some extent, we can now see the emigrations of the Cold War era within a historical framework. At the same time, the literature that has emerged from that period, and from the sometimes extreme conditions of exile, continues to speak to many readers with urgency and immediacy.

But then, texts are not only transportable, they also transport—meanings, experiences, histories, and stories. In her essay, Katarzyna Jerzak speaks movingly about teaching literature of the Holocaust to her American students—a group, she suggests, as innocent as any of historical experience or knowledge of catastrophe. And yet, she tells us, these students respond powerfully to the works of writers like Manea or Grynberg. They respond to the terrible losses these writers describe, the injustices they witnessed, and the thirst for justice. For even though the Holocaust was a primarily Jewish catastrophe, the alchemical magic of writing can convey such extremity to those who have not lived through it, intimating the universal stratum of experience within the particular, and thus carrying the text from the writer's imagination to its far-flung readers and destinations.

For the immigrant writer, the process of coming to know a new world involves the attempt to imagine and to enter into other subjectivities, and the subjectivity of another culture and language. At the same time, literature more than perhaps any other form of human activity can give us insight into other subjectivities, fates, and lives. In that sense, the literature of exile has often acted as a sort of deep bridge across geographical borders, cultural mentalities, and ideological divides. It is a tradition that the essays gathered here help illuminate, and to which their authors have richly contributed.

Contributors

Matei Calinescu emigrated to the United States in 1973 from Communist Romania. He is Professor Emeritus of Comparative Literature and of West European Studies at Indiana University, Bloomington. He was a Guggenheim Fellow (1976–1977) and a Woodrow Wilson Center Fellow in Washington, D.C. (1995–1996). His publications in English include *Five Faces of Modernity: Modernism, Avant-Garde, Decadence, Kitsch, Postmodernism* (1987), *Exploring Postmodernism* (1987), and *Rereading* (1993). He is also the author of numerous books, essays, and articles in Romanian and French.

Morris Dickstein is Distinguished Professor of English at the Graduate Center of the City University of New York. His books include *Gates of Eden: American Culture in the Sixties* (1977, 1997), *Double Agent: The Critic and Society* (1992), *Leopards in the Temple: The Transformation of American Fiction, 1945–1970* (2002), and *A Mirror in the Roadway: Literature and the Real World* (2005), recently reprinted in paperback.

Henryk Grynberg is a Polish poet, novelist, and essayist living in the United States since 1967. In this country, he is best known as the author of *The Jewish War and the Victory* (2001), and *Drohobycz, Drohobycz and Other Stories* (2002), which brought him the 2002 Koret Jewish Book Award.

Geoffrey Hartman is Sterling Professor Emeritus of English and Comparative Literature at Yale University and Project Director of the university's Fortunoff Archive for Holocaust Testimonies. He left his native

Germany in 1939 with the *Kindertransport* and arrived in the United States in 1945. A widely published scholar, critic, and poet, his latest book, *The Geoffrey Hartman Reader* (2004), was awarded the 2006 Truman Capote prize for literary criticism.

Eva Hoffman is a writer and an academic scholar. She was born in Kraków, Poland, and emigrated with her family to Vancouver, British Columbia in 1959. She received her Ph.D. in literature from Harvard University and worked as an editor and writer for *The New York Times*. Her works include *Lost in Translation* (1989), *Shtetl: The Life and Death of a Small Town and the World of Polish Jews* (1997), and *After Such Knowledge: Where Memory of the Holocaust Ends and History Begins* (2004). She lives in New York and London.

Katarzyna Jerzak grew up in Poland, arrived in the United States in 1986, and studied at Brown University and Princeton University, receiving her Ph.D. in 1995. She is Associate Professor of Comparative Literature at the University of Georgia. Her publications include articles on Witold Gombrowicz, Giorgio de Chirico, E. M. Cioran, and Henryk Grynberg. Her book manuscript, "Modern Exilic Imagination," is currently under review, as is her translation of Grynberg's essays.

Dov-Ber Kerler, pen name Boris Karloff, was born in Moscow in 1958 and immigrated with his parents to Israel in 1971. In 1984–2000 he lived in England, where he studied and taught Yiddish language and literature at Oxford University. In 2001, he moved to Bloomington to assume the Dr. Alice Field Cohn Chair in Yiddish Studies at Indiana University. A son of the noted Yiddish poet and literary editor Yoysef Kerler, he has published his own poetry in Yiddish periodicals in Israel, Europe, and the United States, including four collections: *Vu mit an alef* (Where with an Aleph, 1996), *Shpiglksav—getseylte lider* (Words in a Mirror, Selected Pickings; with Yoysef Kerler, 1996), *ELABREK: lider fun nayem yortoyznt* (ELABREK: Poems of the New Millennium, 2006), and *Katoves on a zayt: nekhtike lider* (I Kid You Not: Poems of Yesteryears, 2007).

Norman Manea, Flournoy Professor of European Literature and writer in residence at Bard College, New York, is a Romanian writer who has been living since 1988 in the United States. His work has been translated into fifteen languages. His latest book in English is *The Hooligan's Return* (2003). He has received several important awards, among them the MacArthur Award (United States, 1992), the international literary Nonino Prize (Italy, 2002), and Le Prix Médicis Étranger (2006).

Zsuzsanna Ozsváth, The Leah and Paul Lewis Chair of Holocaust Studies, is Professor of Literature and The History of Ideas at the University of Texas at Dallas. Born in Hungary, she left the country in 1957 and has been living in the United States since 1962. She is author and translator of a number of books and articles, including *In the Footsteps of Orpheus: The Life and Times of Miklós Radnóti* (2001). Her most recent publication is "Trauma and Distortion: Holocaust Fiction and the Ban on Jewish Memory in Hungary," in *The Holocaust in Hungary: Sixty Years Later*, eds. R. L. Braham and Brewster S. Chamberlin (2006).

Lara Vapnyar emigrated from Russia to New York in 1994. She is the author of a well-received book of short stories, *There are Jews in My House* (2003), and the novel *Memoirs of a Muse* (2006). Her stories have appeared in *The New Yorker, Harper's*, and *Zoetrope*. In addition to writing fiction, she is working on a Ph.D. in comparative literature in the CUNY Graduate Center.

Bronislava Volková, Professor of Slavic Languages and Literatures and Director of the Czech Program at Indiana University, has been living in the United States since 1976. She is a bilingual exile poet from Czechoslovakia and the author of nine books of existential and metaphysical poetry. Her selected poems in English were published under the title *Courage of the Rainbow* in 1993. Her most recent publication is a twin retrospective CD, *The Slightest Reminder of Your Being . . . Three Decades of Exile: 1974–2004 / Nejmenší připomínka Tvého bytí . . . Třicet let exilu 1974–2004.*

Index

Alvin H. Rosenfeld is Professor of English and Jewish Studies at Indiana University, Bloomington and founder and former director of Indiana University's Borns Jewish Studies Program. He is author of *Imagining Hitler* (Indiana University Press, 1985) and *A Double Dying: Reflections on Holocaust Literature* (Indiana University Press, 1980) and editor of *Thinking about the Holocaust: After Half a Century* (Indiana University Press, 1997). He chairs the academic advisory board of the U.S. Holocaust Museum's Center for Advanced Holocaust Studies.